Modality, Essence and Possible Worlds

Modality, Essence and Possible Worlds

Indrani Sanyal

Suryodaya Books

Cataloging in Publication Data — DK
[Courtesy: D.K. Agencies (P) Ltd. <docinfo@dkagencies.com>]

Sanyal, Indrani, author.
Modality, essence and possible worlds / Indrani Sanyal.
pages cm
Includes bibliographical references and index.
ISBN: 9788192570266

1. Language and languages — Philosophy. 2. Modality (Logic) 3. Essentialism (Philosophy) I. Title.

P107.S26 2015 DDC 401 23

ISBN: 978-81-925702-6-6

First published in India in 2015

Published by:
Department of Philosophy
Jadavpur University
Kolkata - 700 032

and

Suryodaya Books
"*Suryodaya*", D-36A/1, Mohan Garden
Najafgarh Road, New Delhi – 110 059
Phone: (011) 2535 3435

Distributed by:
D.K. Printworld (P) Ltd.
Regd. Office: "Vedaśrī", F-395, Sudarshan Park
(Metro Station: Ramesh Nagar), New Delhi – 110 015
Phones: (011) 2545 3975, 2546 6019; *Fax*: (011) 2546 5926
e-mail: indology@dkprintworld.com
Website: www.dkprintworld.com

Printed by: Suryodaya Books, New Delhi

To
The memory of my teacher
Pranab Kumar Sen
with deep respect and gratitude

अथाधिविद्यम्। आचार्यः पूर्वरूपम्। अन्तेवास्युत्तररूपम्। विद्या सन्धिः। प्रवचनम् सन्धानम्। इत्यधिविद्यम्।।
athādhividyam । *ācāryaḥ pūrvarūpam* । *antevāsyuttararūpam* ।
vidyā sandhiḥ । *pravacanam sandhānam* । *ityadhividyam* ।

— *Taittirīyopaniṣad*, 1.3.4

Next concerning the Knowledge. The Master is the first form; the disciple is the latter form; knowledge is the linking; exposition is the joint of the linking. Thus far concerning the Knowledge.

— Sri Aurobindo, Taittirīya Upanishad, in *The Upanishads* II, 2004

Contents

	Introduction	1
1.	How Is $(\exists x)$ (x Is Necessarily Greater than 7) Possible?	21
2.	The De Re Modality and Essentialism	65
3.	Modality and Possible Worlds	74
4.	A Transcendental Argument for Essentialism	132
5.	Sen's Views on Reference and Quantification and Their Implications in a Modal Context	169
6.	Pragmatic Ambiguity	187
7.	The Logical Space	197
8.	The Limits of Language and the Unlimited Beyond	224
9.	Some Observations on Builder's Language	245
10.	The Structural Universals: Arguments For and Against	260
	Bibliography	270
	Index	278

Introduction

Modality, Essence and Possible Worlds is a collection of ten essays I have written in different phases of my academic life — from the remotest to the very recent. The essays included in this volume are thematically linked with one another in one way or other, which also led me to come up with a plan for publishing these together under the same title. Essays collected in this volume are documentation of my modest attempts towards negotiation with some of the unmitigated issues frequently raised, discussed and debated in the domain of Anglo-American Analytic Philosophy. The Department of Philosophy at Jadavpur University, to which I belonged in various capacities — as a postgraduate student, as a research scholar and still belong as a teacher, has a long and vibrant history of nearly sixty years of academic pursuit in different domains of specialization. One of the significant trends of the Department was quite obvious with its direct and sometimes mediate engagement with the Anglo-American Analytic Philosophical tradition, which is a distinguishing historical movement of the twentieth century in the domain of philosophy. The analytic philosophy has different layers or phases and all philosophers engaged in this movement belonged to a family by their sincere urge to develop and practise 'analysis' in resolving or dissolving philosophical issues. Terms 'analysis', 'conceptual analysis', 'logical analysis', and 'linguistic analysis' are used to signify the method of philosophy advocated by the analytic movement in philosophy. The nomenclature 'analytic philosophy' is of very late origin, according to a record, it is in vogue sometimes since 1950. Analytic philosophy does not have one unique model of analysis, nor does it stand for any definite viewpoint in philosophy. All analytic philosophers aimed at clarity of expressions and strength of arguments. It is not easy to identify some common areas of their admiration and aversions. It has been supposed that analytic philosophers are united in their anti-metaphysics stance. But this is also not a correct description of an analytic philosopher. There are analytic philosophers who do not consider analytic philosophy as anti-metaphysical in attitude, but rather consider it as a drive to reinstate metaphysics on stronger foundation. Analytic philosophy is a blanket expression, under the cover of which again there are multifarious sub-divisions like philosophy of language, philosophy of logic, philosophy of mind and so on. Many teachers and researchers of the Department of Philosophy at Jadavpur University were devoted to research in the line of analytic philosophy. As students we had also very good exposure to different areas of analytic philosophy. The methodology of analysis, the very germane of analytic philosophy, is still in practice at the Department of Philosophy, Jadavpur University but its practice has reconciled with the changes within the very analytic philosophical tradition by adopting diversifications through multifarious channels. No doubt, the trend persists in its broad spectrum, but admittedly it has taken diverse turns. The great gift of analytic philosophical tradition is its methodology for research. The present volume recounts my commitment to analytic philosophy.

In Chapter One, 'How Is $(\exists x)$ (x Is Necessarily Greater than 7) Possible?' I am primarily trying to discuss about the feasibility of intermingling of quantifiers with modal operators, since the possibility of quantified modal logic has been put to sharp challenge by W.V. Quine. The logic that was born in the year 1946 out of intermingling of quantifiers with modal operators in a particular order has definitely survived, and is certainly fit to be a logic. But in the face of strong opposition by Quine and some others, these questions require a thorough examination. This article has dealt with views of many distinguished philosophers and logicians. The problem of quantification into a modal context has given rise to the following two important questions:

1. Is quantification into a modal context logically feasible?
2. Is quantification into a modal context metaphysically feasible?

To outline the 'logical argument' of Quine, as we may call it, wherein he gives certain formal reasons for rejecting quantified modal logic, is as follows: since it is not possible to quantify over-expressions occupying referentially opaque positions, modal contexts which are also referentially opaque, do not permit quantification. The first essay of this volume deals with this issue step by step, in the first place, by figuring out Quine's objection, second, considering four possible replies to Quine's objection, that do not propose any radical change in the Quinean framework on quantification and third, concluding with the discussion showing the point of convergence of these four solutions. There are logicians who call into question the very notion of quantification as understood by Quine. Ruth Barcan Marcus proceeds to show that quantification is possible in an opaque context by introducing the substitutional interpretation of quantification in the place of Quine's objectual interpretation of quantification. However, in this particular suggestion, I did not get into any discussion, though the nature of substitutional interpretation of quantification has been addressed in my article entitled 'Sen's Views on Reference and Quantification and Their Implications in a Modal Context'. Of the four solutions to Quine's objections that have been discussed in this essay, the first one is from Arthur Smullyan and F.B. Fitch showing that the apparent paradox of reference failure generated in a modal context is due to the scope of ambiguity of the descriptive phrases occurring in a modal context; the second solution suggested by Ruth Barcan Marcus is drawing attention to the distinction between an extensional context and modal context in interpreting the relation of identity. The third solution that has been proposed suggests existential generalization is possible in a modal context, by showing the different kinds of positions that a singular term may occupy in a sentence. The fourth solution provides cue for keeping the reference of a singular term fixed as we pass from this actual world to other possible world. This solution is provided by Jaakko Hintikka.

In Chapter Two 'The De Re Modality and Essentialism' I take up the second issue regarding possibility of quantified modal logic on the ground of its metaphysical feasibility. The summary of the argument is as follows: Quantification into a modal context is possible only if necessity is de re. But there cannot be any de re necessity unless a thing can be said to possess a property necessarily. To say that a thing possesses a property necessarily or essentially is to be involved in essentialism. There is another angle from which again the charge of essentialism may be brought against the possibility of quantified modal logic, but that has not been discussed in the present article. In this article, I have discussed only the first type of essentialism that is involved in *de re* modality and try to defend it against Quine's attacks. One of Quine's main arguments against essentialism is that it is full of contradictions and, therefore, it is a philosophically unaccepted doctrine. Here attempts are made to show how de re modality can be defended against Quine's objections. One way that has been explored is by showing that a thing can be said to be necessarily so-and-so independently of any specification without raising any problem. Another alternative option has also been explored by showing that even if a thing is necessarily so-and-so only under some specification, the modality may still be de re. These two essays are very much outcome of my Ph D dissertation entitled 'Some Philosophical Problems of Quantified Modal Logic' which I did under the supervision of Professor Pranab Kumar Sen.

As a member of the Logic Group under the leadership of Professor Sen, I continued to work with issues surrounding modal logic as such. The result of my research was published under the title, *Modality and Possible Worlds* (Chapter Three). The semantical representation of modal calculi usually involves reference to possible worlds other than our own world and requires postulation of possible objects not found in the actual world. To name a few pioneers in this direction were Saul Kripke, Jaakko Hintikka and

Stig Kanger, all working independently of one another, invoked possible worlds models for the explication of modal notions. The framework of possible worlds has proved to be of immense explanatory value. But it cannot be denied that the notion of possible worlds has given rise to lots of debates and doubts in philosophy. Possible worlds are supposed to be fraught with contradiction, the talk of possible worlds violates the Occam's principle by leading to needless multiplication of entities. In this paper, I have tried to elucidate and explain the ontological status of so-called possible worlds. The thorough discussion about the views of the semanticists, who upheld the model of possible worlds, reveals that these logicians very much differed from one another in representing their views on the subject. In this paper, I have tried to elaborate their views in a definite order by drawing a distinction between the 'modalists' who consider modality as primitive and the 'non-modalists' who do not believe in primitive modality; for them there are no modal entities whatsoever. Now, under the 'modalists' there are two sub-groups, viz. modal possibilists, who consider possible worlds as primitive and modal actualists, who do not consider possible worlds as primitive. The group which considers modality to be primitive, but does not consider possible worlds to be primitive is further sub-divided into (1) realists, (2) conceptualists, and (3) linguists. The realists, in this scheme of division, are those who think that possible worlds exist independently of our knowledge, belief as certain derived entities of the actual world. The conceptualists regard possible worlds as conceptual constructions and the linguists, on the other hand, take possible worlds as certain kinds of linguistic entities. All these alternative proposals adopted for accounting possible worlds have been taken up in this essay. In this connection, I have attempted to clear one confusion: the decision to treat modality as primitive should not be confused with the notion of possible worlds as primitive. In the context of modality its primitiveness implies its being non-reductive and non-derivative. This establishes the difference of my approach from that of others who subject modal notions to further analysis to decipher their physical basis. There is a significant sense in which possible worlds are devices or aids to imagination which help in explaining the notions of possibility, necessity, etc. Also, this paper very strongly refutes possibilism as an alternative account of possible worlds.

'A Transcendental Argument for Essentialism' (Chapter Four) appeared in the Festschrift volume of Amita Chatterjee entitled *Mind and Cognition: An Inter-Disciplinary Sharing*. Since the days of my PhD dissertation on 'Some Philosophical Problems of Quantified Modal Logic', I always felt against Quinean stricture that essentialism is a strong philosophical position. Relentlessly arguing for the possibility of quantified modal logic, more attention was paid in reclaiming its logical feasibility. But gradually it occurred to me that metaphysics of essence is a defensible, respectable philosophical position with immense practical consequences. The logical feasibility for quantified modal logic if substantiated that may be considered as providing a sound argument in defence of essentialism. But we may develop or look for other arguments as well to substantiate the essentialist claims. In course of supervising the PhD dissertation of Dr Karabi Das Mahapatra, presently Associate Professor of Jiagunj College, Murshidabad, on 'The Nature of Identity: The Relativist vs. the Absolutist', myself and Karabi had spent years reading and discussing *Sameness and Substance* of David Wiggins along with the writings of many other philosophers to bring out the best possible viewpoint about the nature of identity. In my later publication *On Essentialist Claims*, I worked in detail on elaborating and analysing different arguments in favour of essentialism nicknaming these as (1) metaphysical argument of Aristotle, (2) epistemological argument of David Wiggins, and (3) semantical argument of Saul Kripke. However, I had still some feeling of incompleteness and the publication of *Sameness and Substance Renewed* by David Wiggins rekindled my imagination to rework on Wiggins's argument. This Festschrift volume gave me an opportunity to revisit Wiggins's argument and to relocate myself in the essentialist vs. non-essentialist debate.

In the first place, in this article, I avoided calling David Wiggins's argument as epistemological argument in favour of essentialism, rather I have called his argument as a transcendental argument. In his *Sameness and Substance Renewed*, Wiggins has claimed to work out, 'the essentialist consequences of the theory of individuation'. I have characterized Wiggins's argument as a transcendental argument on the ground that like any transcendental argument, to account for some actual experiential occurrences for their being as these have been, it asserts the necessity of a conclusion. Wiggins is analysing the cognitive act of individuation and he is thus defending 'indiv?iduative' essentialism as a consequence. Wiggins's type of essentialism depends upon three interrelated observations: first is about the very pattern of the common individuative practices; second is about the principle that supports and explains it; and third is regarding the meaningfulness of such de re constructions as discoverable through individuative practices. Wiggins may be summarized as follows: To conceive anything of x, or to counter-factually conceive anything of x, x has to be individuated; to individuate x is to provide an answer to the question, 'what is x'?; to answer 'what is x', is to say that x is necessarily so-and-so. This is, according to Wiggins, embracing essentialism. In this connection, I have elaborately discussed the thesis of sortal dependency of identity as proposed by Wiggins after his *Sameness and Substance* and his *Sameness and Substance Renewed*. One thing I have tried to emphasize is that Wiggins's approach to essentialism should not be mistaken for conceptualistic or conventional approach to essentialism. For Wiggins is not one with those for whom talk of necessity is just a verbal squeamish. Wiggins has defended essentialism through the trajectory of epistemology, and this approach is not to be viewed as a mark of weakness in logic. Thus, essentialism that is derived from Wiggins is the consequence of the very manner of our epistemic activity of conceiving that makes it possible to account for a connection between the man and the world. This argument as proposed by Wiggins has many strands and in this essay a thorough attempt has been made to bring out all the details of his argument. From Wiggins's model, it is clear that emphasis has been on upholding determinate individuative practices. But there are lots of debates and differences of opinion about the very nature of the individuative practices. This acceptance of individuative practices discussed is based upon a particular theorization of identity as the notion of sortal relative identity. In this connection, ten subsidiary formulations of D-thesis have been elaborately discussed. In the final conclusion, I have definitely tried to argue in favour of Wiggins to substantiate his argument in support of essentialism.

In Chapter Five 'Sen's Views on Reference and Quantification and Their Implications in a Modal Context': *Essays in Honour of Pranab Kumar Sen*, I have tried to elaborate Sen's views on matters relating to reference, predication and quantification with reference to a modal context. The concept of reference is a primordial concept that kept analytic philosophers preoccupied for several years. Reference, no doubt is an important component for verbal communication. The mechanism of language enables us to refer to objects, to single objects and to objects in general. In the case of a normal human adult, reference goes hand in hand with predication. In 'How Is ($\exists x$) (x Is Necessarily Greater than 7) Possible?', it has already been shown that Quine's main argument against the possibility of quantified modal logic rests on the failure of reference of terms occurring in a modal context. One possible rejoinder to Quine would have been to show that there is no reference failure in that context. In this connection, we may note that Quine's way of classifying reference of a singular term as (1) pure reference, and (2) opaque reference (i.e. non-reference) was not satisfactory compared to the distinction proposed by Sen. Sen's position, in a sense has utilized Donnellan's position and has also gone beyond the Donnellian scheme in some of its aspects. In this article, I have tried to develop Sen's position more analytically and systematically to combat Quinean objection. Now Sen's way of projecting non-singular reference of a singular term and its showing of two instances as blind non-singular reference and sighted non-singular reference may, however, be questioned. It seems, however, the whole controversy as to the possibility of quantification in a modal context reduces to the issue as to whether a singular term in a modal context is referential or non-referential. According to Sen, a singular term in a modal context may be referential. Really, the perspective from which Sen handled the problem is different from that of Quine. Quine was looking for the position for a singular term in classifying types of reference, whereas from the same motive Sen was considering the use of a singular term.

Another important contribution of Sen is re-construal of substitutional interpretation of quantification. It was a great contribution of Ruth Barcan Marcus, the pioneer of Quantified Modal Logic, to introduce substitutional interpretation of quantification. No doubt, there are lots of controversies among the logicians themselves as how to interpret quantification. The whole scene as to the nature of quantification may be mapped in the following way:

1. The standpoint of the absolutist who maintains that substitutional quantification to be wholly different from the objectual interpretation of quantification.
2. The standpoint of the non-absolutist is less rigid in maintaining the distinction between the substitutional quantification and objectual interpretation of quantification. Even among the non-absolutists we observe different shades of opinion.
   (a) There are some non-absolutists who maintain that substitutional quantification is ultimately reducible to objectual quantification. They are said to be reductionists in thus eliminating substitutional quantification in favour of objectual quantification.
   (b) The other group does not admit that the only adequate analysis of substitutional quantification is a reductionist one.

John Wallace and Leslie Tharp, whose views are usually known as 'Wallace Tharp Thesis', maintain that substitutional quantification and objectual interpretation of quantification are not two different types of quantification, for, according to that viewpoint substitutional quantification can be reduced to objectual quantification. Another supporter of substitutional interpretation of quantification is Saul Kripke, who also maintains that substitutional quantification and objectual interpretation of quantification can be combined in a system. Sen did not maintain explicitly his allegiance to any particular group. However, according to my understanding of Sen's position, I have tried to provide a separate place for Sen. If quantification is defined, as it is defined by Sen, as a way of obtaining a sentence from sentential function, then substitutional quantification can as well share this characterization. But wherein lies the speciality of substitutional quantification? Sen has rightly emphasized the difference when he says that substitutional quantification is different from the objectual quantification so far as procedures are concerned, whereby a sentence is obtained from a sentential function. This idea might have been implicitly present in the ideas of all substitutionalists and objectualists. But what I have tried to establish is that Sen's endeavour brings out clearly, actual implications behind these assumptions.

Another problem was that of quantification into a modal context as was pointed out by Quine. What elated me most is that by following the strictures of Ruth Barcan Marcus, it is quite possible to argue that quantification is possible in a modal context. But Sen's way of terse analysis helped further to make case for substitutional reading of quantification more plausible. Of course, Sen did not discuss how the substitutional interpretation of quantification is a boon for modal logic. But I found that his way of interpreting substitutional quantification will remove some of the prejudices. If this sort of construal of quantification is accepted then that would remove the impasse created by Quine against quantified modal logic.

Chapter Six 'Pragmatic Ambiguity' originally appeared in the *Rabindra Bharati Journal of Philosophy*. In fact, a seminar was organized by the Department of Philosophy, Rabindra Bharati University on the Philosophy of Pranab Kumar Sen, in which my colleague Dr Upal Datta Gupta read out a paper entitled 'Some Referential Expressions', discussing the views of Pranab Kumar Sen about the role of expressions of the form, 'the-so-and-so' in reference. In that seminar, as a commentator, among other things, I felt the need for supplementing Dr Datta Gupta's paper by placing Pranab Kumar Sen on a longer greater historical platform of contemporary Western analytic tradition. In this particular paper, I have also tried to draw attention to some of the important consequences of this view. In this connection, once again I got the opportunity to readdress the profound philosophical question, in which Sen was particularly interested as to whether all reference is singular? The belief that all reference is singular is nicknamed by Sen as a Russellian tradition. This was pointed out very aptly by Dr Datta Gupta that Sen had put to challenge this tradition and tried to make room for non-singular reference as well. I tried to find an answer to the main issue as to what led Sen to argue for non-singular reference as well? In this connection I had to depend upon Keith Donnellan's paper, 'Reference and Definite Description', which has been acknowledged to be his source of inspiration by Sen himself. In course of this discussion what primarily occurred to me was that an attempt should be made to unearth the insight that lay hidden behind the admission of this distinction between two uses of referential distinction as admitted by Sen. It will not be a blind guesswork to suppose that Sen believes that all that matters in language are not mere syntax and semantics but pragmatics as well. The other important aspect of language, i.e. pragmatics, which is concerned with the acts of language use needs to be considered with due weightage. The strong positivistic bias of the majority of the analytic philosophers prevented them from assigning any importance to the speaker of the language, the person concerned who makes the utterance to mean something in the world. In this paper, I have seen Sen more as a supporter of later Wittgensteinian legacy than the earlier Tractarian model. Sen's putting emphasis on the functioning of language within the active, practical lives of the speakers, makes his approach different from the rigid positivistic bias of the early analytic philosophers. This also draws a line of demarcation between Sen and Quine. The recognition of pragmatic ambiguity had strong philosophical consequences in other respects also. Quine did not entertain the possibility of any pragmatic ambiguity and his failure to realize any difference in the role of singular terms in their referring functions, left just two options open before him with regard to the occurrence of a singular term in a subject position, viz. as either (1) referentially transparent, and (2) referentially opaque. In this paper, I have only dealt with its consequence in the case of quantified modal logic. In fact, in Sen's writing there is a hint for pragmatic ambiguity but he himself has not much clearly and explicitly given his views on the subject. I find the notion of pragmatic ambiguity to be of immense importance and some positive hints may be derived from Indian philosophy by utilizing its concept of *tātparya* especially with reference to the notion of *prakaraṇa*. However, in future I may concentrate on this issue in detail.

One of my very dear philosophers is Ludwig Wittgenstein. As a postgraduate student, I had the opportunity to get introduced to Wittgenstein through *Tractatus Logico-Philosophicus* (*TLP* or *Tractatus*) by Pranab Kumar Sen. Since then to my mind, Wittgenstein seemed to be wonderful; extraordinary was his style of presentation. During my thirty years of teaching career at Jadavpur University, Wittgenstein often remained as subject for my first preference under the Postgraduate/Philosophy of Language (Western Module) Course. In this volume, I am fortunate enough to get the scope for including three of my articles on Wittgenstein. In the first article in this series on Wittgenstein entitled 'The Logical Space' (Chap. 7), I have tried to focus upon the importance of the concept of logical space in Wittgenstein's

Tractarian philosophy. Before entering into a detailed discussion, I owe an apology to the critics who may sternly frown at me for trying to bring back to life what has been long ago aborted by the creator himself. Sixteen years later, in his Preface to *Philosophical Investigations*, he has written:

> . . . since beginning to occupy myself with philosophy again, sixteen years ago, I have been forced to recognize grave mistakes in what I wrote in that first book.[1]

Wittgenstein's apathy towards his earlier approach centred round not only his ideas about the nature of the relation between logic and language, but on the whole perspective that was worked out in *Tractatus*. The Tractarian perspective, however, provided impetus to many thinkers and they jumped upon its ideas to their benefit. Undoubtedly, in spite of its shortcomings as Wittgenstein himself also pointed out, some of its major ideas are captivating and have great importance in the context of philosophical discussions. This seems to me that the interpreters of Wittgenstein have spent pages after pages discussing various knitty-gritty of the Tractarian philosophy but have not paid that much attention towards his notion of logical space. The logical space of *Tractatus* encapsulates his logic, whose sublimity stuck the earlier Wittgenstein: in *Philosophical Investigations*, when he is no longer interested in tracking that sort of logic or dubious about its very existence, still very sincerely states the position of those who were sincerely stuck by the sublimity of logic as follows: 'For there seemed to pertain to logic a peculiar depth – a universal significance.'[2] But no doubt *Tractatus* is a classic of philosophy and it should not be supposed to be easier to master. Wittgenstein himself was aware of three stalwarts of European philosophy — Frege, Russell and Moore who were also mistaken in grasping his thought. In this article, I have tried to reconstruct the major ideas of Wittgenstein with strenuous effort and labour. In the writings

---

1 *Philosophical Investigations*, Preface, p. viii.

2 Ibid., 89, p. 42e.

of early Wittgenstein we come across the idea of analysis to purge out unnecessary messy and polluted elements of language and to get at the core essential logic of the language. Wittgenstein's contribution to heralding a linguistic turn of analytic philosophy has been widely acknowledged by various quarters. In *TLP*, 4.0031, Wittgenstein writes:

> All philosophy is a critique of language.

The surface grammar of language often leads to misunderstanding, unclarities and shambles that bred philosophical problems. The linguistic analysis has been made known as the received therapy for emancipation from this shambolic state by the analytic philosophers of twentieth century definitely receiving inspiration from Wittgenstein's *Tractatus*. Wittgenstein also wrote later in his 'Some Remarks on Logical Form'.[3]

> The idea is to express through appropriate symbolism what in ordinary language leads to endless misunderstandings. That is to say, where ordinary language disguises logical structure, where it allows the formation of pseudo-propositions, where it uses one term in an infinity of different meanings, we must replace it by a symbolism which gives a clear picture of the logical structure, excludes pseudo-propositions and uses its terms unambiguously.

Thus his notion of logical space accommodating logic requires to be clarified, for he was aiming to set the limits of thought, by setting the limits of language, by parcelling out region of sense from that of nonsense.

Chapter Eight, 'The Limits of Language and the Unlimited Beyond', addresses the question that very much bothered as to whether Wittgenstein's search for the limits of language was really a move to seal the domain that falls beyond the limits of language? No doubt, the influence of Wittgenstein was enormous on the group of philosophers surrounding Moritz Schlick (1882–1936) at the University of Vienna, known as the Vienna Circle, and also

---

[3] *Proceedings of the Aristotelian Society*, Suppl. vol. 9, p. 163.

became known as 'Logical Positivism'. But Wittgenstein sometimes drives crazy his interpreters to make sense out of his utterances in the light of the viewpoint of the logical positivist; in this connection, the following propositions from the *Tractatus* are worthy perusal:

> The sense of the world must lie outside the world. . . .
>
> If there is any value that does have value, it must lie outside the whole sphere of what happens and is the case. For all that happens and is the case is accidental.
>
> It must lie outside the world. – *TLP* 6.41

These quotations seem to authenticate the standpoint of those interpreters of Wittgenstein who claimed to have decipered Wittgenstein's abiding craving for mystical values. Naturally, question would arise as to whether these quoted lines match with the frame of mind of a diehard logical positivist?

He says with strong conviction:

> There are, indeed things that cannot be put into words. They *make themselves manifest*. They are what is mystical. – *TLP* 6.522

Wittgenstein has written in his *Notebooks*:

> The urge towards the mystical (*Der Trieb zum Mystichen*) comes of the non-satisfaction of our wishes by the science. – 51 (3)

The logical positivists in their eagerness to include Wittgenstein in their camp, often thought these remarks of *Tractatus*, struggling to make room for mysticism, authentic values – aesthetic, ethical and religious – are to be disregarded as scandalizing freaks. But the question still persists, how to make sense along with Wittgenstein's cry for determinacy of sense – limits of sense, his equivocation about the mystical realm. In the present essay, I have again tried to chart out the course that led to these two sorts of different interpretations of Wittgenstein. To recapitulate his starting point, it is impossible to do so without referring to the basics of his philosophy of language. But finally, I have tried to convince, it was not a self-defeat for Wittgenstein to leave the door ajar for the Unlimited Beyond. This essay tries to voice some of my beliefs about the Tractarian beyond that kept me often preoccupied since the days of my supervising MPhil dissertation entitled 'The Limits of Language' of Tamasa Chattopadhyay.

In Chapter Nine, 'Some Observations on Builder's Language', I have shifted my focus to later Wittgenstein, to his other monumental work *Philosophical Investigations*. The rarest thing in the course of history of philosophy has been achieved by a lone philosopher by initiating two distinct, often supposed to be antagonistic movements within the domain of philosophy, with thousands and thousands of followers in each trail. The second phase of transformation for analytic philosophy, Oxford philosophy, from its stagnant state geared up for a new facelift by no means independently of the influence of Wittgenstein. The kind of philosophy that displaced analytic philosophy in its post-war phase manifested the triumph of the spirit of *Philosophical Investigations* over the spirit of *Tractatus*. Wittgenstein's legacy was a new vision and new methods; the task of philosophy is not to add to the sum of human knowledge, but to enable us to attain a clear understanding of what is already known.

Philosophical Investigations begins by crticizing referential theory of meaning of the *Tractatus* and proposing another alternative model of language. Wittgenstein begins with the idea of a builder's language as a portrayal of a primitive language and its functions without any well-defined syntax or formation rules for sentences. If one does not understand the words of a sentence or their mode of combination, then one will not understand the sentence. In the builder's language the understanding of the utterance, indeed, plays a very crucial role. But how to explain the notion of understanding? According to some, any speaker's ability to use words of his language correctly is explainable in terms of a mental state. Again according to some to understand the meaning is equivalent to have acquired the ability to use the word. According to some thinkers understanding is connected with the formation of mental pictures or images. Wittgenstein does not commit to the view that having mental images is necessary for understanding. Wittgenstein does not deny the popularity of this viewpoint but he argues to establish many deficiencies of this view. In fact, in the context of builder's language, the notion of understanding plays a predominant role. Finally, I fall back upon Wittgenstein's concept of form of life to make clear his notion of understanding. In *Philosophical Investigations*, Wittgenstein rejects the *Tractarian* approach of explaining meaning in terms of truth-conditions. In *Philosophical Investigations*, Wittgenstein's approach is very much anti-essentialist. I offered some pre-version of this paper 'Wittgenstein's Notion of Understanding in *Philosophical Investigations*' as an optional paper in MPhil course for two consecutive semesters during 2011 and 2012 and was also very much profited by my discussion with MPhil students Satyajit Mondal, presently a PhD scholar under Rajiv Gandhi Scholarship Scheme of Government of India and Sumana Bera, presently Associate Professor, Department of Philosophy, Vidyasagar University, Midnapore.

In Chapter Ten, 'The Structural Universals: Arguments For and Against', views of two distinguished analytic philosophers of the twenty-first century — David Mallet Armstrong and David Kellog Lewis — have been thoroughly discussed. Armstrong was committed to a kind of immanent realism, often known as scientific realism whereas Lewis is committed to a kind of nominalism, often referred to as class nominalism. My concern with structural universals is not the result of any ad hoc decision. Demands for an adequate theory for structural universals have come from various quarters. It has come from science, from common-sensical macroscopic account of the world and also from combinatorial theorization about modality. The structural universals, like other universals, are supposed to occur repeatedly, these are instantiated by different particulars, and structural universals include other universals. In the debate between Armstrong and Lewis, Lewis does not accept structural universals whereas Armstrong strongly adduces arguments in defence of structural universals. While supervising the Ph D dissertation entitled "Revisiting Universals" by my student Bhumika Kanjilal, presently Assistant Lecturer at Durgapur Govt. College, I also had the opportunity to discuss with her once again the notion of structural universals along with many other things.

Each essay of this volume has some history behind its origination and I am indebted to many – especially to my teacher Pranab Kumar Sen and to my erstwhile students. My indebtedness to my teacher, direct and indirect, is beyond expression. I am also indebted to my PhD and MPhil scholars, to name a few, Dr Karabi Das Mahapatra, Dr Tamasa Chattopadhyay, Dr Bhumika Kanjilal, Mr Satyajit Mondal and Ms Sumana Bera for I have been enriched by dialogues and discussions with them on some of the themes that are included in this volume. Each essay of this volume, I think, is sufficiently comprehensible for a separate reading. This is not a continuously running text, hence no attempt has been made to eliminate areas of overlap between one article and another. Some slight modifications and changes have been incorporated in the articles wherever need has been felt. Chap. 7 'The Logical Space' has been translated from my previously written essay 'Youktika Parivyapti' in Bengali from *Wittgenstein: Jagat, Bhasa O Cintan*. In this volume while as an author I had to cope with issues relating to modality and quantification, or issues centring limits of expressibility and transcendence or issues relating to making sense of understanding from Wittgenstein's *Philosophical Investigations*, I find the notion of essence, the essence vs. accident debate, the thesis of essentialism obviously supersede other issues. From the Tractarian essentialist and referentialist framework, a shift to later Wittgenstein's conceiving of meaning in terms of use, rekindles the debate as to whether essentialism is to wither away. However, reconsideration of all these issues requires another volume.

This volume, as it has already been pointed out, focuses on my active engagement with some major areas of analytic philosophy. The essays that are included have already been published in some journals or anthologies. The articles entitled 'How Is '($\exists x$) (x Is Necessarily Greater than 7)' Possible? (Chap. 1), appeared in the *Journal of Indian Council of Philosophical Research*, IV(2), Spring 1987 and 'The de re Modality and Essentialism' (Chap. 2), in *Indian Philosophical Quarterly*, XI(3), July 1984. The article entitled, 'Modality and Possible Worlds' (Chap. 3) appeared in *Foundations of Logic and Language: Studies in Philosophical and Non-Standard Logic* ed. Pranab Kumar Sen, Jadavpur Studies in Philosophy, Second Series, Kolkata: Allied Publishers in collaboration with Jadavpur University, 1990. The article entitled 'A Transcendental Argument for Essentialism' projects afresh Wiggins's viewpoint to provide logical defence for essentialism, in the volume *Mind and Cognition: An Inter-Disciplinary Sharing* (the Festschrift volume in honour of Amita Chatterjee, edited by Madhuchhanda Sen, Kuntala Bhattacharya and Smita Sarkar, New Delhi: D.K. Printworld, forthcoming). Two other articles entitled, 'Sen's Views on Reference and Quantification and Their Implications in a Modal Context' (Chap. 5) and 'Pragmatic Ambiguity' (Chap. 6) appeared in *Realism, Responses and Reactions: Essays in Honour of Pranab Kumar Sen*, ed. D.P. Chattopadhyaya, Sandhya Basu, Madhabendra Nath Mitra and Ranjan Mukhopadhyay, New Delhi: Indian Council of Philosophical Research, 2000, and the other in the *Rabindra Bharati Journal of Philosophy*, VI, 2000, respectively.

Chaps. 7-9 deal directly with Wittgenstein, 'The Logical Space' (Chap. 7), appeared in *Wittgenstein: Jagat, Bhasa O Cintan*, an anthology on Wittgenstein in Bengali, ed. Tushar Kanti Sarkar, Indrani Sanyal and Shefali Moitra, Kolkata: Allied Publishers and Jadavpur University 1998; 'The Limits of Language and the Unlimited Beyond' (Chap. 8) appeared in *Philosophy, Science and Analysis* (the Festschrift volume in honour of Sibjaiban Bhattacharya), edited by Dikshit Gupta and Dilip K. Basu, 2015 New Delhi: New Delhi Publishers; and 'Some Observations on Builder's Language' (Chap. 9) appeared in the *Journal of Indian Academy of Philosophy*, 49(1-2), 2010. The article entitled 'The Structural Universals: Arguments For and Against' (Chap. 10) appeared in *Indian Journal of Analytic Philosophy*, II(1), 2007.

I am extremely thankful to all the editors or authorities concerned and institutions from where these anthologies and journals were published for giving me permission for including these articles in my present volume. I express my gratitude to the Director (Academic), Indian Council of Philosophical Research, New Delhi; Editors, *Philosophy, Science and Analysis*, New Delhi; Head of the Department of Philosophy, Jadavpur University, Kolkata; Executive Editor, *Rabindra Bharati Journal of Philosophy;* Editor, *The Journal of Indian Academy of Philosophy*, Kolkata; Editor, *Indian Journal of Analytic Philosophy*, Utkal University, Bhubaneswar; Editors, *Mind and Cognition: An Inter-Disciplinary Sharing*, D.K. Printworld, New Delhi for their kind permission.

I am grateful to Dr Gangadhar Kar, Head of the Department of Philosophy and to my colleagues at the department who have always encouraged me to publish this volume. I am also grateful to the University Grants Commission for providing the financial support for the publication of this volume and to Jadavpur University for providing all sorts of administrative support. I express my deep gratitude to Mr Susheel Mittal for all sorts of ready support. I am also grateful to Mr Rajendra Agarwal of Suryodaya Books, New Delhi for his best effort and cooperation in bringing out this volume in time.

14 March 2015 **Indrani Sanyal**

1

How Is (∃x) (x Is Necessarily Greater than 7) Possible?

THE question raised by the title of this paper may also be put in the following way: how is quantification *into* a modal context possible? No doubt, W.V. Quine's[1] strong opposition to such intermingling of quantifiers with modal operators, as are obtained when a modal operator is placed within the scope of a quantifier, has raised a controversy. Certain considerations — logical and ontological — led Quine to maintain that quantified modal logic is paradoxical. To ask 'how is "(∃x) (x is necessarily greater than 7)" possible?' is to waver between alternatives, for this question reduces itself to two sub-questions, viz.:

1. How is '(∃x) (x is necessarily greater than 7)' logically feasible?
2. How is '(∃x) (x is necessarily greater than 7)' meta-physically feasible?

Here, I would like to concentrate on the first alternative, i.e. how far '(∃x) (x is necessarily greater than 7)' is logically possible. However, it should not be supposed that the discussions regarding the metaphysical justification of quantified modal logic are either unimportant or uninteresting. What one cannot but feel is that the suspicion regarding the logical tenability of quantified modal logic has to be removed first. Of course, the logic that was born in the year 1946 out of intermingling of quantifiers with modal operators in a particular order[2] has definitely survived, and

---

1 W.V. Quine, *Reference and Modality*, pp. 139-59.

2 Ruth Barcan Marcus's paper, 'A Functional Calculus of First Order Based on Strict Implication', pp. 1-16.

certainly is fit to be a logic. Still, in the face of a strong opposition by W.V. Quine as found in many of his writings, this question requires a thorough overhauling. With that objective in view the present essay divides itself into three parts. In the first part a thorough discussion and analysis has been made of the views of W.V. Quine who maintains that quantification into a modal context is either meaningless or false. The second part concentrates on different solutions that have been offered by different logicians and philosophers to show that there is no real paradox in a quantified modal logic. This is followed by a resumé, and that is the concluding part.

I

To outline 'the logical argument' of Quine, as we may call it, wherein he gives certain formal reasons for rejecting quantified modal logic, is as follows: since it is not possible to quantify over expressions occupying referentially opaque positions, modal contexts which are also referentially opaque do not permit quantification.

The principle of substitutivity of identicals is supposed to be a test for deciding referential transparency or referential opacity of a singular term occurring in a sentence. The position for a singular term in a sentence is referential, if and only if the singular term is interchangeable with all its co-referential terms; on the other hand, the position for a singular term in a sentence is referentially opaque if the singular term is not so interchangeable. Now, we can see that the occurrence of the singular term, 'Aristotle' in the sentence "'Aristotle' is a proper name" is referentially opaque. Similarly, in the sentence, "'Tully' contains five letters", the position of 'Tully' is referentially opaque. The person called 'Tully' was also known as 'Cicero', so we see that the terms 'Tully' and 'Cicero' are co-designative terms, since both the terms refer to one and the same person. The principle of substitutivity of identicals cannot be applied to the term 'Tully' occurring in the sentence "'Tully' contains five letters". For the term 'Tully' cannot be replaced by the term 'Cicero' in this sentence. If we substitute 'Cicero' for

'Tully' in the sentence "'Tully' contains five letters", we get the sentence "'Cicero' contains five letters". But in this instance substitution has failed, for the original sentence is true, but the sentence resulting from such substitution is false. The word 'Cicero' contains more than five letters. Thus, from the failure of the principle of substitutivity of identicals it is evident that the position for the singular term 'Tully' in the sentence mentioned above is referentially opaque. In this example, 'Tully' does not refer to the object named by that expression. 'Tully' within quotes is the abbreviation of the expression, 'the word "Tully"'.

A question may, however, arise at this point: how is it that Quine, who so seriously eliminates all singular terms,[3] formulates the criterion for deciding referential opacity in terms of the failure of the substitutivity of co-referential singular terms? Quine himself was aware of some such possible objections. So, in order to avoid reference to singular terms, a second criterion has been formulated by Quine. This second criterion is in terms of miscarriage of quantification. Thus, Quine's revised way of saying that the position for a singular term is opaque, or that it is transparent, is as follows: the position for a singular term in a sentence is referentially transparent, if and only if we can quantify over the term occurring in that position; and the position for a singular term in a sentence is referentially opaque, if and only if we cannot quantify over that term occurring in that position. This reminds us one of the principles of Quine:[4] a word *W* is a name in the semantical sense of the term, if and only if quantification with respect to *W* is a valid form of inference. So it is clear that if a term does not designate, i.e. the position for the term in a sentence is referentially opaque, quantification with respect to that term is not possible.

Let us consider the sentence: 'Tully was a Roman'. By replacing the term 'Tully' by a variable 'x' we get the open sentence

'x was a Roman'.

---

[3] See Quine, *Word and Object*, pp. 181-86.

[4] Quine, 'Designation and Existence', and also 'On What There Is', p. 13.

Now this open sentence is fit for quantification. By adding an existential quantifier to this open sentence, we get the following sentence: '($\exists x$) (x was a Roman)'. Translated in ordinary language, this sentence asserts: 'There is a person x, such that x was a Roman'. This is quite meaningful. So we see that in this instance, quantification with respect to the term 'Tully' is a valid form of inference. This shows that the position of the singular term 'Tully', in the above-mentioned sentence is referentially transparent.

Again, consider the position of the singular term 'Tully' in the sentence: "'Tully' contains five letters". By replacing the term 'Tully' by a variable 'x', we get the open sentence: "'x' contains five letters". Now, when we apply existential generalization to this open sentence, we get the sentence: "($\exists x$) ('x' contains five letters)". This is utter nonsense. For here 'x' within quotes stands for the 24th letter of the English alphabet; and it is in itself a letter, and so it is ridiculous to maintain that it contains five letters. Therefore, we see that quantification is not possible in this case. This is an instance of a false sentence preceded by an irrelevant quantifier. Thus, it is shown that the position of the term 'Tully' in the above-mentioned sentence is referentially opaque.

According to Quine, terms occurring in a modal context constitute another instance of referential opacity. That the terms occurring in a modal context is referentially opaque can easily be shown by using the criterion of the substitutivity of identicals. Though the terms '9' and 'the number of planets' are co-designative, we cannot replace the term 'the number of planets' for the term '9' in the sentence: '9 is necessarily greater than 7'. Here the principle of the substitutivity of identicals fails. It is false to maintain: 'The number of planets is necessarily greater than 7'. There is nothing in the number of planets to make it necessarily greater than 7. In this instance, therefore, we find that the truth-value of that sentence resulting from the substitution is altered. It is a mere contingent matter of fact that the number of planets happen to be 9. There would not be any logical impossibility in its being either more or less than 9. According to Quine, this failure of the substitutivity of co-designative terms establishes the referential opacity of the terms occurring in a modal context.

From all these observations follow the most important view of Quine that quantification into a modal context is not possible. Quine's suggestion is, therefore, that any attempt to quantify into a modal context has to be abandoned. Disregard of this suggestion has been shown to lead either to nonsense or to unintended sense. The sentence, '9 is necessarily greater than 7', yields by the application of the principle of existential generalization: '(∃x) (x is necessarily greater than 7)'. Here, too, the question arises as to what this x is. If '(∃x) (x is necessarily greater than 7)' is true at all, then there is at least one named or nameable object of which it is true that *that* object is necessarily greater than 7. But is there any such object at all, i.e. an object, *any* of whose names could be written in the place of x in the open sentence: 'x is necessarily greater than 7'. There is no such object — 9, for example, is not such an object. If it were, we could replace '9' by its co-referential term, 'the number of planets' in that position. But we cannot do that.

Thus, according to Quine, this quantified formula, '(∃x) (x is necessarily greater than 7)', would have been true if we could say that there is a number x, such that irrespective of how it is specified, it is necessarily greater than 7. The proposition, '(∃x) (x is necessarily greater than 7)', would not violate the principle of the substitutivity of identicals, if it can be shown that x, i.e. 9, has necessary greaterness than 7, independently of any particular mode of characterization. The point is that we cannot say that x, i.e. 9, is necessarily greater than 7 irrespective of any specification, for when we specify 9 as the number of planets and say that this number is necessarily greater than 7, then what we say is false. Quantification to be possible: demands that there be an object x which is so-and-so irrespective of any particular manner of specification. To say that an object x, which is so-and-so irrespective of any particular manner of specification, is to embrace essentialism, and this Quine finds to be metaphysically objectionable.

Thus, Quine maintains that '($\exists x$) (x is necessarily greater than 7)' is either meaningless or false. But the arguments which he puts forward are not conclusive. In the first place, it should be noted that being meaningless and being false are not the same thing. The question of truth and falsity is relevant only with respect to a formula that is meaningful. The way in which Quine argues does not show the construction to be meaningless. Quine occasionally says that quantification in modal contexts is meaningless, but he does not succeed in showing, nor does he try to show, that a quantified modal formula is meaningless, *because* it is not a well-formed formula.

Now, we have to consider in detail how far Quine's objections against quantified modal logic are acceptable. It is not, however, much difficult to see that Quine's arguments against quantified modal logic rest on a number of assumptions, either explicit or implicit. In the first place, Quine takes the objectual interpretation of quantification to be the only legitimate interpretation of quantification. Second, he takes modal context to be referentially opaque, since there is a failure of substitutivity of co-referential terms. He assumes the relation of contingent identity to be sufficient as the basis of the substitutivity of co-referential terms in any context whatsoever. The fourth point to note is that, according to Quine, substitution and existential generalization always go hand in hand. None of these assumptions is beyond doubt. The proponents, on the other hand, have tried to show that a de re modal statement, if properly understood, is free from the logical difficulties Quine finds in it. In the next part, I propose to discuss some solutions that have been offered by different proponents of this particular development of modal logic. Those who seek to defend quantified modal logic do not offer, however, any unanimous solutions. Their solutions differ according as they call into question one or the other assumption of Quine. The proponents of this move may be classed broadly into two groups. Some are quite radical in their attitude, who call into question the very notion of quantification as understood by Quine. This is the approach sometimes taken by Ruth Barcan Marcus[5] and Jaakko Hintikka.[6] On the other hand, there are some who seek to establish that quantified modal logic is possible, even if we agree with Quine that the objectual interpretation of quantification is the *only* interpretation of it.

II

Quine rejects the possibility of quantified modal logic, as we have already discussed, on the ground that the positions — occupied by the singular terms in a modal context — are referentially opaque. For, according to Quine, quantification in a context is possible only if it is referentially transparent. Ruth Barcan Marcus, to begin with, is one of those who do not accept the Quinean thesis that quantification is not possible in a modal context. Marcus proceeds to show that quantification *is* possible in an opaque context by interpreting quantification in an altogether different way from that of Quine. This is possible largely because, in the case of functional calculus, no clear-cut uniform interpretation regarding the nature of quantification is available. The logicians differ among themselves in at least two ways on the question, 'how to construe quantifiers', and accordingly we have two ways of interpreting quantification, viz.:

1. The objectual interpretation of quantification or, in short, the objectual quantification; and
2. the substitutional interpretation of quantification or, in short, the substitutional quantification.

Quine prefers the objectual interpretation of quantification. This is because only the objectual interpretation of quanti-fication is supposed to preserve a close link with reality. The famous dictum of Quine,[7] as we know, is: 'To be is to be the value of a variable'.

---

5 Marcus, 'Interpreting Quantification', pp. 252-59.

6 J. Hintikka, *Models for Modalities*.

7 See Quine's paper, 'Designation and Existence', in *Readings in Philosophical Analysis*, ed. Feigl and Sellars, p. 50.

For, according to Quine,[8] a word *W* designates, if and only if existential generalization with respect to *W* is a valid form of inference. A consequence of Quine's theory is a first-order predicate calculus where only individual variables are admitted and which is not committed to the existence of property variables or proposition variables. Quine has shown that a singular term occurring in a modal context fails to refer to any object. And, for this reason, the existential generalization is not possible with respect to that term. Let us recapitulate the main points of Quine's argument once more. Now, 'x is necessarily greater than 7' is a sentential function. According to Quine, from this sentential function mentioned above we cannot infer '$(\exists x)$ (x is necessarily greater than 7)'; i.e. we cannot infer that there is something, which is necessarily greater than 7. For, here, the question arises: what is this object? Is it 9, i.e. the number of planets? But to suppose this is to conflict with the fact. Hence Quine concludes that quantification is not possible in a modal context.

Marcus, however, does not find any reason for upholding the objectual interpretation of quantification to be the only possible interpretation. Rather, Marcus considers the substitutional interpretation of quantification to be one of the fruitful interpretations of quantification. What is novel about this substitutional interpretation of quantification? Like the objectual quantification, the substitutional quantification is also a way of obtaining a sentence from a sentential function. But the objectual quantification and the substitutional quantification are different so far as procedures are concerned by which a sentence is obtained from a sentential function. The difference between these two sorts of interpretation of quantification will be evident if we carefully consider some examples. Suppose there is a sentential function 'x is human'. Now, in the case of the objectual quantification either by adding a universal quantifier or an existential quantifier, we may obtain the following two sentences:

---

8 Quine, 'Designation and Existence', in *Readings in Philosophical Analysis*, ed. Feigl and Sellars, p. 50

1. For all x, x is human.
2. For some x, x is human.

Or to put it in symbols

1′. $(x)\ (Hx)$.

2′. $(\exists x)\ (Hx)$.

On the other hand, in the substitutional quantification, as its very name suggests, stress is on the substitution instances. The substitutional quantification is a way of obtaining sentences from a sentential function by describing it in terms of its true substitution instances. In the case of the substitutional interpretation of quantification, the universal quantifier '(x)' and the existential quantifier '$(\exists x)$' are interpreted respectively as follows:

1. All substitution instances of 'Fx' are true.
2. Some substitution instances of 'Fx' are true.

Given a sentential function 'x is human', we can characterize this sentential function in either of two ways:

1. All substitution instances of 'x is human' are true sentences.
2. Some substitution instances of 'x is human' are true sentences.

Thus, we see all or some of the substitution instances of a given sentential function, may be said to be true. However, to say that all or some substitution instances of a sentential function are true is to presuppose that there are actually substitution instances, all of which or some of which are true. Now, given any sentential function, say, 'Fx', we have to see what the substitution instances are that can be derived from it. The substitution instances of a sentential function are the result of replacing the variable occurring in that sentential function by a name. Sometimes, it may happen that all the substitution instances of a sentential function are true. If, in terms of *all* of those true substitution instances, the sentential function is described, we get the sentence: 'All the substitution instances of the sentential function "Fx" are true'. Again, it may sometimes happen that some of the substitution instances of a given sentential function are true. Naturally, in this case, the sentence that is obtained by characterizing the sentential function is different; here, we get the sentence: 'Some substitution instances of the sentential function "*Fx*" are true'. What we have said can be expressed more elaborately by saying: there is a name (or at least one name) such that, when the name is written in place of the variable "*x*" in the sentential function, '*x* is human', the result is a true sentence.

A careful observation from what has been said so far will reveal an important point of distinction between the objectual quantification and the substitutional quantification. In the case of the objectual quantification, we are required to use the sentential function to get a sentence; whereas, in the case of the substitutional quantification, a sentence is obtained by characterizing the sentential function in terms of its true substitution instances.[9] This is somewhat like using a word, say, 'table' to obtain the sentence 'the table is brown' and also characterizing the word 'table', as 'having five letters' to obtain the sentence 'the word "table" has five letters'.

It may be objected that the substitutional quantification has no link with reality, hence it is futile to interpret quantification substitutionally. In the case of the substitutional quantification, our concern is only with some linguistic entities. Therefore, those sentences that are obtained through substitutional quantification have nothing to do with reality. Such objections are, however, based on certain misconceptions, because all the sentences that we obtain by the substitutional quantification are the result of the characterization of the sentential function in terms of its true substitution instances. Therefore, we see that in this case prior to characterizing a sentential function in terms of its true substitution instances we must have some idea as to whether the resulting substitution instances are true or not. The moment we talk about the truth and falsity of the substitution instances the context of

---

[9] Section II of P.K. Sen, 'Variables and Quantification'.

reality definitely comes in. If we are confined to linguistic entity only, the question of truth and falsity cannot arise at all. Therefore, those who think that the substitutional quantification is devoid of reference to reality are mistaken. The substitutional interpretation of quantification itself can be of two sorts.[10]

1. It is possible that substitution is taken in a purely linguistic or syntactical manner. The whole of our previous discussion is about this type of substitution.
2. But it is also possible, as Marcus points out, substitution is understood in terms of such ontological categories as individuals and properties within the framework of substitutional quantification.

P.K. Sen elaborates the technical details of the substitutional quantification taken in its second sense. We have already noticed that the sentence, 'There is some substitution instance of the sentential function "x is human" which is a true sentence', says the same as 'There is a name such that when the name is written in place of the variable x in the sentential function "x is human" the result is a true sentence'. In this case, we can understand substitution instances in terms of some ontological categories so that it is not totally devoid of any reference to object. This is as follows:

> There is an individual (or at least one individual) such that, when the name of that individual is written in place of the variable x in the sentential function 'x is human', the result is a sentence which is true.[11]

At this point, however, an important question may arise: are these linguistic and non-linguistic versions of the substitutional quantification equivalent? This is quite doubtful. These two sentences that we have obtained from the sentential function 'x is human' by the substitutional quantification would be logically equivalent, only if we can maintain: (a) for every individual there is a name; and also (b) for every name there is an individual.

---

[10] Section II of P.K. Sen, 'Variables and Quantification'.

[11] Ibid.

Similarly, the two sentences that we may obtain from the sentential function, 'Socrates *F*' by the substitutional quantification are logically equivalent, only if we could establish a correlation between properties and predicates.

From the above discussion, the following points emerge: first, we see that the substitutional quantification can be understood in two ways — either as being concerned exclusively with linguistic entities or as having some extra-linguistic reference as well. Second, however, we see that if substitution is taken as linguistic characterization it is beyond all controversy; but when substitution is understood in terms of ontological categories it is not equally uncontroversial. Third, we see that substitution, even if understood in terms of linguistic entities alone, cannot be said to be totally devoid of extra-linguistic reference. For, in this case, there is a reference to truth. And the notion of truth fails to make any sense unless it is taken to involve some extra-linguistic reference.

What is more important for our purpose is that, if we interpret quantification substitutionally, we can easily apply it to a modal context as well. Quine's main objection is that a modal context exhibits referential opacity, so quantification is not possible. But when quantification is interpreted substitutionally, we need not maintain any distinction between positions that are referentially transparent and the positions that are referentially opaque. If quantification is thus understood, we can have existential generalization with respect to a word *W* even if it does not designate any object. So, Marcus thinks that, though a modal context is referentially opaque, we can have existential generalization in this case. Hence, for Marcus, the supposed paradox is really non-existent. Let us consider the following sentential function: 'x is necessarily greater than 7'. From the above sentential function we can obtain by substitutional quantification: 'there is some substitution instance of the sentential function, "*x* is necessarily greater than 7" which is a true sentence'. What can be the substitution instance here? We can see that there is a name such that when it is written in place of the variable x in the sentential function 'x is necessarily greater than 7', the result is a sentence which is true. Thus, if we write '9' in place of x in the sentential function mentioned above, we get '9 is necessarily greater than 7'. Hence we find that there is at least one substitution instance of the sentential function, 'x is necessarily greater than 7' which is true. So, Marcus concludes that we can have quantified modal logic.

This substitutional interpretation of quantification is not merely an ad hoc device on the part of Marcus to save quantified modal logic. Marcus discusses in detail in her paper 'Interpreting Quantification'[12] the different advantages of this substitutional interpretation of quantification.

Quine, however, does not find the substitutional view of quantification to be so smooth sailing as its supporters claim it to be. According to Quine, there are some serious drawbacks of the substitutional quantification. To quote Quine:[13]

> To take it as substitutional would require assuming in our language a name, or some uniquely designating expression, for every individual, every creature or particle, however, obscure and remote; and this would be artificial at best.

Second, Quine points out that if there be any unspecifiable object, the substitutional quantification is bound to fail. According to classical mathematics, as Quine argues, the real numbers are non-denumerably infinite, but there can be only denumerably many expressions — be it simple or complex; so, if quantification is construed substitutionally, we cannot have quantification over real numbers. But, Quine points out, if quantification is interpreted objectually, there would not be any difficulty in having quantification over real numbers.

Let us consider how far Quine's argument against the

---

12 See Marcus, 'Interpreting Quantification', pp. 254-55.

13 Quine, 'Reply to Professor Marcus', in *The Ways of Paradox and Other Essays*, pp. 182-83.

substitutional quantification is acceptable. So far as the first argument of Quine is concerned, we can see clearly that it depends on certain presuppositions: in the first place, Quine presupposes that for substitutional quantification to be valid every object should have a name. Second, Quine thinks that, even if it is possible to assign a name to every object, that would be an artificial device. Now, what is a substitutional quantification? Given a sentence frame '*x* is human', we obtain by the substitutional quantification the sentence:

> Every substitution instance of 'x is human' is true.

When we are called upon to explain further what do we mean by the 'substitution instance', we express it as follows: it is the result of writing any name in place of the variable *x* in the open sentence '*x* is human'. So it appears that Quine is right in so far as he holds that for substitutional quantification to be valid every object should have a name. But why Quine calls it 'to be an artificial device' is not clear. In a sense, all names are given artificially. Let us consider a naming ceremony. Supposing a man wants to name his baby. His wife say: 'Let us call him "John"'. The man agrees. Thus, the baby is named 'John'. But can we maintain that because this naming ceremony is an artificial way of conferring a name on an object, viz. a baby, this name 'John' is no name at all? Perhaps, Quine would also not like to maintain anything like this.

We may now turn to a consideration of Quine's second objection to substitutional quantification. The objection can be formulated in the form of an argument as follows:

PREMISE 1: Since there can be only denumerably many names which can be substituted for *x*, there can be only denumerably many substitution instances of ϕx.

PREMISE 2: Objects of some domains are non-denumerably many, e.g. real numbers.

CONCLUSION: If there is a quantification over objects in such a domain, say, over real numbers, this quantification cannot be interpreted substitutionally.

Here, too, Quine's objection rests on certain questionable assumptions. In the first place, Quine maintains that real numbers are non-denumerably many. But the idea of non-denumerable infinity itself is controversial. However, for the sake of argument, we may grant this premise to Quine. Still, Quine's conclusion is not acceptable.

Quine further assumes that names of objects are to be as numerous as the objects themselves, if the objects are to be nameable at all. Quine supposes that there must be a one–one correspondence between objects and names like this:

$$0_1 \qquad N_1$$
$$0_2 \qquad N_2$$
$$0_3 \qquad N_3$$
$$0_4 \qquad N_4$$

But we can see that it is gratuitous to suppose that this must be the case. We should not demand that there be any such one–one correspondence between names and objects. It is not necessary to assign names to all individuals at a time. We can, and usually do, name objects as and when necessary, though we do not *have* to use a new name each time. Rather, it is often the case that we call different objects by one and the same name. 'John' may be the name of a boy of age four, of an old man and also the name of my neighbour's pet dog. We are not assigning here a different name to each object. In fact, a realistic view of the relation between objects and names is not that it is one–one, but that it is many–one.

Further we can see that

1. every substitution of ϕx is true, i.e.:
2. for all *S*, if *S* is (used as) a substitution instance of ϕx, then *S* is true.

To say 1 or 2, it is not necessary that we should be able to assign a different name to every object. It seems that Quine does not take seriously the difference between being able to assert 1 or

2, and being able to assert the following:

$$\phi a \cdot \phi b \cdot \phi c \cdot \phi d$$

We may elaborate our point as follows.

The quantified sentence 'every substitution instance of ϕx is true' can be read as 'for all S, if S is a substitution instance of ϕx, then S is true', where S is a variable ranging over sentences as values and the quantification over S itself, by contrast with the quantification over x, is objectual. Thus understood, the quantified sentence is not committed to the actual existence of any substitution instance of ϕx, although it is committed to the actual existence of sentence, just as the quantified sentence, 'for all x, if x is a freely moving body, then x, never comes to a rest', is *not* committed to the actual existence of freely moving bodies, although it is to the actual existence of individuals. Thus, under this interpretation, a universal *substitutional* quantification over real numbers, or any non-denumerably infinite set of objects, will be taken to make a *conditional* assertion to the effect that 'if a sentence is a substitution instance of ϕx with respect to any of these non-denumerably infinite objects, *then* the sentence is true. *This* conditional assertion can be true, even if there does not *actually* exist a substitution instance of ϕx with respect to each of these non-denumerably infinite objects. Therefore, we can see that we do not have any ground for accepting Quine's view.

We must acknowledge, however, that our treatment of substitutional quantification has not been adequate. But this need not detain us, for defending substitutional quantification is only one of the ways of defending quantification in modal contexts.

Hintikka, too, does not find any real paradox in quantified modal logic. He endeavours to find out actually what is meant by saying that quantification is not possible into a modal context. What are the obstacles on the way of having quantified modal logic? To find an answer to this question, we need to discuss, first, a positive instance where quantification is possible. This will enable us to elaborate the conditions, on fulfilment of which quantification would be possible. While arguing for quantified modal logic, Hintikka does not subscribe to an altogether different sense of quantification from that of Quine. What he wants to point out is that the objectual quantification has been unnecessarily linked up with certain other presuppositions. This will be clear if we closely analyse the Quinean argument to dethrone quantified modal logic. Quine discovered a close link between a name and existence. For, according to Quine, from the semantical point of view, not every singular term which has the grammatical form of a designator is a name, but only those expressions which do actually designate are so. Variables replace names and are replaceable by names. So Quine further concludes that a word *W* designates if and only if existential generalization with respect to *W* is a valid form of inference. So, according to Quine, quantification is not possible with respect to any and every singular term. We can apply quantification only to those terms that really designate some object or other. According to Quine, quantification is not possible with respect to empty singular terms or such terms which, because of the very peculiarity of the context in which they occur, fail to refer to the object. Thus understood, quantification has an existential presupposition. This 'existential presupposition is', as Hintikka puts it, 'a presupposition to the effect that a singular term to be substitutable by a variable, must stand for what exists'.[14]

Hintikka considers this existential presupposition to be one of the unwarranted assumptions made about quantification, and he wants to dissociate this 'existential presupposition' from the notion of quantification. This existential presupposition of quantification may not raise any problem so long as we are confined to the descriptive uses of the language. Unfortunately, however, we do not always remain confined to the realm of the descriptive uses of the language. Rather, sometimes we like to say what would have happened if a particular individual did not exist, and there is nothing illogical in our saying some such thing. Hence we see that the need

[14] Hintikka, 'Existential Presuppositions and Their Elimination', p. 27.

for eliminating existential presupposition is the need for talking about individuals that do not exist in the actual world.

However, even if we succeed in dissociating the existential presupposition of quantification, that would not by itself solve the problem of combining modality with quantification. Those who believe that quantification has an existential presupposition demand further that the substitution value of a bound individual variable must be a singular term which refers to some well-defined individual or object. Hintikka calls this 'the uniqueness presupposition'[15] of quantification. The point becomes clear if we consider Quine's argument for the impossibility of quantification in a modal context. Quine argues that we cannot apply existential quantification to the open sentence, 'x is necessarily greater than 7'. By applying existential quantification we shall obtain the sentence, '$(\exists x)$ (x is necessarily greater than 7)', which, in plain words, states that there is some (unique) object which is necessarily greater than 7. But this cannot be maintained in a modal context. Quine supposes that the presupposition of uniqueness pertains to the very notion of quantification; and since this presupposition of uniqueness cannot be fulfilled in a modal context, it is held that quantified modal logic is not possible. Hintikka, however, wants to dispense with this presupposition of uniqueness as well in a modal context. To quote Hintikka:

> What one needs in the theory of modal logics is in my opinion quite literally a presuppositionless logic or 'free logic' (to use this unfortunate label), namely a logic without[16] presuppositions of uniqueness.

Why is it that there is a failure of the presupposition of uniqueness in a modal context? Hintikka sees very clearly that there is an *ambiguity in reference* of a singular term occurring in a modal context. And this ambiguity in reference of a singular term presents serious problems to modal logic. The problem is that,

---

[15] Hintikka, 'Existential and Uniqueness Presupposition', pp. 125-26.

[16] Hintikka, op. cit., p. 114.

as Hintikka shows clearly, there are at least two distinct ways in which a singular term refers to its object. A singular term (occurring in the subject position of a sentence) may have either a simple (or unique) reference or multiple reference. When a singular term refers to one and the same individual in different possible worlds, that singular term is said to have unique reference. A singular term *x* will be said to have an unique reference if that singular term *x* refers to an object, say, *a*, not only in the actual world *W*, but also in all other possible worlds $W_1, W_2, W_3, \ldots, W_n$. We may represent Hintikka's notion of unique reference picturesquely as follows:

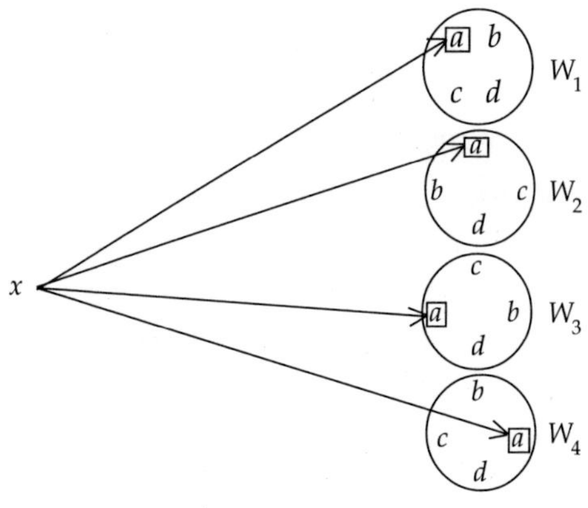

In this diagram, *x* stands for the singular term, '→' indicates reference of the singular term, and *a* has been put in a square to indicate that it is the referent of *x* in different possible worlds. W_1, W_2, W_3 and W_4 are different possible worlds.

But this is not the only way in which a singular term may refer to its object. Often a singular term refers, but not to one and the same individual in different possible worlds. When a singular term has multiple references, the referent of the singular term is not fixed. Or, to put it more technically, under circumstances of its multiple references, the referent of the singular term cannot be said to be any well-defined individual. Hintikka's notion of multiple references can be represented as follows:

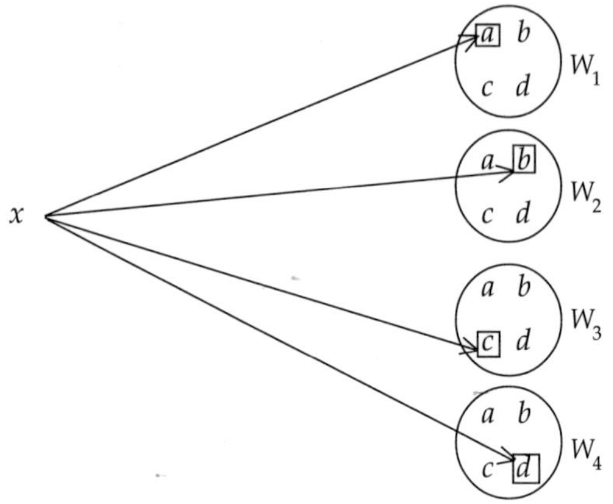

In this diagram, x stands for the singular term, '→' represents reference. Letters that are in squares stand for the referent of x in different possible worlds, and W_1, W_2, W_3 and W_4 represent different possible worlds.

Hence we see that a modal statement in which a singular term occurs may have either unique reference or multiple references. So such modal statements must also admit of alternative interpretations accordingly as the referring function of the singular term is understood.

Thus, the controversial sentence, 'the number of planets is necessarily greater than 7', is amenable to two alternative interpretations accordingly as the singular term, 'the number of planets', has either unique reference or multiple references. Now, in this world of ours, the number of planets is 9. Hence we see that, in this actual world, the singular term, 'the number of planets', refers to 9. If this singular term refers to 9 not only in this actual world, but also in W_2, W_3 and W_4, then the reference of the singular term can be said to be a well-defined individual.

But we have already pointed out that there is another alternative way of referring to a singular term. It is true that, in this actual world, the number of planets is 9. But, in other possible worlds, the number of planets may be four, five or any other number. So the term 'the number of planets' may refer to 5 in W_2, 4 in W_3, and so on. Thus, the term 'the number of planets', refers to different things in different possible worlds. Therefore, we see that a singular term may have multiple reference, and, thus, fail to have uniqueness of reference. It is this fact that a singular term sometimes refers to more than one object that creates the paradox. Two terms, say, a and b, may refer to one and the same individual in the actual world, thus making the identity $a = b$ true, but may fail to refer to the same object in some other world. In this case, a and b can fail to be intersubstitutable. The terms, 'the number of planets' and '9', refer to the same individual in the actual world, and this makes the identity 'the number of planets = 9' true in the actual world. But, in some other world, where the number of planets is either more or less than 9, the terms, 'the number of planets' and '9', will not be intersubstitutable for one another in that world. Hence the identity 'the number of planets = 9' also fails to be true in that world. Therefore, we see that multiplicity of reference of a singular term is an obstacle on the way of having quantified modal logic, because that demands that the identity be true in all possible worlds, not only in the actual. At least, this is the way in which Quine argues. For, as we have already pointed out, there is, according to Quine, a presupposition of uniqueness associated with quantification. Under the different courses of events that are possible in different possible worlds, the term, 'the number of planets', would refer to different numbers. Hence we cannot go from a statement, however true, about these different individuals to a statement that says that there is some (unique) object, of which the property of being necessarily greater than 7 is true.

So Hintikka suggests that the condition for the quantifier has to be modified, and this uniqueness presuppositon of quantification has to be eliminated. If we eliminate the uniqueness presupposition of the quantification, then it will no longer be required to maintain that the substitution value of a bound individual variable be some well-defined individual. In that case, we can as well take any individual that is not well defined to be the substitution value of the bound individual variable. So even when the term 'the number of planets' refers to different individuals in different worlds, there is no difficulty in having quantification. For when we say

$$(\exists x)\ (x \text{ is necessarily greater than } 7)$$

we mean only that there is some object (non-unique, i.e. an object which may be different in different worlds) of which the same is true.

These are the arguments by which sometimes Hintikka and sometimes Marcus try to defend quantified modal logic. But one should not fail to notice here that these defensive arguments, either of Marcus or of Hintikka, propose some vital changes in the framework from which Quine opposes. Quine actually does not say anything about the possibility or impossibility of substitutional quantification in a modal context. Neither Quine is eager to develop a presuppositionless logic of quantification as proposed by Hintikka. Hence it may be asked by some whether these logicians really succeed in refuting Quine's arguments. However, even if any such objection is raised, we need not be at a loss to defend modal logic. That is, even by retaining objectual interpretation of quantification along with its uniqueness presupposition, we can show that '($\exists x$) (x is necessarily greater than 7)' is neither meaningless nor false.

All the hues and cries about the paradox in a quantified modal logic were raised, because Quine and other anti-modalists failed to notice that there are some basic differences between an extensional point of view and a modal point of view. Generally speaking, Arthur Smullyan,[17] F.B. Fitch,[18] Hintikka,[19] Marcus[20] and many others capitalized over this weakness of Quine. In particular, Smullyan and Fitch draw our attention to the fact, which Quine failed to notice, that a proper description behaves differently in a

---

[17] A.F. Smullyan, 'Modality and Description', pp. 35-43.

[18] F. B. Fitch, 'The Problem of the Morning Star and the Evening Star', pp. 81-95.

[19] Hintikka, *Models for Modalities*.

[20] Marcus, 'Extensionality', pp. 44-51.

modal context from an extensional context. Again Marcus, Hintikka and Prior[21] find that the principle of substitutivity, on the basis of which substitution of co-referential terms is made, in a modal context, has to be founded on a stronger notion of identity than in an extensional context.

Smullyan, Fitch, etc. salvaged quantified modal logic by showing that the apparent paradox is due to the scope–ambiguity of the descriptive phrase occurring in a modal context. In the cited example, we find that a descriptive phrase occurs with a modal operator in the same sentence. So, unless the scope of the descriptive phrase is clearly stated, ambiguity persists, and the alleged paradox arises. As shown earlier, the critics of quantified modal logic argue that, in this case, from the propositions:

1. 'the number of planets =9', and,
2. 'it is necessary that 9 is greater than 7',
3. we derive the conclusion: 'it is necessary that the number of planets is greater than 7'.

Smullyan does not deny that this conclusion is false. Rather, he traces back the falsity of this conclusion to the scope–ambiguity of the descriptive phrase, viz. 'the number of planets' occurring in the conclusion. Whether the occurrence of the description is primary or secondary in this instance has to be made explicit. In the absence of any clear statement regarding the scope of the description, its occurrence in a sentence is amenable to more than one interpretation. The intended sense of the sentence may not be conveyed, if we consider any one of the alternatives at random. Actually, this is what happens in a modal context. Thus, the conclusion, 'it is necessary that the number of planets is greater than 7', may mean any one of the following:

(a) As a matter of fact, the number of planets is such that it is necessarily greater than 7.

---

21 A.N. Prior, 'Is the Concept of Referential Opacity Really Necessary?', p. 195.

(b) It is necessary that the number of planets is greater than 7.

In (a), the description, 'the number of planets', has a primary occurrence and has a wider scope in the sentence. But in (b), it is clear that the same description, 'the number of planets', has a different kind of occurrence, a secondary occurrence, having a narrower scope in the sentence.

The critics of quantified modal logic overlook this ambiguity lurking in the conclusion: 'it is necessary that the number of planets is greater than 7'. They take the conclusion at its face value. But thus interpreted, i.e. when a description occurring in a proposition is given a narrower scope, the proposition is false. Smullyan shows that the argument to be valid should stand as follows:

1. The number of planets = 9.
2. It is necessary that 9 is greater than 7.
3. Therefore, as a matter of fact, the number of planets is such that it is necessarily greater than 7.

Thus we see that in this instance the proposition containing the descriptive phrase and a modal operator is true, provided the description has a primary occurrence.

But why do some people fail to notice that a descriptive phrase occurring with a modal operator induces scope–ambiguity? It would not be totally justified to say that, since these critics are accustomed to extensional logic, they fail to notice that a description may sometimes induce scope–ambiguity, for none of the extensionalists denies that the descriptive phrase, 'the present King of France', induces scope–ambiguity. It is realized by Russell and Whitehead that it is necessary to indicate unambiguously the scope of a description in each of such cases. An example may illustrate the point: 'The present King of France is not bald'.

Two interpretations of this sentence are possible as the description, 'the present King of France', has either a primary occurrence or a secondary occurrence.

(a) 'The present King of France is not bald' may be read as, 'it is not the case that the present King of France is bald'. In this case, x in the propositional function, 'x is bald', is substituted by 'the present King of France is bald', and then the result is denied. So, in this case, the scope of the description does not cover the whole of the proposition in which it occurs. This is a secondary occurrence of the description, hence it is narrower in scope. Here negation enjoys a wider scope. In this interpretation of description, the above-mentioned proposition is true.

(b) Another interpretation of this description is possible. This interpretation provides a primary occurrence to the description and thus understood the sentence may be read as: 'the present King of France is such that he is not bald'. According to this interpretation, the description, 'the present King of France', has a wider scope. But in this reading of the scope of the description, the above proposition is false.

But in the truth-functional context, the scope of the description is not at all important when (ιx) (Fx) exists. The description where (ιx) (Fx) exists may be said to be a proper description. 'The present prime minister of India' is a proper description, whereas 'the present king of India' cannot be said to be a proper description. If a description is a proper description and is contained in a truth-functional proposition, then it does not induce any scope–ambiguity. With respect to a truth-functional proposition containing a proper description, it is irrelevant whether we interpret that description as having either a primary occurrence or a secondary occurrence therein. For a truth-functional proposition containing a proper description has the same truth-value in either interpretations. Bertrand Russell and A.N. Whitehead maintain[22] in their *Principia Mathematica*:

> It will be seen further that when $E!$ (ιx) (Fx) we may enlarge or diminish the scope of (ιx) (Fx) as much as we please without altering the truth-value of any proposition in which it occurs.

---

22 *Principia Mathematica*, vol. I, p. 70.

Under these circumstances (ιx) (Fx) behaves like a logically proper name.

Let us concentrate on the following examples for further clarifications. 'The present prime minister of India' is a description and, indeed, a proper description. 'The present prime minister of India is not bald' is an instance, where a proper description occurs in a truth-functional context. We can interpret this proposition containing a description in two ways by giving either a primary occurrence or a secondary occurrence to the description.

1. When we give a wider scope to the description, 'the present prime minister of India', we obtain the following proposition: 'The present prime minister of India is such that he is not bald'. In this proposition the description, 'the present prime minister of India', enjoys a primary occurrence. This proposition is true.
2. The descriptive phrase, 'the present prime minister of India', has a secondary occurrence, for it is given a narrower scope in the proposition: 'It is not the case that the present prime minister of India is bald'. But in this interpretation also the above-mentioned proposition is true.

Now, what is so far stated and explained on behalf of the extensionalists is uncontroversial. It is a fact that a description, when it is not a proper description occurring in a truth-functional context; does induce scope–ambiguity; whereas a proper description occurring in a truth-functional context does not at all lead to scope–ambiguity. From the above observations regarding the behaviour of descriptions occurring in a truth-functional context, they were led to generalize that a proper description does not induce any scope–ambiguity in any context whatsoever. In this, they are, however, not at all justified. In fact, no parallel can be drawn between a proper description occurring in a truth-functional context and a modal context. That even a proper description can induce scope–ambiguity is something of which extensional logicians were not aware. So Quine and others, failed to see from their extensional point of view, that a proper description like 'the number of planets' induces scope–ambiguity. Possibly on this account they did not take into consideration the implications of scope–ambiguity of the terms like 'the number of planets' in modal context. This, I think, is one of the greatest achievements of Smullyan and Fitch to draw our attention to the difference between an extensional point of view and a modal point of view. In a modal context whether a description is proper or not is immaterial for any and every description does induce scope–ambiguity. This account of scope–ambiguity as given by Smullyan and Fitch cannot, however, be regarded as complete. For they did not discuss anything about the proper name and its occurrence in a modal context. Saul Kripke[23] utilizes the notion of scope–ambiguity. According to Kripke, Smullyan and Fitch are right in so far as what they have said. But Kripke felt that there are certain other features of the Russellian theory that need to be rectified in order to accommodate quantified modal logic. Kripke thinks that Russell is mistaken in his view regarding the nature of ordinary proper names.

For Russell ordinary proper names are more like descriptions. In the first place, both descriptions and ordinary proper names may lack denotation. But logical proper names are, according to Russell, such that they can never lack denotation.

In the second place, when an ordinary proper name or definite description does not lack denotation there is no scope–ambiguity. A logically proper name, on the other hand, never lacks a denotation, so there is no scope–ambiguity. That is why a logically proper name can be taken in either of two ways, i.e. we can give it either a wider-scope interpretation or a narrower-scope interpretation. And, in either interpretation the proposition containing a logically proper name is true. This reflects, according to Russell, that the logical behaviour of a description and an ordinary proper name is the same. That is why Russell maintained that ordinary proper names are 'truncated descriptions'.

---

[23] Saul Kripke, 'Naming and Necessity'.

Kripke, however, does not accept the Russellian view that ordinary proper names are 'truncated descriptions'. Kripke considers Russellian view to be entirely wrong. According to Kripke, it is not the case that ordinary proper names induce scope–ambiguity. It is only a description that does so. The same thing can be put in other words by saying that descriptions induce de re/de dicto ambiguities in a modal context, while proper names, including the ordinary ones, do not. This notion of scope–ambiguity is, in fact, closely related to the de re/de dicto modal distinctions. Because there is scope–ambiguity in a modal context, we have two interpretations of modal propositions either as de re or as de dicto. When a description has a wider scope, the modal operator has a narrower scope. Let us consider our example again: 'the number of planets is necessarily greater than 7'. If it is taken to be true as meaning 'the number of planets is such that it is necessarily greater than 7', the definite description, 'the number of planets', is understood to have a wider scope. Here we are saying of *the number*, which is (i.e. happens to be) the number of planets, that it has the property of being greater, and necessarily greater, than 7. This is, therefore, a clear instance of de re modality. The Latin phrase de re implies that in this variety modals qualify the thing about which something is said.

When a description has a narrower scope, the modal operator has a wider scope. To take an example; 'it is necessary that the number of planets is greater than 7'. In this instance, the description, 'the number of planets', has a narrower scope. Here a modal property attaches to the whole of the proposition. Such, a case as this is known as a de dicto case. Kripke thinks that this sort of de re/de dicto ambiguity is not present in cases of proper names. This is because names are rigid designators; but descriptions are not generally rigid designators. What does it mean to be a rigid designator? According to Kripke, a rigid designator is such that if it denotes anything, then it denotes that thing in every possible world (in which the thing exists). But descriptions, and so the description, 'the teacher of Alexander', may denote Aristotle in one world but some other person in another world.

So, according to Kripke, a proper name, being a rigid designator, has no sense, and thus only refers to an object. As a result, the occurrence of a proper name in a modal sentence admits of only one, viz. the de re interpretation. Michael Dummett,[24] however, does not agree with Kripke in maintaining that names are rigid disignators. We have already hinted at the semantical role of rigid designators: rigid designators do not induce de re/ de dicto ambiguity. In order to establish his point, Dummett seeks to present certain counter examples to the Kripkean theories that proper names are rigid designators. In this connection, Dummett refers to those names which have corresponding descriptions exhausting everything that we know about the bearer of the names.

Therefore, it appears reasonable to maintain that not all names but some names are 'disguised descriptions'. In this connection, we can point out that Russell's view that proper names are 'disguised descriptions' appears to be at least partially true. Under this circumstance, a need may be felt for modifying Kripke's thesis. According to this modified form, the conclusion seems to be that not all names are rigid designators; some names are non-rigid designators; and they do induce de re/de dicto ambiguity. Kripke, however, does not favour this sort of modification. Keith S. Donnellan, in one of his latest papers, 'The Contingent A Priori and Rigid Designators' very nicely synchronizes the view of Kripke with that of Dummett. Donnellan discusses two alternative ways in which a name can be introduced: (a) a name can be introduced as a rigid designator by using a description; and (b) a name can be introduced as a mere abbreviation of a description.

There is an excellent elucidation of this point in the article, 'The Necessary and the a Priori' by P.K. Sen. A description by means of which a proper name is introduced can be said *merely to fix the reference of a proper name* and not to give its meaning, only if

---

[24] Michael Dummett, *Frege: Philosophy of Language*, appendix to chap. 5.

it is not *essential* that the proper name should be introduced by means of the description which is actually used to introduce it. If it is essential that the proper name should be introduced by a certain description, i.e. there is not other means by which it could be introduced, then we cannot say that the description *merely* fixes the reference of the name. In fact, if the name is essentially introduced by a description, the description does give the name its meaning, and in that case, the name can be said to be a 'disguised description'. Donnellan, however, admits that, in an actual case, it is difficult to decide whether a name has been introduced by means of a description as a rigid designator or as an abbreviation of a description. There is no conclusive argument to establish which the point is. There is nothing like general linguistic intentions, so that the point can be decided from a mere look at the proper names. In the absence of any explicit stipulation for whether or not the name shall be taken as a rigid designator, one is at liberty to take it in either way. These two possibilities, that the name is a rigid designator and that it is an abbreviation of a description, yield difference 'in the predicted status of a certain sentence'. But this is not a 'usable difference' as Donnellan himself remarks. To quote Donnellan:

> . . . it would be indeterminate whether a name introduced by means of a description is a rigid designator or an abbreviation so long as the name continues to be pegged to the description.

This observation, however, does not cast any doubt on the thesis that names in general are rigid designators.

Now, let us try to sum up the main conclusion we have arrived at in this section. Beginning with Smullyan we have traversed a long path. And by now it seems quite clear that we have found a definite answer to the supposed paradox of quantified modal logic. This notion of scope–ambiguity proves to be a wonderful tool in the hands of the modal logicians. It is Smullyan who deserves the special credit for drawing our attention to the peculiar behaviour of descriptive phrases, especially in quantified modal context. But Smullyans' answer to the supposed paradox is incomplete. What are we to say when the same paradox is shown to be involved in a proper sentence? Kripke, as we have seen, tackles this problem quite successfully from his own special point of view.

From the above discussion, two important points emerge:

1. We can have de re modal propositions with descriptions. Smullyan hits rightly on this point.
2. We can have de re modal propositions with proper names. In this respect, the contribution of Kripke to our understanding of quantified modal logic is enormous.

So we see that the very possibility of quantified modal logic is nothing but the possibility of de re modal proposition. A de re modal proposition can be either with a description occupying the subject position or with a proper name occupying the same position. Hence we see that quantified modal logic is possible.

Ruth Barcan Marcus also notices that extensional logic and modal logic are different; so an extensional point of view cannot be co-extensive with a modal point of view. This simple truth has been ignored by those who seek to explain a modal context from the point of view of an extensionalist. Those who make a fuss over the paradoxes of quantified modal logic forget the limitations of the extensionality principle and make it the basic principle of substitution in modal contexts as well. This is really objectionable. In this case, two completely distinct issues have been mixed up, and as a consequence of that the supposed paradox arises in quantified modal logic. In fact, the following two issues need to be clearly distinguished:

(a) If identity is taken to mean the relation of material equivalence and if the principle of substitution is defined in terms of the above sense of identity, then the question as to whether the principle of substitution does apply to modal logic cannot arise at all.

(b) If we want to discuss the question as to whether the principle of substitutivity can be applied to modal logic, then the notion of identity cannot be so restricted as to take it to be the same as the relation of material equivalence (which, by its very essence, excludes non-truth functional and intentional contexts).

Coming to save quantified modal logic, Marcus adopts the second alternative course described above. She feels the need for redefining the concept of identity, i.e. she sees that our conception of the relation of identity has to be changed in such a manner that it is freed from the narrower point of view of the extensionalists. In fact, she attempts to defend quantified modal logic by exposing the absurdity of adopting the point of view of an extensionalist in modal logic.

Hence she brings in the concept of necessary identity. Marcus remarks:

> That principle seems intuitively obvious to me for if the notion of necessity makes any sense, what could be more obvious than that necessarily a thing is the same as itself. . . .[25]

Hence we see that the relation of necessary identity is presumed to function as identity in quantified modal context. But how does it solve the puzzle and the paradox? From the first observation of Marcus follows the second, which is of no less importance. If the relation of identity is taken to mean the relation of necessary identity, the principle of substitution has to be recast accordingly. Naturally, the earlier formulation of the principle of substitution, as it is presented by the extensionalists, is bound to be unsatisfactory. In a modal context, the relation of strict equivalence or necessary identity has to be made the basis for the substitution of any two co-designative terms. Marcus reformulates the principle of substitution as follows:

> Given $P \equiv Q$, P is not everywhere interchangeable with Q, but only in restricted non-modal contexts. Given $N(P \equiv Q)$, then the substitution theorem is unrestricted.[26]

---

25 Marcus, 'Comment', p. 132.

26 Marcus, 'Extensionality', p. 50.

It should be noted that, in this formulation, Marcus also makes an extraordinary use of the notion of strict equivalence, supposing it to hold also between terms as well as propositions. However, as in the case of the relation of material equivalence, so also in this case, this unconventional sense of the relation of strict equivalence is not totally unrelated to its ordinary sense. It appears that, according to Marcus, the terms t_1 and t_2 are strictly equivalent, if and only if all sentences, which are obtainable from each other by a simple replacement of t_1 by t_2 or t_2 by t_1, are strictly equivalent. So we see that, in some contexts, material equivalence is enough for identity, i.e. in those contexts we can assert $t_1 = t_2$ on the ground that the relation of material equivalence obtains. Again, in some contexts, strict equivalence alone is enough for identity, i.e. in those contexts we can assert $t_1 = t_2$ is only on the ground that the relation of strict equivalene obtains. So it is not at all difficult to see that there is a difference between the substitution conditions that are required for the relation of material equivalene and those required for the relation of strict equivalene.

It is not only Marcus but also Kripke, Prior, Hintikka and many others felt the need for the relation of necessary identity as the basis of substitution in a modal context. Prior demands that there be a genuine identity behind the substitution that is being done in a modal context.

From the writings of Smullyan and Marcus what is clear is that substitution need not present any problem to a modal context. Even so, supposing substitution fails in a modal context that does not stand on the way of existential generalization. What I propose to discuss in the present section is that the supposed association of existential generalization with substitution is a myth. To elaborate this point some clarification is sought regarding the different kinds of positions that a singular term may occupy in a sentence. This also opens up another way to show that quantification is possible in a modal context. We can indicate different uses of a singular term in a sentence in the following chart:

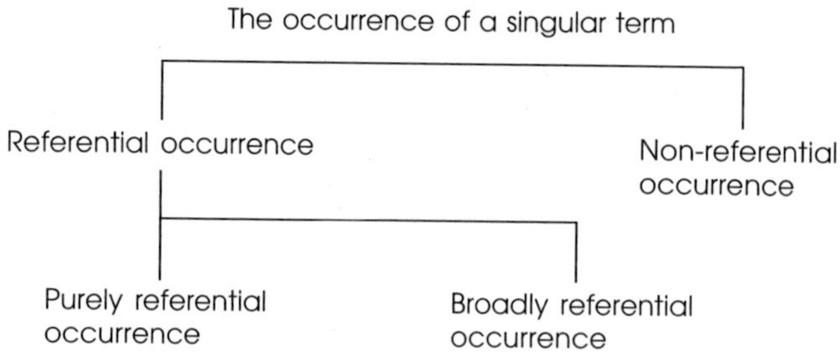

A term can be said to be used purely referentially when its one and only use is to refer to the object to which it is supposed to refer. Thus in the sentence, 'Giorgione is a chess player', the term 'Giorgione' refers to the person Giorgione. The only function that is being performed by the term 'Giorgione' in this sentence is that of referring. It does not have any other role to play. So this can be characterized as a purely referential use of the term 'Giorgione'.

This purely referential use of the term 'Giorgione' can be contrasted with the 'non-referential' use of the same term in another sentence. Let us consider the sentence: '"Giorgione" contains 9 letters'. This occurrence of the term 'Giorgione' is in sharp contrast with its earlier use. In this case the term 'Giorgione' does not refer to the person Giorgione, it refers to itself; and we are saying something about the term itself. This use of the term 'Giorgione' is said to be non-referential, for in this use the term does not refer to the person Giorgione at all. Thus we can put the matter as follows: a term is said to be used non-referentially when it is not used to, and does not refer to, the object.

But, apart from these two uses, there can be a third use of a singular term. Though Quine himself hinted at this use of a singular term, he failed unfortunately to realize the great importance of this use of the term, and thus remained unaware of the different implications of this third sort of use of a singular term. We can collect an example of such an intermediate use of the term 'Giorgione' from Quine himself. "'Giorgione' was so called because of his size"[27] is one such example of an intermediate use of the singular term.

[27] Quine, 'Reference and Modality', p. 140.

Now we know that 'Giorgione' and 'Barbarelli' are co-referential terms. But in the above sentence we cannot substitute the term 'Barbarelli' for the term 'Giorgione'. For, if we so substitute, we obtain the sentence, 'Barbarelli is so called because of his size', and that is certainly false. Now a question may arise as to why the principle of substitutivity fails to apply in this case. If a context is non-referential, then, of course, the principle of substitutivity of co-referential term would fail. But we cannot call the occurrence of the term 'Giorgione' in the sentence, 'Giorgione was so called because of his size', to be a non-referential occurrence. For here the term 'Giorgione' does refer to the person, to Giorgione. The sentence does not mean: the term 'Giorgione' was so called because of his size. Here we are not saying anything about the term, we are saying something about the person. As we have already pointed out, Quine himself characterized such occurrences only as not being purely referential. So we find that there is a sort of occurrence of a singular term that is neither non-referential nor purely referential. We may coin the term 'the broadly referential use of a singular term' to mean this sort of occurrence of a singular term. If we analyse the role of the singular term in this sentence, its difference from the earlier two roles will be evident. We have already seen that we cannot substitute Barbarelli' for the term 'Giorgione' in the sentence, 'Giorgione was so called because of his size'. Now, why is this so? The phrase 'so called' is a device of natural language to avoid repetition. We can, however, recast the above sentence to bring out clearly its logical force. Thus recast, the sentence stands as follows: 'Giorgione was called "Giorgione" because of his size'. In this sentence, "Giorgione' refers to the person Giorgione and *also* conveys certain other information as to why Giorgione was called 'Giorgione'.[28]

---

[28] Connected with the distinction between the purely referential use and the broadly referential use, there is a difference between two kinds of predication. Pranab Kumar Sen made me aware of this point. A comparison can be drawn with Donnellan's distinction between a referential use of a description and on attributive use of a description as found in his 'Reference and Definite Descriptions'.

This really opens up the way to delinking existential generalization from substitutivity.[29] Once we see that failure of substitutivity does not necessarily imply failure of reference, it is not too difficult to see that it does not necessarily imply failure of existential generalization either. However, in the particular example of broadly referential use as we have discussed existential generalization fails. It is true that from 'Giorgione was so called because of his size' we cannot infer '$(\exists x)(x$ is so called becuase of his size)', since it is not clear what 'so called' would mean in this quantified sentence. However, in the present case also, we can secure existential generalization, by paraphrasing 'Giorgione was so called because of his size' into 'Giorgione was called "Giorgione" because of his size'. From the latter sentence we *can* derive $\exists x)$ (x was called "Giorgione" because of his size)'.

Hence we see that there are instances in which existential generalization is possible, in spite of the fact that substitution of co-referential terms is not. This lesson may be carried to modal context as well. Let us consider the sentence: '9 is necessarily greater than 7'. Here the occurrence of the singular term '9' is said to be referentially opaque. Quine argues that in this instance inter-substitution of two co-referential terms '9' and 'the number of planets' is not possible for such substitution yields falsity. Since the context is thus referentially opaque, the singular term mentioned herein does not refer to any object as such, and so Quine finally concludes that existential generalization is not possible in a modal context either.

The point that emerges clearly from the preceding discussion is that the way in which Quine analyses the proposition '9 is necessarily greater than 7' is not correct. In the light of what we have said so far, we see that merely from the failure of the principle of substitutivity it does not follow that the context is referentially opaque; for, we have already shown that substitution is possible provided the singular terms occupying the subject position have a 'pure reference' to the object. Hence from the failure of the

[29] This is suggested by Pranab Kumar Sen.

substitution of co-referential terms we may conclude that a modal context is such that a singular term does not have a pure reference to the object. But it is totally unjustified to jump from this to the conclusion that since an occurrence of a singular term in a sentence is *not purely* referential, it *cannot be* referential at all. Such a conclusion would have been valid if there were only two possibilities regarding the occurrence of a singular term in a sentence. But we have tried to establish that with respect to the types of occurrence for a singular term our choice is not restricted to two; to recollect there are at least three possibilities, viz.

(a) the purely referential occurrence;

(b) the broadly referential occurrence; and

(c) non-referential occurrence.

We may concede this much to Quine that the occurrence of the term '9' in the sentence '9 is necessarily greater than 7' is not purely referential. But, certainly, here the occurrence of the term '9' is *not* non-referential or opaque either. We can take this occurrence of 9 to be broadly referential. In this case, it cannot be said that the term '9' has no reference altogether; what we can find is that the term '9' has a broadly referential use, for it *does* refer to the number 9. The term is here not used purely to refer to the object, but does some other function; it indicates or suggests, though not actually states, *why or how* 9 is greater than 7.

But we do not find any problem in these instances about existential generalization. We can well apply the rule of existential generalization. The assertion that a condition is satisfied by some named individual implies the assertion that the condition is satisfied by *at least one* individual. Now when a singular term is said to have a broadly referential occurrence as it does not fail to refer, there is no reference failure either. We can put the matter as follows: since the assertion of necessary greaterness than 7 is true of a named object, the assertion of necessary greaterness than 7 is true of *at least one* object. This amounts to saying: '($\exists x$) (x is necessarily greater than 7)' is neither meaningless nor false. Therefore, we see that de re modal sentences are possible.

III

Let us recapitulate some of the main points once more to see where do we stand. To establish that quantified modal logic involves a paradox Quine has offered two distinct arguments. One is what we have called 'the logical argument' and the other is what we have called 'the metaphysical argument'. In the present essay, as I have already made it clear, my concern is only with 'the logical argument' of Quine. So far as this 'logical argument' of Quine is concerned, we find that Quine gives certain formal reasons for rejecting quantified modal logic. To put it very briefly, Quine's argument is as follows: since a modal context is referentially opaque, we can neither apply the principle of substitutivity of co-referential terms nor the principle of existential generalization. But from what we have said so far it is clear that this argument of Quine fails. The proponents of quantified modal logic have shown conclusively, in my opinion, that there is no real paradox in quantified modal logic. They have succeeded in showing that a de re modal statement, if properly understood, is free from logical difficulties found by Quine. In this connection, I have discussed some of the following solutions that have been offered by different logicians and philosophers:

1. It has been shown that by accepting a substitutional interpretation of quantification one can have quantified modal logic. In this connection, the name of Ruth Barcan Marcus comes first to the mind.
2. Jaakko Hintikka wants modal logic to be one of the free logics in the sense of being especially free from existential presupposition and uniqueness presupposition. He shows that, thus understood, quantified modal logic is possible.
3. Occurrence of a singular term in a de re modal statement leads to ambiguity according as it is taken to have a purely referential use or a broadly referential use. The supposed paradox arises, if this ambiguity in the referring function of a singular term is overlooked and the failure of substitutivity

of co-referential terms is taken to mean only referential opacity.

4. Smullyan and Fitch salvaged quantified modal logic by showing that the apparent paradox is due to the scope ambiguity of proper descriptive phrases occurring in a modal context.
5. Again Dagfinn Follesdal has argued that a modal context is referentially transparent if a singular term keeps its reference fixed as we pass from the actual world to other possible worlds.
6. Some have shown that substitution of co-designative terms does not fail in a modal context if we take the relation of necessary identity as the basis of the substitution. This is the way in which Marcus, Prior, Kripke, Hintikka and many others argue.

There may be many other solutions. But I have considered some of these major solutions, and I think that these are enough to refute Quine's charge against quantified modal logic. Some of the solutions that I have discussed show quantification to be possible in a modal context by totally changing the Quinean notion of quantification. In this connection, we can recollect Marcus' suggestion to interpret quantification substitutionally or that of Hintikka to modify the conditions of quantifiers by eliminating the presupposition of uniqueness supposed to be associated with the notion of quantification. However, as these arguments propose some vital changes in the framework within which Quine moves, it may be argued by some that these proponents of quantified modal logic have not really succeeded in refuting Quine's arguments. But, if any such objection is raised, we need not be at a loss to defend modal logic. For, among the solutions that I have discussed, only the first and the second are of this type.

We can also discover a point of affinity among the remaining four solutions. Apparently, these are four *distinct* solutions. At least, it does not appear to be the same to say that we can have quantified modal logic:

1. if a singular term occurring in a de re modal proposition is taken to have a referential use;
2. if the singular term keeps its reference fixed as we pass from this actual world to other possible worlds;
3. if we take the scope of a definite description occurring in a de re proposition to be larger than that of the modal operator; and
4. if we take the relation of necessary identity as the basis of the principle of substitutivity in a modal context.

What I propose to establish further is that these four solutions that have been offered to solve the supposed paradox of quantified modal logic are basically the same.

Let us begin with Quine's example: '9 is necessarily greater than 7'.

The possibility of quantified modal logic is bound up with a de re understanding of this modal proposition. For the questions that are asked again and again are whether we can substitute the term '9' by the term 'the number of planets' to get the sentence, 'The number of planets is necessarily greater than 7', and whether we can infer from the above proposition by existential generalization '$(\exists x)$ (x is necessarily greater than 7)'. According to Quine, as we know, cannot, because these resulting propositions are false. On the other hand, following Marcus, Prior, Smullyan, Fitch, Hintikka, Kripke, Follesdal and many others we find that the propositions — 'the number of planets is necessarily greater than 7' and '$(\exists x)$ (x is necessarily greater than 7)' — are true.

If we carefully observe these four different solutions, we can see that all of them agree in some common points. These solutions agree in holding that the charge of paradox arises against quantified modal logic mainly because of the de re/de dicto ambiguity of the proposition 'the number of planets is necessarily greater than 7'; and most of them maintain, at least by implication, that the paradox is further caused by the fact that even as a de re proposition it suffers from another ambiguity.

Following Donnellan, it can be shown that the singular term, 'the number of planets', may either have a referential use (or purely referential use) or an attributive use (or so-called broadly referential use). Why did Quine suppose that the substitutivity of co-designative terms fails in a modal context? If a singular term is said to have an attributive use, then the attribute of being so-and-so is important. But when a definite description can be said to have a referential use, it is enough if the singular term succeeds in referring to the desired object. In that case, even if the description misfits the object, that does not matter much. Quine's error lies in his failure to realize that even in its de re interpretation, the proposition, 'The number of planets is necessarily greater than 7', is ambiguous. In its attributive use the phrase, 'the number of planets' is supposed to be necessarily greater than 7 *as* being the number of planets. So, we see, in this case the attribute of being the number of planets is all important. Certainly, the number of planets cannot be said to be necessarily greater than 7 by virtue of being the number of planets. For it is only a contingent matter of fact that the number of planets happen to be nine. So, in the case of an attributive use of the singular terms, substitution of co-designative terms, viz. 'the number of planets' and '9', is not possible. If a singular term had one use and that was its attributive use only, then we would have no other alternative than accepting the thesis that the substitution of co-designative terms is not possible in a modal context. But, fortunately, that is not the case. Furthermore, it would be noted that, though in this instance the substitution fails, there is no failure of existential generalization. A singular term may also have a referential use. When a singular term like 'the number of planets' is taken in its referential use, we can have both substitution and existential generalization. When the term 'the number of planets' is used referentially, it refers to a particular object which the speaker has in his mind in using the description. Thus, in this case, the speaker has a particular object in mind, viz. 9. Even if the number of planets is 10 in our actual world, we can substitute the term 'the number of planets', by the term '9'. If assertion of necessary greaterness than 7 is true of a named *object*, then assertion of necessary greaterness than 7 is true of the same object under a different name or description, and also the assertion is true of *at least one object*. That is, '$(\exists x)$ (x is necessarily greater than 7)' is true. We can express our modal proposition unambiguously to bring out the referential use of the description as: 'the number that just happens to be the number of planets is necessarily greater than 7'.

This immediately reminds us of Smullyan who deserves credit for showing that the supposed paradox arises for Quine failed to notice that proper descriptive phrases induce scope–ambiguity in a modal context. According to Smullyan, the proposition, 'the number of planets is necessarily greater than 7', may be read either as:

1. it is necessary that the number of planets is greater than 7, or as
2. the number of planets is such that it is necessarily greater than 7.

In proposition no. 1, the descriptive phrase 'the number of planets' has a narrower scope and the modal operator has a wider scope. When the proposition is interpreted in this way, thus by giving the descriptive phrase a secondary occurrence, it is certainly false. For, as we know, it is only a contingent matter of fact that the number of planets is 9. If it were the case that whenever a descriptive phrase occurred in a modal proposition the modal operator should have a secondary occurrence, then we would have no other alternative than accepting Quine's position as final. Luckily, however, this is not the case. A descriptive phrase occurring in a modal proposition may also have a primary occurrence in that proposition. Thus, when the description is given the wider scope as in the proposition no. 2, no such paradox arises. For here the intended interpretation is as follows: as a matter of fact, the number of planets is such that it is necessarily greater than 7. From this we can obtain by existential generalization the proposition: $(\exists x)$ (x is necessarily greater than 7). If Quine asks once more; 'what is this object x?' then we can answer '9', i.e. the number that happens to be the number of planets.

Third, Quine has argued that in a modal context we cannot substitute the term, 'the number of planets', for '9'. But this argument fails to take note of the ambiguity lurking in the identity proposition 'the number of planets = 9'. This identity statement can be taken to express either contingent identity or necessary identity. In modal logic we have to consider an individual as a member of different possible worlds. The term, 'the number of planets', may refer to 9 in W_1, to 8 in W_2, to 7 in W_3 and so on. If it does so, we cannot say that there is a necessary identity between the number of planets and 9. Neither can we say in this case that the reference of the term, 'the number of planets', is fixed. What we have here is clearly an instance of multiple reference of a singular term, and we cannot say that here is any well-defined object which is necessarily greater than 7; and this is why existential generalization fails in this case. But this phrase, 'the number of planets', can be so understood as to have a unique reference. If, on the other hand, the phrase, 'the number of planets', refers to 9 not only in the actual world, but also in all other possible worlds, we can say that the phrase, 'the number of planets', has a unique reference; and, in that case, we can also say that there is a necessary identity between 'the number of planets' and '9'. Thus, the intended interpretation of the proposition, 'the number of planets is necessarily 9', is the 'the number which happens to be the number of planets is 9 in all possible worlds'. That is, here the stress is on *the number*, that happens to be the number of planets *qua the number of planets*. And, for *this* reason we can substitute the term, 'the number of planets', for '9'. Since there is a well-defined individual that satisfies the given condition we can maintain: '(∃x) (x is necessarily greater than 7)'.

Thus we see that the main conclusion of all these solutions is the same. According to these different solutions, we can have intersubstitution of co-designative terms and can apply the principle of existential generalization to a modal proposition like '9 is necessarily greater than 7', if the intended interpretation of this sentence is 'as a matter of fact, the number *that* numbers the planets is necessarily greater than 7'. And we can have this interpretation of the modal proposition, provided that we take the singular term, 'the number of planets', to have a referential use; and that is so when the occurrence of the descriptive phrase has a larger scope and when consequently we can assert a necessary identity between 'the number of planets' and its co-referential term, the reference of the term 'the number of planets' now being fixed in all possible worlds including the actual. In other words, it is only then '$(\exists x)$ (x is necessarily greater than 7)' is possible, and we can have quantified modal logic.

2

The De Re Modality and Essentialism

THE critics of quantified modal logic are not willing to accept it even when it is shown that quantified modal logic is not at least logically impossible. For quantified modal logic, even if it is possible, leads to essentialism. According to some, the doctrine of essentialism is a quite troublesome doctrine. However, we can see that this notion of essentialism is rather ambiguous. The critics who bring the charge of essentialism against quantified modal logic are not always clear as to what they mean by essentialism and how does it come into quantified modal logic. While discussing quantified modal logic we can notice that the charge of essentialism actually has arisen against quantified modal logic from two different considerations.

Quantification into a modal context is possible only if necessity is de re. But there cannot be any de re necessity unless a thing can be said to possess a property necessarily. To say that a thing possesses a property necessarily or essentially is to be involved in essentialism.

Again the charge of essentialism may be brought against quantified modal logic from some other considerations. One way to make de re modality intelligible is by providing a semantics of possible worlds. This semantics of possible worlds raises fascinating questions of trans-world identity. This problem of trans-world identity has been sought to be resolved by appealing to the notion of essence. This, we may say, is the second possible way in which essentialism comes into quantified modal logic. In this essay, I will discuss mainly the first type of essentialism that is involved in de re modality and try to defend de re modality against Quine's attacks.

Now let us discuss the first type of essentialism and try to see how it comes into quantified modal logic. To say, '$(\exists x)$ (x is necessarily greater than 7)' is to suppose x, i.e. 9, has necessary greaterness than 7 independently of any particular mode of characterization. When we say that an object x is such that, whether we describe it as this or that, it is necessarily possessed of a particular property, we say that this property is the essence of the object concerned. Let us suppose that 9 is an object which is necessarily possessed of the property of being greater than 7. Now, if it is necessarily possessed of the property of being greater than 7, whether we describe 9 as the successor of 8 or as the number of planets, we can say that 9 is necessarily greater than 7 independently of any mode of characterization, or that 9 has some essence. Since it is an essence of 9, the object, to be necessarily greater than 7, we can substitute the term '9' by the term 'the number of planets', and, in that case, the application of the principle of existential generalization does not present any problem. If '$(\exists x)$ (x is necessarily greater than 7)' is true, then there is at least one object of which it is true that *it* is necessarily greater than 7. And if we admit that 9 has some essence, then 9 can be such an object whose name can be written in the place marked by x in 'x is necessarily greater than 7'. But Quine considers this to be too high a price that one has to pay for quantified modal logic. Quine is very much opposed to such a point of view as this which supposes that an object can have a necessary property independently of any specification, for, he feels, this leads to the metaphysical jungle of Aristotelian essentialism.[1] According to Quine, being necessarily so-and-so and possibly so-and-so are not any characteristics of any object itself. It is not a necessary property of 9 itself that it is greater than 7. Because if 'being greater than 7' were a necessary property of 9, it would have remained a necessary property throughout. But when we refer to the same object not as 9 but as the number of planets, Quine maintains, we

[1] W.V. Quine, 1976, 'Three Grades of Modal Involvement', in *The Ways of Paradox and Other Essays*, Harvard University Press, p. 176.

can no longer say that it is a necessary property of the number of planets to be greater than 7. That the number of planets is 9 is one of the contingent facts regarding celestial bodies.

One of Quine's main arguments against essentialism is that it is full of contradictions and, therefore, it is a philosophically unacceptable doctrine.

Quine[2] invites us to imagine a person who is *both* a mathematician and a cyclist and to see the bewilderment that is the outcome of essentialism. Let us suppose that there is a mathematician.

We can say that a mathematician is necessarily rational but not necessarily (i.e. is only contingently) two-legged. Again suppose there is a cyclist. We can say that a (well-formed) cyclist is necessarily two-legged but not necessarily (i.e. is only contingently) rational. Now, let us suppose that there is a person whose name is Paul K. Zweir,[3] who is both a mathematician and a cyclist. Which attribute of this individual is to be considered as necessary and which one as contingent in this case? This presents a problem. For we know:

1. All mathematicians are necessarily rational but not necessarily two-legged.
2. All (well-formed) cyclists are necessarily two-legged but not necessarily rational.

Now, since Paul K. Zweir is both a mathematician and a cyclist we may infer the following:

3. Paul K. Zweir is necessarily rational but not necessarily two-legged.
4. Paul K. Zweir is necessarily two-legged but not necessarily rational.

From 3 and 4 by the rules of simplification and adjunction we obtain two contradictory propositions.

---

2 Quine, *Word and Object*, The MIT Press, p. 199, 1960.

3 This name is due to Alvin Plantinga. See his *The Nature of Necessity*, Oxford University Press, 1974, p. 24.

5. Paul K. Zweir is necessarily rational and not necessarily rational.
6. Paul K. Zweir is necessarily two-legged and not necessarily two-legged.

Hence Quine finds that the talk of necessary and contingent attributes is futile without reference to some background grouping. From all these observations follows the most important tenet of Quine that no variable occurring inside an opaque construction can be found by a quantifier from outside.

To decide how far Quine's objection can be justified we have to start from where Quine stops. We cannot accept Quine's contention that since quantified modal logic is involved in essentialism, it is worse for it. We shall try to show here how de re modality can be defended against Quine's objections.

One way is to show that essentialism is not troublesome, i.e. to show that a thing can be said to be necessarily so-and-so independently of any specification without raising any problem.

Another alternative way is to show that even if a thing is necessarily so-and-so only under some specification, the modality may still be de re.

Let us consider very briefly how far the first approach to the said objection can be successful. In fact, in usual discussions of essentialism several issues are confused. I do not think that here it would be out of place to mention the names of some philosophers who tried to show that Quine's objection is unacceptable. R.B. Marcus in her paper, "Essential Attribution" tries to sketch out certain salient features of the doctrine of Aristotelian essentialism. A more formal account of essentialism can be given following Marcus[4] and T. Parsons.[5] These authors focus on the point that Quine's characterization of essentialism is not adequate. Further we can show that Quine is wrong in supposing that essentialism involves

---

[4] R.B. Marcus, 1967, 'Essentialism in Modal Logic', *Nous*, March, **I**(1): 91-96.

[5] T. Parsons, 1974, 'Essentialism and Quantified Modal Logic', in *Reference and Modality*, ed. L. Linsky, Oxford University Press, p. 75.

a contradiction. In this respect, names of Marcus[6] and Plantinga[7] are worth-mentioning, people who show by purely logical considerations that there is no real contradiction in the case of quantified modal logic. We have already discussed the example of a mathematician cyclist to show how contradiction may be supposed to arise in the case of quantified modal logic. The argument that is presented by the anti-essentialists involves this following important step:

1. Cyclists are necessarily two-legged.
2. *a* is a cyclist.
3. Therefore, *a* is necessarily two-legged.

The first premise of this argument, however, is ambiguous. That this proposition, 'cyclists are necessarily two-legged' can be read either de dicto or de re seems to have been overlooked by the anti-essentialists. In its first interpretation, i.e. if the premise is read de dicto, stands as follows.

1A. Necessarily, all cyclists are bipedal.
2. *a* is a cyclist.
3. Therefore, *a* is necessarily bipedal.

This first premise, viz. 'necessarily all cyclists are bipedal' is equivalent with a proposition of the form '$A \supset B$'. But there is no rule of inference like, '$A \supset B$', 'A, and therefore B', though an analysis of the above step in the anti-essentialists' argument shows that it proceeds by some such rule of inference. It is this which shows that the anti-essentialist argument is invalid.

On the alternative reading of the first premise of the argument which presents it as a de re statement, the argument stands as follows:

1B. All cyclists are necessarily two-legged, *a* is a cyclist, therefore, *a* is necessarily two-legged.

---

6 R.B. Marcus, 'Essentialism in Modal Logic', pp. 92-93.

7 Alvin Plantinga, *The Nature of Necessity*, pp. 23-26.

Thus understood, the first premise of this argument is doubtful for the essentialists find it difficult to accept this premise. That, the essentialists do not mean to say that whatever is a cyclist is necessarily two-legged. For, we cannot say of any particular individual that he is necessarily two-legged or anything else. Such assertions, which have a tone of fatalism, are not exactly what the modal logicians want to make. It is essential in the sense that if a particular individual is once a cyclist it is impossible that he should not be two-legged.

Apart from these formal considerations, certain informal philosophical arguments can be put forward to show that there is no contradiction in essentialism.[8] Let us consider the following propositions:

1. *Z* is necessarily bipedal and Z is not necessarily bipedal. This proposition can be shown to be logically equivalent with the following proposition:
2. *Z* is necessarily possessed of the property of being bipedal and is not necessarily possessed of the property of being bipedal.

Now, the question is whether there is any actual contradiction in Proposition 1. There can be a contradiction in Proposition 1, if and only if there is a contradiction in Proposition 2, for Proposition 1 is equivalent to Proposition 2. Again this proposition, 'z is necessarily possessed of the property of being bipedal and *z* is not necessarily possessed of the property of being bipedal', is comparable with the following proposition:

3. *A* resembles *B* and *A* does not resemble *B*.

Apparently, Proposition 3 involves a contradiction. But if we carefully analyse the implicit suggestions of this proposition, no such contradiction arises. To make it evident that there is no contradiction in this case we are to draw a distinction that exists between two types of predication, of which one may be called an

[8] This is suggested by Pranab Kumar Sen.

'absolute predication' and the other a 'relative predication'. A predication can be said to be absolute when it is about the subject absolutely without reference to anything else. This proposition, '*A* resembles *B*' appears to be an instance of absolute predication. But actually it is not so, and the problem is really due to this misunderstanding of the nature of the predication. We do not, in fact, mean to say that *A* resembles *B simpliciter*. What we really mean is that *A* resembles *B in some respect*. So what we have here is not an instance of absolute predication, rather it is an instance of relative predication. Similarly, when we say that *A* does not resemble *B*, what we mean to say is that *A* does not resemble *B in some respect*. Supposing there are two balls, of which one is red and the other is blue. Looking at these balls, one may remark, 'The first ball resembles the second ball, and also the first ball does not resemble the second ball'. No doubt this also appears to involve a contradiction. But if we carefully notice the type of predication that has actually been made in this case, we find that the contradiction vanishes. For in this case, what we really mean to say is that the first ball resembles the second ball so far as the shape is concerned, and the first ball does not resemble the second ball so far as the colour is concerned. Thus we see that there is no real contradiction. When this sentence is properly and unambiguously analysed all chances of contradicion do vanish. Apparent contradiction ceases to exist when it is made clear that a predication is neither an absolute predication nor a relative predication in the *same respect*; it is a relative predication about an object in different respects.

The lesson that we derive from Proposition 3 can be carried over to Proposition 2. Similar considerations will help us to dissolve the apparent contradiction in Proposition 2. In fact, we can see that there is no absolute predication in Proposition 2 but only a relative predication. Let us consider the first half of 2, viz., 'Z is necessarily possessed of the property of being bipedal'. What we mean to say here is: 'Z is necessarily possessed of the property of being bipedal in some respect'. And what we mean to assert in the second half, viz., 'Z is not necessarily possessed of the property of being bipedal' is 'Z is not necessarily possessed of the property of being bipedal in some other respect'. To put it more elaborately, the whole sentence stands as follows:

> Z is necessarily possessed of the property of being bipedal in so far as he is a cyclist and *z* is not necessarily possessed of the property of being bipedal in so far as he is a mathematician (and not a cyclist).

Hence we see in this case that there is no contradiction at all. And we have already pointed out that Proposition 2 is logically equivalent to Proposition 1. So it is clear that if there is no contradiction in Proposition 2, there is also no contradiction in Proposition 1.

But one may object that this is coming back to Quine. Quine himself said again that we cannot talk about necessity without reference to some background grouping. But there is an important difference between Quine's approach and that of ours, which we proceed to explain now. Let us suppose, '*A* is necessarily *O* relative to its specification as *Z*'. Can we infer from this: '*A* is not necessarily' *O*?' Quine appears to infer just this. But this sort of argument cannot be correct. From 'Z is necessarily bipedal relative to his specification as a cyclist' it does not follow that *z* is not necessarily bipedal.

The underlying presumption here seems to be that a specification of an object as such and such distorts the real nature of the object. Actually, however, there need not be any gulf between being specified as a cyclist and being a cyclist. 9, specified as the successor of 8, is necessarily greater than 7. It would be entirely wrong to argue that '*since* 9 is necessarily greater than 7, as specified as the successor of 8, therefore, 9 cannot *be* necessarily greater than 7.

The difference between our point of view and Quine's is, thus, this: Quine believes that if something necessarily has a property relative to a certain specification then it does not really have that property necessarily. We want to maintain that if a thing necessarily has a property relative to a certain specification, then unless the specification distorts the nature of the thing, the specification is made in terms of a real aspect of the thing, and if the thing necessarily has a property in that respect, then there is no reason why the thing itself should not really have that property.

The important point that emerges from the above discussion is that absolute predication is not necessary for de re modality. Quine is wrong in supposing that there is an opposition between a relative predication and de re modality. Modality does not cease to be de re when it is relativized.[9] This doctrine of relative predication enjoys a double benefit for it explicitly avoids the supposed contradiction of essentialism and at the same time saves de re modality.

---

[9] This is suggested by Pranab Kumar Sen.

3

Modality and Possible Worlds

THE semantical representation of modal calculi usually involves reference to possible worlds other than our own world and requires postulation of some possible objects not found in the actual world. Saul Kripke,[1] Jaakko Hintikka[2] and Stig Kanger,[3] working independently of one another, invoked possible worlds models for the explication of modal notions. No doubt, this framework of possible worlds has proved itself to be of immense explanatory value. The notion of possible worlds is often found helpful in discourses involving counterfactuals, meanings and intensional abstract entities. But at the same time it cannot be denied that this notion of possible worlds is at the root of innumerable confusion and controversy. In the present study, I want to find out some of the several philosophical implications of the semantical treatment of modal logic. Since there are multiple types of modal systems, it is not possible for me to venture into the details of every variety of modal calculus. For the time being, I mainly confine myself to the consideration of those modal calculi that represent the normal modal systems. The aim of the present inquiry is to consider and elucidate the ontological status of the so-called possible worlds as implied by the model theory of modality.

---

1 In Saul Kripke, 1971, 'Semantical Considerations on Modal Logic', in *Reference and Modality*, ed. Leonard Linsky, London: Oxford University Press. 1971.

2 In Jaakko Hintikka, 1969, *Models for Modalities: Selected Essays*, Dordrecht-Holland: D. Reidel.

3 Stig Kanger, 1957, *Provability in Logic*, Amsterdam: Almqvist and Wiksell.

I

In spite of its advantage, this model-theoretic approach to modal logic has often been viewed with suspicion in many quarters. One of the most serious charges against the notion of a possible world is that it involves a contradiction. The proponent of a possible world framework is committed to the existence of unactualized possibilia. It is supposed that this framework of possible worlds pledges one to hold that there exist things — possibilia — that do not actually exist. Obviously, if it is implied by the semantics of modality that there exist things that do not exist, then it involves a contradiction. Second, it has been maintained that the talk of possibilia violates Occam's principle, for it involves needless multiplication of entities. Third, as pointed out by Quine, the so-called possibles are disorderly elements because they baffle the principle of individuation. Possible worlds are thus supposed by many to be ghostly, insubstantial and incomprehensible.

One of the ways to dissolve the whole issue about possible worlds is to provide a substitutional interpretation of quantification.[4] These logicians may be taken to advocate a nonstandard semantics for modal calculus. This substitutional interpretation of quantification itself has given rise to lots of controversy among logicians. It is, however, not within the scope of the present study to consider this non-standard approach to the semantics of modal logic. Here, I mainly deal with those logicians and philosophers who either explicitly or implicitly accept the standard objectual interpretation of quantification in modal contexts and its corresponding semantical account.

The semantical treatment of modality, which is often referred to as the model theory of modality or as the possible worlds model as presented by Kripke and others, we have already pointed out, has generated a great controversy among logicians and

---

[4] Ruth Barcan Marcus, 1962, 'Interpreting Quantification', *Inquiry*, 5: 252-59; also see Pranab Kumar Sen, 1980, 'Variables and Quantification', in *Logic: Induction and Ontology*, Jadavpur Studies in Philosophy, vol. II, New Delhi: The Macmillan Co. of India, pp. 56-91.

philosophers. Hence, the primary question remains: what are these possible worlds in the possible worlds models and what are their relation with modality?

First, let us see whether our understanding of the general notion of a model can throw some light on the nature of possible worlds. It cannot be denied that the idea of representing modal calculus model theoretically has been derived from the mathematicians. The notion of a model is a creation of mathematicians. This notion has proved useful in scientific discourse, and so its use has also become quite frequent. The logicians too have found it useful to talk in terms of models. But it is not easy to provide a precise and uniform definition of a model. In mathematics, we find that models represent a certain structure. To a mathematician a model stands for a sort of domain of entities which satisfies the axioms of a given theory. In any axiomatic system of mathematics the main concern is to vindicate the logical relation of the axioms of that system to their consequences. But such axiomatic representation often needs to be supplemented by a model theory for providing justification and interpretation of different formalized theories. Hence the demand for a model-theoretic representation cannot be avoided in mathematics.

The same thing we can observe if we consider the history of the development of the different systems of modal calculus. No doubt, the axiomatic development of modal calculus enabled us to understand better the relations between different modal axioms and their consequences. But, at the same time, a need was felt for justification and interpretation of different formalized modal systems and this could not be ignored. Thus, the possible worlds models may be considered as a study in the foundations of modal calculus.

In presenting a semantical account of modal calculus, Kripke uses the term 'model structure',[5] whereas Hintikka uses the term,

---

[5] Kripike's 1971, 'Semantical Considerations on Modal Logic', in *Reference and Modality*, ed. Leonard Linsky, London: Oxford University Press.

'model systems'.[6] Roughly speaking, the model structure of Kripke is the same as the model systems of Hintikka. In order to be a model structure, a structure must exhibit certain characteristics. The first requirement for a model structure is that it must have some constituent elements or objects in some definite order or in relation with one another. So, the model structure which is supposed to provide an interpretation of modal calculus is viewed to be a non-empty set consisting of certain elements.

In order to understand the nature of this model structure we have to be clear about the elements and their relations which constitute this model structure. The strict formalist may suppose that one's admission of elements and their relation need not necessarily commit one to anything regarding the nature of such elements and their relations. This non-commital attitude regarding the nature of the elements and their relation is not to be found either in Kripke or in Hintikka. Second, it is to be noted that the concept of model structure carries no sense without reference to some formal system. Third, we must not forget that the notion of satisfiability is the pivotal concept in a model-theoretic approach. A distinction is to be drawn between a model structure and a model structure of α. The set of formulas of α is then called satisfiable if it has such a model. Tarski has also maintained that a possible realization in which all valid sentences of a theory T are satisfied is called a model of T. The concept of satisfaction is inseparably related with the concept of interpretation. Thus, when we speak about a model structure of a modal calculus we are, in fact, in search of some interpretation, which makes a given set of formulas true.

Thus, relying on these three important features of a model structure we may attempt to provide a definition of a model. Thus, we can say that x is a model for y if and only if the following conditions are met:

---

[6] Jaakko Hintikka's 1969, 'Modality and Quantification' and 'The Modes of Modality', in *Models for Modalities*, Dordrecht-Holland: D. Reidel, pp. 60, 72.

1. *x* is a set of elements (objects) and relations.
2. *y* is an axiom or a set of axioms in a formal system.
3. *x* satisfies *y*, i.e. *x* turns all the axioms and logical consequences of *y* into true statements.

The question that becomes very important at this point is what are the elements (objects) mentioned in this model for modality? To provide semantics for some of the systems of modal logic, as we have already noted, Kripke introduces the notion of a (normal) model structure. A model structure (m.s.) is an ordered triple (*G*, *K*, *R*), where *K* is a fixed set, *R* is an accessibility relation on K and $G \in K$. Kripke adds, *K* is the set of all possible worlds, and *G* is the real world. Hence we find that the non-empty set *K*, which is referred to as the set of possible worlds, is one of the elements contained in the model structure of Kripke. The possible worlds are supposed to be the intuitive counterparts of these model sets. This is the reason why the model-theoretic representation of modal logic is often nicknamed as possible worlds semantics.

Before we proceed further, a brief account of some of the salient features of the Kripkean semantics would not be out of place here. In the Kripkean semantics, if H_1 and H_2 are two possible worlds, then $H_1R\,H_2$ means that H_1 is 'possible relative to' H_2, or H_1 is accessible to H_2. Now, what does it mean to say that a world is accessible to another world? There is no single answer to this question for there is no one system of modal logic. Different systems of modal logic differ from one another because of the difference between the axioms they respectively contain or between the calculi they incorporate. Different systems of modal calculus may be viewed as representing different notions of necessity and possibility. The system *S*-5, for example, is best understood as a system which captures the logical notion of necessity. Because of this, the accessibility relation itself is not fixed, it varies from system to system. In a semantic representation of the system Hughes and Cresswell[7] call *T*, which is a weak

[7] See *An Introduction to Modal Logic*, London: Methuen & Co.

system, the accessibility relation is taken to be reflexive in nature. We can say that the weakest form of the accessibility relation is the one in which it is only reflexive. As we ascend higher up in the scale to stronger systems of modal logic, more and more conditions are imposed on this accessibility relation. Thus, the accessibility relation is transitive, as well as reflexive, in Lewis's system *S*-4. In the Brouwerian system the accessibility relation is supposed to be reflexive and symmetric. If it is required that the relation of accessibility be transitive and symmetric, as well as reflexive, i.e. an equivalence relation, we obtain a system which is equivalent to Lewis's system *S*-5.

In the Kripkean semantic representation of modal logic, it is quite clear that each model set is constructed according to certain conditions and each contains a number of basic sentences plus sentences compounded from those sentences according to certain rules. A model assigns to each atomic formula P (i.e. a propositional variable) a truth-value T or F in each world $H \in K$. Thus, in the case of propositional modal logic a model ϕ on an m.s. (G, K, R) is a binary function $\phi(P, H)$ where P varies over atomic formulae and where H varies over elements of K, whose range is the set $\{T, F\}$.

Truth-values for non-atomic formulae in the above model is determined by the following conditions:

$V((A\&B), H) = T$ iff $V(A, H) = T$ & $V(B, H) = T$

$V(\sim A, H) = T$ iff $V(A, H) = F$

$V(\Box A, H) = T$ iff $V(A, H') = T$ for every $H' \in K$ such that HRH'; otherwise $V(\Box A, H) = F$.

In other words, such propositions as 'it is necessary that *P*' are true in the actual world if the proposition *P* is true in the actual world and also true in every other possible worlds accessible to the actual world; otherwise, the proposition, 'It is necessary that *P*' is false.

From the consideration of the model structure of modal calculi it is clear that in order to clarify the logic of modality we have to consider several possible worlds in relation to each other and not just one world at a time, as we can do in explaining the semantics of ordinary non-modal propositional calculus.

In a semantical representation of quantified modal logic some more conditions than are mentioned above are to be imposed on a model set. Introduction of quantifiers requires that a domain of individuals be associated with each world wherein these individuals exist. In Kripkean semantics, in addition to the notions already mentioned, the notion of assignment plays an important role. An assignment is a function which assigns to each individual constant of the language an element of the domain, and to each n-adic predicate of the language an ordered n-tuple of elements of the domain. The idea behind this assignment is that the domain represents the set of objects about which we are talking in our language. The assignment function confers on the individual constants of the language their denotations in the domain; and this assignment function confers on the predicate expressions of a language their extensions in the domain. We are now in a position to define a quantificational model structure (G, K, R) together with a function ψ which assigns to each $H \in K$, a $\psi(H)$, called the domain of H. According to Kripke, $\psi(H)$, intuitively understood, is the set of all individuals existing in H. However, $\psi(H)$, i.e. the set of all individuals existing in different *H*s need not be the same. The population of each world may be different. There are systems of modal calculus whose semantical representation suggests that the domain of the actual world is narrower than U (i.e. union of all domains assigned to the members of K). In this system, it is conceivable that some new objects exist in the possible world. That means, it makes room for objects that do not actually exist. Hence comes the idea of a non-existent object. These are some of the logical implications that Kripke derives from the semantical representation of some of the systems of quantified modal logic. The system *S*-5, which is supposed to capture best the logical notions of necessity and possibility, does not admit the possibility of quantification over objects that do not exist in the actual world.

Hence, in this system, it is impossible to quantify over non-existent objects. While developing semantics for *S*-5, Kripke does not give up the principle of bivalence. Kripke puts a restriction on the objects over which we quantify. We quantify only over actually existing objects. Hence the problem of non-existing individual does not arise with regard to this particular system of quantified modal logic. The notion of non-existing possible individuals has also raised lots of debate among the logicians and philosophers. But finding that this notion of a possible individual is not necessarily tied up with our understanding of modality I omit any discussion on it for the present.

A careful consideration of Kripke's semantic representation of modal logic, just discussed, clearly reveals the following.

In the first place, we find that Kripke interprets modality in terms of possible worlds. Second, by admitting possible worlds to be one of the constituent elements of this framework, he is committed to the existence of possible worlds.

However, there may be sceptics who do not agree with my observations. The feasibility of the framework of possible worlds may be questioned at least from three different considerations. First, theoretical considerations regarding the nature of semantics may lead one to question the feasibility of the semantics of possible worlds. Second, one may doubt whether Kripke has seriously committed himself to the reality of possible worlds. Third, one may try to explain the objectivity of modal statements without reference to possible worlds, by presenting the semantics of modal logic without any such reference.

It is quite common among some philosophers, Alvin Plantinga, for instance, to draw a distinction[8] between a formal semantics or pure semantics on the one hand and applied or depraved semantics on the other. Let us try to be clear about this distinction between a formal semantics and an applied semantics. It is only when we

---

[8] Alvin Plantinga, 1974, *The Nature of Necessity*, Oxford, Clarendon Press, pp. 126-131.

are clear about the exact nature of the distinction that we shall see what the implications of making such a distinction are. Plantinga, however, does not provide any clear-cut criterion on the basis of which such a distinction can be drawn. He just cites certain instances to show where the semantics can be said to be formal, and where it can be said to be applied. According to him, Kripke's formal semantics 'as such has no obvious connection with modal notions of all'.[9] Furthermore:

> . . . it is not to the pure semantics as such that we must look for the promised insight into our modal notions — not, at least if we take the semantics seriously rather than as a heuristic device.

Instead there is an applied semantics which can be naturally associated with Kripke's pure semantics:

> In the intended applied semantics, therefore, a model structure will not be just any triple (*G*, *K*, *R*) where *G* is a member of *K* and *R* is reflexive; *K* will be a set of possible worlds (not chessmen) — possible states of affairs of certain kind — of which *G* is a member.[10]

In either case of semantics, be it formal or applied, an interpretation is given. But the mode of interpretation in two cases is widely different. One may interpret certain given signs by reference to certain other signs. Thus, the model structure (*G*, *K*, *R*) which is an ordered triple may be interpreted by reference to certain signs. The ordered triple (*G*, *K*, *R*) when interpreted in terms of any other ordered triple, the minimum requirement for an interpretation may be said to have been fulfilled. Of the given model structure (*G*, *K*, *R*) it is required that *K* is a set of which *G* is a member and on which *R* is a relation. Now, we can interpret it, as it has been shown by Plantinga, in terms of the ordered triple (*G*, *K*, *R*), where K could be, for example, a set of chessmen, *G* the king which is a member of *K* and *R* the relation *as large as*. Or, we may interpret the ordered triple, (*G*, *K*, *R*), say, in terms of *K*

---

[9] Alvin Plantinga, 1974, *The Nature of Necessity*, op. cit., pp. 126-27.

[10] Ibid., p. 127.

which is a set of school children, *G*, the set of students reading in class VII, and *R*, the relation of the same age as. So, we find that sometimes an interpretation may consist in just associating certain signs with certain given signs. Something like this is supposed to occur in the case of pure semantics. But when a specific meaning is attached to the symbols and formulas of a formal language we step into the sphere of applied semantics.

This is how Plantinga explains the difference between two types of semantics. Taking the hint from Plantinga, we may try to grasp the difference between these two types of semantics by help of a logical formula as our example. Supposing there is a logical formula, say, $(PVQ) \rightarrow S$. Now, we may semantically interpret this formula in either of two ways. The given formula may be interpreted to be 1 iff it is not the case that (PVQ) is 1 and S is 2, otherwise it is 2. It appears that the above way of interpreting does not commit one to any ontological entity, for here just certain signs are being associated with certain other signs. But sometimes, we may not be satisfied with this sort of interpretation. In that case instead of speaking in terms of certain signs we may use meaningful expressions. We may interpret the above formula $(PVQ) \rightarrow S$ in terms of true proposition, false proposition, non-exclusive sense of disjunction and logical implication. In that case, it would be another way of taking semantics. What is offered here is an instance of applied semantics.

Besides Plantinga there are some other logicians who too are in favour of this distinction. The motive for drawing this distinction between a pure semantics and an applied semantics especially in the case of modal logic is not difficult to understand. This distinction may be, in the first place, over-emphasized by those who want to establish that the Kripkean semantics for modal logic does not necessarily imply the framework of the possible worlds. There are some logicians, who in their blind faith in formalism, may even go to the extent of identifying semantics proper with formal semantics. To them the so-called applied semantics, which has some link with intuition, is a pseudo-semantics. They are of the opinion that Kripke presents a formal semantics for modal logic as a purely set-theoretical construct. This sort of semantical representation is adequate for establishing validity and consistency of the modal systems. They are of the opinion that there is nothing in this set-theoretical presentation of Kripke that commits him to the existence of possible worlds. It is, however, clear why these people find interest in giving a purely formal semantical treatment to modal logic. For, if semantics is given in this manner then the difficult and obnoxious issues regarding possible worlds and possible individuals would not arise at all. These formalists think that from the set-theoretic model structure as presented by Kripke it is not at all evident how seriously he is speaking about possible worlds. They do not attach much importance to intuitive considerations. They regard Kripke's talk of possible worlds as 'convenient but dispensable imagery'. To them applied semantics is really a depraved semantics. They look upon those intuitive explanations which are derived from applied semantical considerations as merely aids to imagination, as heuristic devices to make formal semantics more agreeable.

One may consider semantics in its purely formal aspect and totally disregard its informal ramifications. But one thing will be definitely lacking in such presentation and that is insight into the real significance of our modal reasoning. A purely formal presentation of the semantics of modal systems fails to capture the essential nature of such systems. Plantinga feels that a formal semantical account by itself is not sufficient to represent modal reasoning; rather it leads to a kind of sophistry. If the semantics for modal logic is considered purely in its formal aspect, the ontological issues regarding possibilia may not arise. But on that plea one cannot remain confined to purely formal semantical considerations alone. Plantinga reminds us, 'To accept pure semantics, therefore, is not as such to acquiesce in any philosophical doctrine at all'.[11]

---

[11] Alvin Plantinga, 1974, *The Nature of Necessity*, op. cit., p. 129.

Moreover, I think that it is very much doubtful how far Kripke and some others engaged in providing semantics for modal logic can be understood in such a purely formal way. Certainly, it is to misunderstand Kripke to regard him as one of the formalists. For we have already seen from our earlier discussion that he provides an intuitive account of his model structure side by side its set-theoretical representation. Hence, this much at least is clear that we cannot assume that Kripke is totally disregarding any informal and intuitive account of our modal thinking.

Susan Haack[12] also admits the importance of 'depraved' semantics and she is in favour of taking the 'intuitive account somewhat more seriously' as a picture or metaphor, or a heuristic device, to make pure semantics a little more 'palatable'. With a view to avoiding circularity, it is suggested by Haack that an informal intuitive account of any formal semantics should be given in a language which is epistemologically independent of its formal reading. This notion of epistemological independence, as introduced by Haack, however, is not sufficiently clear. Neither do we find any attempt on the part of Haack to make it quite clear. Perhaps, she wants to lay emphasis on the point that our understanding of a formal language should not hinge upon its intuitive reading. Furthermore, it seems that this sort of demand for an epistemological independence of an informal language of its formal rendering is too strong a demand to be fulfilled. It is undeniable that this notion of epistemological independence is quite vague for in this case no criterion has been furnished for determining epistemological independence of one account of a language from that of another. With this notion which lacks in precision, it is quite difficult to vindicate epistemological independence of an intuitive reading of a language from that of its formal reading. For further complexity may arise from the fact that the formal account of a language and an informal account of the same may either agree or disagree. When a formal account of

---

[12] Susan Haack, *Philosophy of Logics*, Cambridge: Cambridge University Press, pp. 188-89.

a language comes into conflict with its intuitive account we generally disregard its formal account as counter-intuitive. On the other hand, when a formal account of an argument and its informal intuitive account agree with each other then either the formal rendering of that language or the intuitive account of that language is deemed to be satisfactory. But, if there is an agreement between an informal account of a language and its formal account, should we say that the principle of epistemological independence of one account of a language from that of its other has been preserved? To me it seems, that there should not be any problem in expressing the same thing in different languages. However, my inclination is not to subscribe to the view that pure semantics and applied semantics are two distinct types of semantics.

Our ordinary intuitive way of understanding is often found to be ambiguous, vague and even to lead to paradoxes. One of the motives behind the construction of any formal system whatsoever is to remove these deficiencies from our intuitive understanding and thus achieve exactitude and consistency in thought. Formal systems thus aim at polishing our intuition. Similarly, modal logic may also be considered as an attempt to formalize with precision our intuitive ways of modal reasoning. Therefore, if we fall back on applied semantics then we are once again relying on intuition to clarify a formal language which was supposed to systematize some of our intuitive reasonings. Prior to the construction of any formal system the logician must have adequate knowledge of the subject matter which he is going to couch in a formalized manner. No set-theoretical construction, or any other formal construction whatsoever, can ignore the intuition inherent in such constructions. It seems to me an unwise decision to encourage a bifurcation within semantics. Since, apparently, it is the insight about possible worlds which has stimulated the very construction of the modal calculi, in the semantic representation of that logic there has to be some room for possible worlds. Any consistent set of axioms and rules may be provided with a model by reference to which the consistency of that set of axioms may be judged. The same is true of a consistent set of axioms and rules of modal logic. But just having a consistent system in respect of a model cannot satisfy a true logician. Modal logic to be worthy of its name cannot ignore the suggestions of the prelogical idea of possible worlds. To quote from Hintikka,

> It seems to me that the best way of achieving conceptual clarity in modal logic is to view all the use of modal notions as involving a reference usually, of course, only a tacit one, to more than one possible state of affairs or course of events, in short to more than one "possible world".[13]

But that is not the end of all controversy. Some may still argue that there is no point in saying that the semantical considerations for modal logic should necessarily be in terms of possible worlds. Even though one may accept some of the points made in support of the semantics of possible worlds, one may not be willing to accept the semantics of possible worlds itself. There are some semanticists who try to present a semantical account of modal logic by dispensing with the notions of possible worlds, possible individuals, etc. Mondadori and Morton[14] try to establish the objectivity of modal statements without assuming some modal entities like possible worlds. They have a particular notion of objectivity in mind. When a particular branch of study is said to be objective, it is said to be so because each statement made in that branch of study is either determinately true or determinately false independently of our being able to decide what it is. (That is, they take a Dummettian view of objectivity.) Hence they are of the opinion that the objectivity of modal statements does not imply modal realism in the sense that it demands that there be a realm of independently existing modal entities.

But the problem is that in the case of mathematical statements

---

[13] Jaakko Hintikka, 1969, 'On the Logic of Perception', in *Models for Modalities*, Dordrecht-Holland: D. Reidel, p. 153.

[14] See their 'Modal Realism: The Poisoned Pawn', in *The Possible and the Actual*, ed. Michael Loux, Ithaca and London: Cornell University Press, pp. 235-52.

it is not so difficult to state in what the objectivity of the statements consists. But the case is more complicated with regard to the modal statements. However, Mondadori and Morton try to provide an account of modal objectivity. In the first place, they state some of the negative conditions for the objectivity of a modal statement. A modal statement cannot be said to be objective if its truth-value depends on what people believe or just agree about. The modal statement 'Humphrey might have won the election' is objective if its truth or falsity depends just on whether the object named is as it is said to be, independently of our beliefs or conventions. 'To put it differently, such a sentence is objective if there is a property, such that the sentence is true if and only if the object has it.'[15] Now the question is, what are these modal properties? Thus when we say 'Humphrey might have won the election' is true according to this view, we are required to show that the individual Humphrey does possess the property in question. They are of the opinion that these modal sentences are true due to certain physical facts. So what are called modal properties, which account for the truth or falsity of modal statements, are not something totally different and secluded from the physical facts. But sometimes it may be difficult to say which particular facts are actually accountable for the truth or falsity of the modal statements. Hence in order to identify those physical facts one must have some knowledge about some of the physical events which are sufficient to render the relevant possibility into an actuality. What these philosophers try to show is that, ultimately, there are no modal facts over and above physical facts.

> Modal properties are possessed by physical objects, as a matter of objective-independent fact . . . We think that the contrast between modal and non-modal properties is not an ontological one.[16]

It may seem that these people have actually succeeded in dispensing with modal properties. But on deeper reflection it

[15] See their 'Modal Realism: The Poisoned Pawn', op. cit., p. 238.

[16] Ibid., p. 249.

appears that by referring just to specific physical facts one cannot account for the truth of a modal statement. An account exclusively in physical terms totally annihilates the distinction between a factual statement and a modal one. This exclusively physicalistic account of modal properties is not at all acceptable. Of course, it is also not acceptable that there are different strata of ontological realms to which modal properties and non-modal properties belong. Modal and non-modal properties do not belong to different ontological realms. But it will not be equally justified to conclude from this that the modal properties are in no way different from the non-modal properties. Modal properties are in the actual physical world; the actual physical world provides the basis of modal properties. Still modal properties are something different from the physical properties.

The possible worlds' semantics fascinates me and, I think, not without reason. The idea of possible worlds is quite suggestive, and illuminating, in explaining modal locutions. Modal notions and the idea of possible world stand in an inseparable correlation. The important question here is how exactly this correlation is to be understood. Two alternatives are possible. Either we take the possible worlds as given and derive the logic of modality on its basis; or, we take the logic of modality as basic and develop the manifold of possible worlds out of the actual world. The first way of looking at the matter appears to be mistaken. But it cannot be denied that there are some who look upon this correlation precisely in this way. To these philosophers possible worlds are real. A careful consideration of the matter will, however, reveal that the correlation that exists between the possible worlds and modality is to be understood in the reverse order. It is modality which is to be regarded as primitive. We invoke the notion of possible worlds to analyse and explicate meanings of modal statements.

II

The possible worlds semanticists, or the people, who uphold the feasibility and comprehensibility of the possible worlds' framework and believe in the meaningfulness of modal logic, miserably fail to represent a common school of thinkers with certain uniform and uncontroversial tenets. Rather, these people widely differ from one another as to the nature and status of the things that are possible worlds. My scheme of classification of the semanticists who commit themselves to possible worlds, in one way or another, is as follows:

Realism about possible worlds is possible both from the perspective of a possibilist and an actualist. For David Lewis, one of the strongest proponents of modal possibilism, the reality is out and out modal. Lewis clinches firmly to modal realism, the view according to which there are innumerable real worlds of which this particular world we inhabit is one. Worlds in this

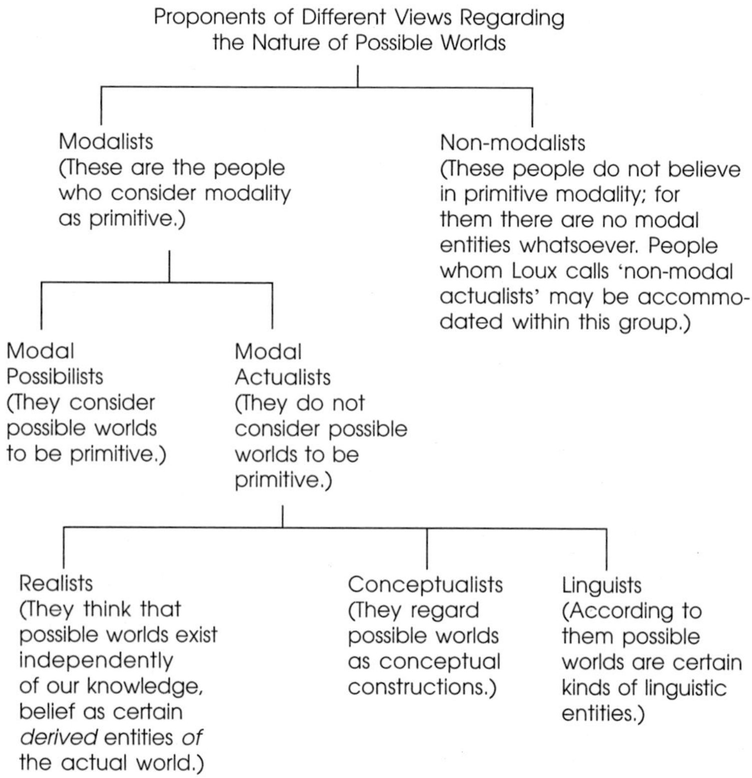

plurality of full-blooded worlds are not empty. Rather, it is by reference to the contents of these worlds and their orders of arrangement, one world is distinguished from the other. For Lewis, these possible worlds are all real, they are like 'remote planets'.[17] There is no network of any sort whatsoever interlinking these varied worlds. To quote Lewis, 'each world represents the way a world could be'.[18] Indeed, there are many ways a world could be, and accordingly this leads Lewis to postulate a plurality of worlds. Of these varied ways a world could be, our world is only one. In other words, every way a world could be is a different possible world. For this reason he holds that possible worlds, which are the ways the world could be, cannot be linguistic entities. Lewis has no hesitation in accepting that these possible worlds are really out there in their own right.

According to Lewis, our world is the actual world. But Lewis provides an indexical analysis of actuality. According to him, the reference of the term 'actual' varies from one context of utterance to another. All worlds can be actual in relation to itself. Thus the word 'actual' means the same as '*this* worldly'. Lewis does not believe in absolute actuality. In Lewis's system, we find that the notion of actuality has been reduced to a relative concept. 'All worlds can be actual at itself'.[19] This world is actual to us, because as inhabitants of this world we call it, 'our world'. But because we call this world actual world or our world that does not mean that this world in any way is in a privileged position. This world, i.e. the actual world for us, has no difference from any (other) possible world so far as its worldness is under consideration. In other words, this world is on a par with all other possible worlds.

These worlds are not empty. But it has already been pointed out that according to Lewis the contents of these possible worlds are different. This explains why, according to Lewis, each individual is strictly confined to that particular world. Hence there are no

---

17 David Lewis, 1986, *On the Plurality of Worlds*, Oxford: Basil Blackwell, p. 2.

18 Ibid., p. 3

19 Ibid.

trans-world individuals in the theory of Lewis. But from this, it does not follow that according to Lewis, all individuals are world-bound. Rather, he tries to blend world-boundedness of an individual with its trans-worldliness in a peculiar way by introducing the notion of counterparts. Lewis's strategy here is to hold that each individual is world-bound, but an object existing in one world can have a counterpart in some other world. Now, if an object *x* of this world has a counterpart *y* in another world, then *x* and *y* are said to have counterpart relation. In the system of Lewis, we thus find an endeavour to replace the relation of identity by the relation of counterparthood. How do we determine which object is a counterpart of it in some other worlds? Lewis provides the following answer. 'A counterpart of an object resembles the object closely in content and context in important respects.'[20]

From this metaphysical perspective Lewis proceeds to consider formalization of modal talks. Thus, naturally we notice in the case of Lewis a departure from the usual practice of formalizing modal talks. In this connection, it should be noted that the extensional bias of Lewis led him to develop a parallel system of modal logic to counter the development of quantified modal logic of extensional types. Lewis nicknames this alternative approach to formalize modal talks as the counterpart theory of modality.

The counterpart theory of Lewis evolves out of the standard quantification theory. The domain of discourse of the counterpart theory is far more extended than the domain of discourse of the standard predicate calculus. The domain of discourse here includes an every possible world and everything in every possible world. In this connection, Lewis provides an elaborate schema for translating the sentences of modal language into the language of counterpart theory.

It must be admitted that in the case of Lewis, we observe a departure from the usual approach to the framework of possible

---

[20] D.K. Lewis, 1979, 'Counterpart Theory and Quantified Modal Logic', in *The Possible and the Actual*, ed. Michael Loux, Ithaca and London: Cornell University Press, p. 112.

worlds. Lewis does not rely on possible worlds, which according to him are real, existing independently of our knowledge or belief about them, just for elucidating the semantics of modal logic. Lewis thinks that for the semantical representation of modal logic we need not invoke realism about possible worlds. Lewis belongs to the group of those who believe that for the semantical analysis of modal logic any set-theoretical construct is enough. Hence there is no doubt that Lewis does not adhere to the doctrine of modal realism to defend the semantics of possible worlds. The position is rather reverse in the case of Lewis. Modal realism is the basis which provides the support to possible worlds semantics. To quote Lewis:

> So for me, the metalogical results are applicable because I believe that there exist frames which afford correct interpretations of the modal operators.[21]

Lewis's ontology of possible worlds, however, has been held to be incredible in many respects. Modal realism of Lewis and its associate tenet of counterpart relation as embodied in counterpart theory of Lewis is wholly unconvincing and counter-intuitive. Moreover, this doctrine of Lewis fails to capture our ordinary modal notions. For, according to this theory we are supposed to interpret de re modalities in terms of individuals which are represented by their counterparts, i.e. by other objects in the domain of other possible worlds, other than their ownself. This interpretation clearly fails to explain the very meaning of any de re locution. The counterpart theory by its very definition is totally incapable of picking up an unique individual in all possible worlds. When it is said, 'Aristotle could have been unwise', we are entertaining a possibility about Aristotle *himself*. We are thus, just debating what could have happened to Aristotle. On the other hand, the counterpart theorist like Lewis would say that when we are saying, 'Aristotle could have been unwise', we are implying that there are real possible worlds where the counterparts of Aristotle exist and who are unwise. Thus, according to this theory,

---

21 David Lewis, 1986, *On the Plurality of Worlds*, Oxford: Basil Blackwell, p. 20.

it amounts to saying that another individual in the domain of another world is unwise. If that is the explanation then how can we justify our claim that we are saying something of the same individual, Aristotle? For, from the beginning it has been taken for granted that the counterpart of an individual is not identical with that individual. Allen Hazen, a staunch supporter of counterpart theory, tries to provide some arguments in favour of Lewis. Hazen proposes a bifurcation between two types of sentences, viz. the sentences that are expressed in ordinary language and the sentences that are expressed according to the technical language of Lewis. The sentences belonging to the second group should be considered to be outside our natural language. Now, if we stick to this difference we should also agree that there is some difference in our understanding of those sentences. Our intuitive way of understanding sentences that predominates in ordinary language may not be of any help in our understanding of sentences that are expressed in the technical language of counterpart theory. In this view then, Lewis is just laying down a schema for translating certain sentences expressed in ordinary language in a technical way. This, however, cannot be accepted as a convincing argument in favour of Lewis.

Realism of Lewis violates the law of parsimony by needless multiplication of entities. Haack calls realism of Lewis an 'Ontological Slum'.[22] However, Lewis does not concede to the charge of being unparsimonious in entifying possible worlds. Lewis agrees that one ought not to admit new kinds of entities unnecessarily for qualitative parsimony is what Occam's razor urges one to follow. But he sees nothing wrong in admitting more entities of an already-allowed sort. Lewis thinks that since possible worlds are things of the same kind as the actual world, admission of their existence as real entities cannot lead to any violation of any ontological principle.

The doctrine of plurality of real worlds, as preached by Lewis,

---

22 Haack, 1977, 'Lewis's Ontological Slum', *The Review of Metaphysics*, Issue No. 119, March, XXX(3): 415.

is really bizarre. One of Lewis's convictions is that the actual world and the possible worlds are things of the same kind. According to Lewis possible worlds are ways things could have been; and the actual world is the way things are. Now, according to Lewis possible worlds and the actual world both exist. But it does appear to be a contradiction to say that the ways things could have been do exist. For with regard to those things which do actually exist why should we say they *could have been*? Does it amount to saying something like 'if I could have been the prime minister of India then I do exist as the prime minister of India'? Of course, if that were the case and all the instances of could-have-beens were existent then nobody would ever have any reason for feeling frustrated. In Lewis's theory modal distinctions totally collapse. If 'ways things could have been' exist and 'ways things are' exist too then how do we draw a distinction between a possibility and an actuality? So the question is, how far is Lewis's conviction that the ways things could have been also exist defensible? Lewis, as we have already seen, provides an indexical analysis of actuality. And he argues that the use of 'actual' with reference to the actual world is an indexical; simply because we are at this world, we call it actual. To an inhabitant of another world, which we call a possible world, that other world too will be an 'actual world' because that inhabitant happens to be at that world. So, according to Lewis, though the actual world and the possible worlds are things of the same kind, it is only with regard to the actual world that we say that it 'actually exists' and possible worlds as real entities 'exist'. He concedes that possible worlds other than the actual world do not actually exist (for *us* at least), because possible worlds are not, located here in our world.

No doubt, Lewis introduces a terminological revolution by insisting on a distinction between 'existence' and 'actual existence'. But, in fact, we find that he is putting old wine in a new bottle. On analysis, it is clear that by 'exists' Lewis means 'is possible' and by 'actually exists' he means 'exists'. Hence, it appears, that though Lewis begins with the conviction that the actual world and the possible worlds are things of the same kind, he cannot really stick to his conviction. When Lewis says that other worlds exist but they do not actually exist, he is implicitly implying that such worlds are only possible. There is no denying the fact that this objection weakens the full-blooded realism of Lewis.

Tom Richards is of the opinion that Lewis's possibilism is incomprehensible. One of the reasons for its being incomprehensible is the fact that Lewis's concept of possible worlds has no definite criteria for individuation and identity. Lewis encompasses 'the way things are' and 'ways things could have been' within the fold of the totality of existents and thus seeks to annihilate their distinction. Now, the question is, how do we then identify and individuate our world as distinct from other possible worlds? In Lewis's view, all the worlds are real, so we should fail to distinguish our world from other possible worlds on the basis of the distinction between existents and possibilia.

Thus, it appears to me that the modal possibilism of Lewis is caught between the horns of a dilemma and in either case full-blooded realism of possible worlds is to be sacrificed. For, either he will have to accept the distinction between existents and possibilia or he will have to reject it.

There is another variety of modal realism with regard to the nature and status of possible worlds and possible individuals that we find in the case of some of the modal actualists. Realism that has been supported by the modal actualists is, however, quite modest in its claim. Hence this form of realism may be called 'modest realism' to distinguish it from the robust realism of Lewis. We can mention the names Plantinga[23] and Robert Stalnaker[24] as the supporters of this form of modal realism.

The actualist view is by far the most common view, but it has been developed in various ways. The fundamental point of the

---

23 Alvin Plantinga, 1974, *The Nature of Necessity*, Oxford: Clarendon Press, also Plantinga, 1979, 'Actualism and Possible Worlds', in *The Possible and the Actual*, ed. Michael Loux, pp. 253-73.

24 Robert Stalnaker, 1979, 'Possible Worlds', in *The Possible and the Actual*, ed. Michael Loux, pp. 225-34.

actualist view is to show that all the manifold of possibilia are to be found in the actual world. Hence, while analysing the nature of possibilia, Plantinga and Stalnaker are of the opinion that possible worlds and possible individuals are not to be found anywhere outside the actual world. These possible worlds belong very much to this concrete real world of ours.

According to Plantinga, these possible worlds are a kind of states of affairs. Plantinga begins his discussion with certain examples of states of affairs, without attempting to provide any definition whatsoever of states of affairs. 'Quine's being a philosopher', 'Quine's being a politician', 'Mr. Thomas's being ten feet tall', 'nine's being an odd number' — these are all examples of states of affairs. Among these different states of affairs, we may observe a certain point of agreement or disagreement. The states of affairs that consist in Quine's being a philosopher and nine's being an odd number have some agreement in the sense that both of these states of affairs do actually obtain. But the states of affairs that consists in Quine's being a politician or Mr. Thomas's being ten feet tall do not actually obtain. Hence these states of affairs which could have obtained but do not actually obtain are called possible states of affairs. For Plantinga, it is these possible states of affairs which constitute the so-called possible worlds. These possible states of affairs also differ from some other states of affairs like Mr. Thomas's squaring the circle or Mr. Thomas's going against the force of gravitation. These latter states of affairs are logically or causally impossible. For this reason such states of affairs are called impossible states of affairs. Thus in Plantinga's system we can take states of affairs as a genus which subsumes actual states of affairs, possible states of affairs and impossible states of affairs. Thus, according to Plantinga, there are both possible and impossible states of affairs. Of those different kinds of states of affairs, the states of affairs which are possible constitute his possible worlds.

It should be noted that Plantinga desists from calling any and every possible state of affairs a possible world. A possible state of affairs that is complete or maximal is said to be a possible world. From Plantinga's discussion, it appears that he takes the notions of 'possible' and 'state of affairs' as primitives. Plantinga however explains what he means by saying that a state of affairs is maximal or complete. A single uncompounded state of affair is not a possible world. A totality of different states of affairs when maximal constitutes a possible world. Now, a combination of states of affairs *S* to be maximal must satisfy certain conditions:

Let *S'* be any state of affairs.

1. *S* should include *S'* if it is not possible that *S* obtains and *S'* fails to obtain.
2. *S* should preclude *S'* if it is not possible that both obtain.

Thus *S* is maximal if for every state of affairs *S'*, *S* includes *S'* or *S* precludes *S'* on the grounds stated above. In that case, as Plantinga would say, *S* is a possible world, say *w*, as it is a maximal possible state of affairs. We may try to clarify Plantinga's idea of inclusion and exclusion of states of affairs with the help of certain illustrations. Thus, Sudipta Sen Gupta's being one of the Indians to visit Antarctica includes Sudipta Sen Gupta's being an Indian. It also includes Sudipta Sen Gupta's being an explorer in Antarctica. So in this case we find that a state of affairs includes many other states of affairs. Similarly, this particular state of affairs of Sudipta Sen Gupta's being one of the Indians to visit Antarctica precludes Sudipta Sen Gupta's not being an Indian, and not being an explorer to Antarctica. We can now define a maximal, or complete, state of affairs as one which includes all states of affairs which it does not exclude. Of course, the actual world is one of the possible worlds, and in its capacity as a possible world, it must also be said to be a maximal state of affairs in the sense just defined. Among the varied possible worlds only that world which obtains is the actual world. Plantinga also argues that there is exactly one actual world, i.e. that exactly one possible world obtains. Hence, Plantinga cannot say, as Lewis does, that this world is actual in relation to the inhabitants of this particular world who happen to call their world as 'our world'. Plantinga outright rejects indexical analysis of actuality. To deny that there is more than one actual world, Plantinga thinks, is to admit something which is 'repugnant to the intellect'.[25]

Plantinga introduces a technical term 'books'[26] to elucidate further his notion of the possible worlds. Plantinga is also inclined in favour of the view that states of affairs and propositions do not constitute two altogether different realms. Rather he is favourably inclined to hold that propositions and states of affairs are inextricably connected. In fact, for Plantinga, the proposition *that Socrates is snub-nosed* is no different from the state of affairs of *Socrates's being snub-nosed*. For we can say that the proposition that Socrates is snub-nosed entails the state of affairs of Socrates's being snub-nosed; and again the state of affairs of Socrates's being snub-nosed entails the proposition that Socrates is snub-nosed. Now, for any possible world *w*, and for any proposition *p*, *w* entails *p* or the denial of *p*. The set of all propositions *S* which includes all those propositions which are members of *S* as they are entailed by *w*, is called by Plantinga 'a book'. So each world has its book. The book on a world *w* is the set of propositions true in *w*. To say that a proposition is true in a world is to say that if *w* had been actual *p* would have been true.

Thus, we can say the following things, following Plantinga:

1. A possible world w corresponds to a unique set of propositions.
2. A state of affairs corresponds to one proposition.
3. A set of states of affairs corresponds to a set of propositions.
4. A set of propositions = a book.

Therefore, we can say a possible world *w* corresponds to a book.

---

25 In Plantinga, 1979, 'Actualism and Possible Worlds', in *The Possible and the Actual*, ed. Michael Loux, p. 259; also in Plantinga, 1974, *The Nature of Necessity*, pp. 45-46.

26 In Plantinga, 1979, 'Actualism and Possible Worlds', in *The Possible and the Actual*, ed. Michael Loux, p. 269.

How to describe these possible worlds? These possible worlds are described mainly in terms of two things:

- First, in terms of individuals or objects that exist in a possible world.
- Second, in terms of properties that objects have in a possible world.

However, it is needless to mention that the objects or individuals that exist in possible worlds are not all of the same type. Some objects are such that they exist in all possible worlds. For example, number seven is an object that exists in all possible worlds. Again there are objects which do not exist in all possible worlds. To say that an object x exists in a world w is to say that if w had been actual, x would have existed; or in other words, to say that x exists in w if it is impossible that w obtains and x fails to exist.

Second, Plantinga speaks of properties that objects have. Plantinga's view of properties is quite different from some other views about properties. The view which has been mostly criticized by Plantinga is referred to as the canonical conception of properties. According to this canonical conception of properties, properties are a kind of set-theoretical entities: they conceive properties as functions from possible worlds to sets of individuals. But Plantinga observes that there are certain difficulties in this conception of properties.

One of the guiding principles about sets is that all sets have their extensions essentially. In other words, no set could have lacked any member it has, or had any it lacks. If an individual which is a member of a set does not exist then the set that contains that individual does not exist. The set S of philosophers, for example — the set whose members are all the philosophers there are — would not have existed if Quine did not exist. Second, no two distinct sets have the same members. For if the set S and the set S' have the same members then the set S and S' are said to be identical.

The point that Plantinga wants to emphasize is that sets and properties are not the same thing for these important characteristics of a set cannot be ascribed to properties. All properties do not have their extensions essentially. By saying this Plantinga wants to imply that a particular property *P* could have been exemplified by an individual that does not in fact exemplify it.

The second point of distinction between properties and sets is that, unlike sets, distinct properties could have the same extension. Thus, for example, the properties of being cordate and being renate belong to exactly the same individuals, but these are different properties.

Hence Plantinga rejects this canonical conception of properties. It has already been shown that in giving semantical representations of different modal systems, Kripke holds that we will have to admit that the domains of objects that are found in the different possible worlds are not the same. Some new individual may be added to the domain or some other individual may be removed from the domain of a possible world. This fact, however, cannot be explained if one sticks to the view that properties are a kind of set-theoretical entities. Plantinga observes that if one sticks to the view that properties are functions from possible worlds to sets of individuals certain logical anomalies will result.

A universally quantified formula of the form $(x)Fx$ is taken to be equivalent with the statement that every member of the domain *D* has *F*. But, as Plantinga argues, these two propositions cannot be shown to be equivalent for these two propositions may not be true and false at the same time in the same world. Supposing there is a world w_1 which has as its domain *D*, and that there is another possible world w_2 which includes all the members of the domain *D* of w_1 plus some other new members. Now in this possible world w_2, since it has been assumed all the members of *D* are *F*, the statement 'All the members of *D* are *F*' is true in the world w_2. But since w_2 includes other individuals as well, over and above all the members of *D*, it is quite likely that those individuals may not be *F*. Then in that case the statement that $(x)Fx$ cannot be said to be true in that particular possible world.

This argument of Plantinga is however not at all convincing. For if we only make the statements which seem to be nonequivalent in a more guarded way, no such logical difficulties would arise.

The second argument forwarded by Plantinga, however, is more convincing. In this argument Plantinga relies on the notion of identity of sets. As has been already pointed out, two sets are said to be identical when they contain the same members. Now, it has been supposed, sometimes a particular individual, say Aristotle, may not exist in another possible world. Let us call that possible world w_2. Then the domain of the world w_2 cannot be said to contain Aristotle as its member. But in another possible world, say w_1, where Aristotle exists, the domain of that world w_1 is said to contain Aristotle. In that case the sets representing the domains of w_1 and w_2 cannot be said to be identical.

Furthermore, a set *S* can only be said to exist in a world *w* where all its members do exist. In this case a careful observation will reveal that there are two underlying assumptions:

1. For any world *w*, there is a set $\psi(w)$ that contains just those objects that exist in *w*.
2. If *D* is the domain of *w*, then w has essentially the property, of having *D* as its domain.

Given these two assumptions, it follows that *w* can exist only if $\psi(w)$ exists.

Supposing, Socrates belongs to $\psi(w)$, then, if we suppose that there is another domain where Socrates does not exist, it is obvious that the set representing the domain where Socrates exists cannot be identical with the set representing the domain where Socrates does not exist. So if $\psi(w)$ does not exist then *w* cannot exist. So, Plantinga concludes that we are required to maintain that possible worlds are necessary beings. But Plantinga's point is to show that since possible worlds are necessary beings, we cannot uphold the canonical conception of properties. According to Plantinga, domains of objects are not necessary beings as it has been supposed by the supporters of the canonical conception of properties. On Plantinga's view these domains are contingent beings. Hence they may or may not exist. But so far as the possible worlds are concerned, they are necessary beings. Hence, from this, it follows that possible worlds do not essentially contain their domains.

But it is not clear as to what point Plantinga is actually trying to make here. What is more difficult to understand is that in order to explain modal notions he rather openly invokes some other modal notions. Hence, it cannot be denied that his attempts to explain what the possible worlds are suffer a setback as he himself gets involved in a vicious circle. He goes on to say that possible worlds are necessary beings, that the domains of possible worlds are not necessary beings, without providing any account whatsoever for his calling a possible world a necessary being or the domain of objects in a possible world as not necessary beings. However, it is not too difficult to explain these additional characterizations about the nature of possible worlds and their domains. If a possible world consists of possibilities regarding the objects of the actual world, then it must necessarily exist; the reason being that if it is possible for *x*, which is *F*, to be *G*, then it is also necessary that it is so possible. That Nixon might not have been the president of the US in 1972 is not a contingent matter of fact, but a matter of necessity. In this connection, one may be reminded of Wittgenstein's observations: whatever is possible is necessarily possible.

From the very beginning we have made it clear that Plantinga is an actualist. Now for any actualist, and so also for Plantinga, a possible world does not exist outside the actual world. In his view the domain of objects in a possible world is a subset of the domain of objects in the actual world. But the difficulty is this that no actualists deny that there could have been an object distinct from any that exists in the actual world. If a possible world is contained within the actual world then how can one say that there could have been an object distinct from all which exist in the actual world? If the domain of a possible world is, in every case, a *subset* of the domain of the actual world then, certainly, there cannot be any individual in a possible world which is not also an object in the actual world. This follows from the very definition of a subset. We are thus faced with a paradox.

Plantinga solves this paradox by referring to the notion of essences. According to Plantinga, as we have already noted, there are some necessary beings. Properties, propositions and possible worlds are necessary beings according to Plantinga. But the individual to which a particular property belongs is a contingent being. This too is something that Plantinga can, perhaps, maintain: to say that the being of an individual is contingent is to say that and individual existing in the actual world does not exist in some possible world. I prefer to call Plantinga's actualism, a kind of realism. He wants to assert independent and eternal existence of properties, propositions and possible worlds. His properties and possible worlds have some sort of affinity with Platonic ideas.

Now, let us turn again to the main line of Plantinga's argument. If individuals are contingent beings then Socrates, since he is an individual, is also a contingent being. So Socrates can exist or cannot exist. But his property, i.e. Socrateity, if we call it so, is a necessary being. This property exists in all the worlds. If Socrates had not existed then this property, viz. Socrateity, would not have got any occasion for being exemplified. But from the fact that a certain property is not exemplified it cannot be inferred that the property in question does not exist at all. It is essential for the property of Socrateity that if it is at all exemplified it must be exemplified by Socrates; while being actually exemplified by Socrates is accidental to it.

Some essences are exemplified in a particular world, now the essences that are exemplified in a particular world, say w, constitute a set of essences. A set of essences (which are exemplified) is thus associated with each particular possible world. $\psi E(w)$, the set of essences exemplified in w, is associated with the possible world w.

We have already noted earlier that Plantinga has said that

domains of possible worlds comprise typically contingent beings. But now it seems that he admits that $\psi E(w)$ is the essential domain of w. Is he not contradicting his earlier stand? Perhaps, to avoid any such misunderstanding he maintains a bit cautiously that worlds do not in general have their domains essentially. $\psi E(w)$ is *the essential domain* of a possible world. Properties are, according to Plantinga, necessary beings, so properties exist in every world. So, there is no problem in maintaining that essential domains are necessary beings. Second, if $\psi E(w)$, i.e. essential domains are necessary beings then the respective worlds have those domains essentially. We have *UE* which is the union of all $\psi E(w)$, i.e. essential domains for all worlds.

Properties are sometimes exemplifed and sometimes not. So essences which are properties are also sometimes exemplified or sometimes not. Hence, there is no difficulty in thinking that there may be some essences which are unexemplified. So $\psi E(w)$ of a world w may contain essences all of which are not exemplified. What Plantinga wants to maintain seems to be something like the following: while the existence of individuals exemplifying properties is contingent, the existence of the properties themselves is not contingent, but *essential*. So, if the domain (of entities) in a world is divided into two sub-domains — one comprising the individuals and the other the properties, then this domain contains both contingent and necessary beings. It is also clear that the properties (essences) must belong to all possible worlds: it may well be that a particular object does not exist in a possible world. But even in that world it is possible that the object might have existed there. But if the object were to exist there, it had to exemplify a certain essence, and an object cannot exemplify an essence in a world in which it does not exist.

Plantinga should have said from the beginning that $\psi E(w)$ represents the set of essences that are associated with a particular world. But when he introduced the notion of $\psi E(w)$ he said that the set of essences exemplified in w is $\psi E(w)$ carrying the impression that it represents the set of only those essences that are exemplified in *w*. But that this is not his intention is clear from his subsequent discussions where he maintains, 'probably there is a world *w* whose essential domain $\psi E(w)$ contains an essence that is in fact exemplified and so *UE*, i.e. the union of $\psi E(w)e$ for all worlds, can contain some unexemplified essence'. So, it must be admitted that Plantinga is bit careless while introducing the notion of $\psi E(w)$.

We may once again turn to the earlier problem. It was regarding how to explain the proposition 'there could have been an object distinct from each object that actually exists' from the point view of an actualist. On the canonical conception of the properties this is true provided there is an individual *x*, of μ such that *x* does not exist in the actual world say α, but does exist in some possible world distinct from the actual world α. Thus on this view there are things that do not actually exist. But the actualists cannot agree with this thesis. For Plantinga, the above-mentioned proposition is true if and only if there is an essence that is *exemplified in some world but not exemplifed in fact*: in other words, if and only if there are unexemplified essences. To quote from Plantinga,

> As actualists we may state the matter thus: although there could have been some things that don't in fact exist, there are no things that don't exist but could have.[27]

Stalnaker too does not support strong modal realism of Lewis. If we consider possible worlds not just as heuristic aid to imagination, the notion of possible world has to be explained and its use justified. Stalnaker also does not believe in robust realism of Lewis. But he is in search of a moderate form of realism about possible worlds. According to the moderate realism of Stalnaker, possible worlds do exist. In this regard his moderate realism is not different from the robust realism of Lewis. According to Lewis as well, as we have already seen, possible worlds exist, even though they are not said actually to exist since to actually exist is to exist in the

27 In Plantinga, 1979, 'Actualism and Possible Worlds', op. cit., p. 272.

actual world. But Stalnaker does not maintain with Lewis that other possible worlds are also things of the same sort as the actual world. Stalnaker subscribes to the view that the actual world is just another name for reality.

But, at the same time, Stalnaker does not defend the position taken by Robert Adams. Adams in his zeal to avoid the extreme realism of Lewis proposes eliminative reduction of possible worlds to something else. Stalnaker does not want to reduce possible worlds to some other entities. Possible worlds, i.e the ways things could have been, have been sought to be accommodated within the actual world by Stalnaker. For this reason, we can call Stalnaker an actualist. But we should also note that he is a realist so far as modalities are concerned. For him possible words are actually existing abstract entities. Like Plantinga, Stalnaker too believes that abstract entities can actually exist without being instantiated. For Stalnaker possible worlds are really properties. He thinks that properties that are possible worlds are basic, i.e. primitive.

Stalnaker maintains that while possible worlds are ways, things might have been the actual world is the way things are. And he maintains further that the way things are is a *property*, or a *state of the world*, not the world itself. Now, as he believes in the existence of uninstantiated properties, he concludes that the way things might be, can, like any other property, exist without being instantiated. Thus in his modal realism he can easily maintain that there are possible worlds but deny at the same time that there exists any world that is like the actual world. Although the possible worlds are real, and neither reducible to other entities nor are notational short cuts, they are less than the actual world.

Thus we see that Stalnaker's realism is more consistent that that of Plantinga. In Plantinga's system we are committed to the existence of possible worlds and within those possible worlds he admits properties. Thus it becomes difficult to understand his notion of possible worlds. But in Stalnaker we find an explicit identification of possible worlds with properties of a certain kind.

Nicholas Rescher's actualism with regard to possible worlds

and possible individuals, on the other hand, is conceptual in consequence. Possible worlds are supposed to be mind dependent, but they are common to many minds. Rescher is a realist so far as the actual world and actual object are concerned. But that is the limit of his realism. He does not agree with Lewis by extending his realism to cover the realm of unreal possibles. Rescher is also not a Berkeleyan for he does not subscribe to the view that the real and the unreal alike require minds for their existence. Rescher is not a Platonic realist either. For he does not preserve any separate realm for the possibilia lying outside the realm of the actual world and yet accessible to mind. Nor does he maintain that the world contains two compartments for existence — one for the actual individual and the other for the merely possible. All possibilia — be it a world or an individual — are nothing but the objects of certain 'intellectual processes'.[28] The very being, the very existence of the possible worlds and possible individuals is 'thought of, assumed or conceived'[29] by the mind. Hence as hypothetical entities the possible worlds or possible individuals are not objectively real; and in Rescher's opinion whatever is not objectively real is devoid of all ontological status. Hence he pronounced zero ontological status for non-existent possibles.

However, Rescher who dooms non-existent possibles to zero ontic status, at times shows enough eagerness to restore some ontological basis to such non-existent possibles. No doubt there appears to be some sort of contradiction in his views regarding the possibilia. How can one provide any ontological foundation to something which is believed to be without any such ontological status? What seems to me is that Rescher had two different questions in his mind when he was maintaining such conflicting views regarding the ontic status of the possibilia. We should not forget that Rescher is an actualist and unlike a possibilist, he cannot grant any ontological status to the possible worlds over and above

---

[28] Nicholas Rescher, 1975, *A Theory of Possibility*, Oxford: Basil Blackwell, pp. 197-98.

[29] Ibid.

the actual world. Perhaps with a view to stressing this difference and to imply that possible worlds do not have any realm of their own outside the actual world, he said they are of zero ontological status. But at the same time as an actualist he cannot ignore the existence of possible worlds and individuals as ghostly entities. Out of the manifold of actual world he thus furnishes the data for the possibilia, and, so, like entities belonging to the actual world, possibilia must have some ontological basis or foundation. According to Rescher, non-existent possibilities have an 'amphibious ontological basis'.[30] Now, as it has already been pointed out, on Rescher's view, non-existent possibles are mind-dependent. Of the various operations an intelligent mind is capable of, conceiving or assuming is one; and on this particular operation of mind depends the origin of the non-existent possibles. But we cannot account for these operations of mind like conceiving or assuming without reference to language. Language is essentially at the root of such operations. So, ultimately both mind and language are said to furnish the ontological foundation for the non-existent possibles. Non-existent possibles do not exist in the primary sense of the term 'existence'. Unrealized possibilities exist in the secondary and derivative sense of the term. Thus, what we can observe in the case of Rescher is that he takes the actual, real world as the starting point. This real world is not the product of imagination. It is given to us through our experience. The possible world, and possibilia in general, are, on Rescher's characterization, constructions from the actual world through the process of hypothetical alteration of the characteristics of the real within, of course, the limits of admissibility. Hence this much is clear that there is an empirical foundation as well behind the possibles. Furthermore, not anything and everything can be a possible. There are certain principles of compossibility as mentioned by Rescher. A collection of possible individuals duly combined with one another constitutes a possible world. However, not every

---

[30] Nicholas Rescher, 1979, 'The Ontology of the Possible', in *The Possible and the Actual*, ed. Michael Loux, p. 174.

collection of possible individuals constitutes a possible world. It is quite possible that individuals which are by themselves possible lead to some sort of mutual incompossibility when combined with one another. A set of severally possible individuals must therefore satisfy certain conditions in order that they do not become mutually incompossible. With this end in view, Rescher enumerates three different kinds of incompossibility.

1. Logical Incompossibility

Each of the severally possible individuals possesses certain differentiating or individuating marks. If their individuating marks contradict one another, a kind of logical incompossibility among the possible individuals is created, and that stands in the way of their constituting possible worlds.

2. Nomic incompossibility

This sort of incompossibility results when all or some of the natural laws are violated by the combination of possible individuals. However, it is quite controversial as to how far natural laws are to be kept unaltered in the construction of a possible world.

3. Metaphysical incompossibility

This third type of incompossibility may result, as pointed out by Rescher, from either of the following two:

(a) from the violation of the principle of the identity of the indiscernibles; and

(b) from description splitting.

In this context, the principle of the identity of the indiscernibles, as understood by Rescher, requires that two distinct actual individuals in the possible worlds should not *generally* share a common description. The second principle requires that distinct possible individuals should not stand for one actual individual. With the help of the term 'surrogate', as introduced by Rescher, which means possible individual with the same prototype, we may state the principle of metaphysical incompossibility more clearly. In a possible world a surrogate cannot stand for two distinct actual individuals, or two surrogates cannot stand for one actual individual.

But the above account of this constructive process for arriving at possible worlds cannot be said to be quite complete, if nothing is said about the possible individuals that lie at the root of this construction. In Rescher's theory the class of possible individuals can be viewed as a genus embracing within its fold actual individuals, unrealized actual variants and supernumeraries. The latter two categories taken together comprise the realm of the unactualized possibility. Rescher arrives at this triple domain theory of individuals on the basis of individual descriptions. Rescher begins with the assumption of predetermined identity of individuals obtained by description in terms of their purely qualitative features and by experiential encounter in terms of their placement within spatio-temporal matrix. The full individuating characterization of an actual individual is only to be had through a pair of data $< d, l >$, the first member of which, i.e. *d*, is a description of the individual (which need not be a complete description, but may be partial) and whose second member *l* represents an ostensive indicator. Hence it is clear that in the case of actualia in order to seek a logically secure criterion for individuation the description has to be supplemented by ostension through experiential confrontation or confrontability. Actual objects occupy different spatial positions; that alone enables us to distinguish two qualitatively same objects. Rescher lays great emphasis on this ostensive basis for identification and calls it 'the concretizing mechanism of identification'[31] to distinguish it from the description which is called by him 'abstractive mechanism of identification'.[32]

Starting from the actual individual Rescher arrives at the notion of unrealized actual variants. Now, while speaking about the actual

---

[31] Rescher, 1975, *A Theory of Possibility*, pp. 45-46.

[32] Ibid.

individual he was speaking about the actual description of the individual. Earlier it was pointed out that the actual description of the individual is given generally in terms of its actual properties, its necessary properties (i.e. those among its actual properties which are to be regarded as essential to it), its possible properties (those properties which it lacks but could possibly have), and its dispositional properties.

However, side by side we can have potentially variant descriptions of the actual. The peculiarity of a potentially variant description of an actual is that it differs from it in only inessential respects; but so far as the essential respects are concerned, there is no difference between the actual and a potentially variant description. It includes all of the same essential properties, be they absolute or dispositional. The crucial feature of this conception of a variant description is that the self-same individual can exist in descriptively different versions. Thus through the description which describes the variant (i.e. possible but unrealized) alternative of the actual individual Rescher arrives at the conception of an unrealized possible individual.

However, in the process of thus giving descriptions in terms of possible variations of the actual individual, we shall arrive at some description which in the very logic of the situation cannot qualify as describing the actual individual. Such descriptions are then considered as reality disqualified. If anything is to realize such a description, it must be some 'merely possible' individual, one altogether outside the range of the actual and its variations. Such individuals which are wholly new, instead of old individuals in new descriptive guises, will be considered as supernumeraries. Thus the actual individual remains the starting point throughout. It is from the consideration of the actual that the whole descriptive machinery proceeds. We even arrive at the conception of the supernumerary or the merely possible through that of the actual individual.

For Rescher, the principle of individuation does not present any problem at all. The principle is presented as follows:

1. An actual individual is completely specified by the combination of its merely qualitative (non-essentialistic) description as given by its property set *P*, plus its ostensively locative indicator *i*.

   $< P, i >$

   with *i* as effectively identity decisive.

2. Actually attached non-existent possible individuals are individuated simply and purely on the basis of their actual prototype, regardless of any descriptive considerations beyond those of essentialistic qualification

   $< P, \varepsilon >$

   with *P* alone as identity decisive.

3. Actually detached merely possible individuals (super-numeraries) are individuated on the basis of their *E*-descriptions (essentialistic descriptions = C.D.S.) alone.

   [$< P, \varepsilon >$, ✡]

   with *P* and ε as jointly identity decisive since ✡ indicates the 'null-prototype' or the 'null-individual'.

From the above account we get an idea of how possible worlds and possible individuals are ultimately generated by human mind with the help of the language that it possesses. This conceptualistic trend, so far as the possibility are concerned, is also present in the writings of Saul Kripke. Kripke has made it clear that possible worlds are not things we discover or observe with a powerful telescope. They are constructions which we make for ourselves.

There is a third position as to the nature of possible worlds. There are some actualists, in the sense defined earlier, often referred to as the reductionists, who are the upholders of this third position. The reductionists are so called because they reduce the talk of possible worlds to a talk about some linguistic entities. But since the reductionists thus seek a reinterpretation of the values of the variables, it should not be supposed that they are not interested in the framework of possible world. On the contrary, we should see that they find the talk about possible worlds quite illuminating. The reductive enterprise of these actualists consists in countering the ontology of possible worlds of the realists.

Here one thing is to be borne in mind. When I am using the expression 'linguistic entities', I mean it to be understood rather widely. The expression 'linguistic entities' covers sentences which are actually written or uttered, or anything that may result in such sentences. However, it should not be supposed that all the philosophical nuances between sentences and propositions are thereby overlooked or ignored. I must apologize for this sort of looseness in characterizing this third position, but I find it unavoidable. As these actualists present some sort of linguistic entities as world-surrogates or 'ersatz'[33] worlds, Lewis calls this position 'Linguistic Ersatzism'. But even among the linguistic ersatzists we may observe that there are ample differences as to the exact nature of these linguistic world-surrogates. However, a rough and ready characterization of the above position would be as follows.

One of the common practices of most of the reductionists is to reduce possible worlds to maximal consistent sets of sentences or propositions. The maximal consistent set of sentences or propositions is such a consistent set of sentences or propositions as one to which no further sentence or proposition could be added without causing the set to become inconsistent. Richard Jeffrey calls such maximal consistent sets of sentences 'complete novels'.[34] Robert Adams, who makes it clear that he wants to reduce talk about possible worlds to talk about sets of propositions, calls such a maximally consistent set of propositions a 'world story'.[35] A world story is, as Adams puts it in his 'Theories of Actuality', 'is a set which has as its member one member of every pair of mutually

---

33 David Lewis, 1986, *On the Plurality of Worlds*, pp. 142-65.

34 Richard Jeffrey, 1965, *The Logic of Decision*, New York: McGraw-Hill, 2nd edn., 1983, Chicago: University of Chicago Press, sec. 12.8.

35 Robert Adam, 1979, 'Theories of Actuality', in *The Possible and the Actual*, ed. Michael Loux, p. 204.

contradictory propositions, and which is such that it is possible that all of its members be true together'. Each world, be it possible or actual, has its world story. But the world story of the actual world differs from that of a possible world. The difference between these two world stories consists in this that in the case of the actual world all the members of its world story are true; but in the case of the possible worlds some of the members of the world story are false propositions. To Adams, however, to say that a proposition is true in an actual world is not the same as saying that a proposition is true in a possible world. Truth in a possible world is fundamentally different from truth in an actual world. The truth of a proposition in an actual world may be explained in terms of some sort of correspondence between a proposition and an object or state of affairs having an independent ontological status. But the truth of a proposition in a possible world is not to be supposed to be a relation between a proposition or sentence and an object or state of affairs having an independent ontological status. The truth of a proposition in a possible world is a matter of the relation of consistency among propositions. Adams also, has an explanation to account for this difference between the notion of truth of a proposition in an actual world and that in a possible world. According to him, the possible worlds are constructed out of the set of propositions which are true in it, and so according to him, the truth of a proposition in a possible world is consistency among propositions rather than correspondence with an independent reality. Thus, it is quite clear that according to Adams, possible worlds are constructions out of the propositions. However, Adams also seems to be quite aware of certain difficulties inherent in his theory because of the controversy as to the nature and status of propositions. He identifies possible worlds with sets of language-independent propositions, i.e. sets of abstract but actual entities having sentence-like semantical properties. To quote from Adams:

> . . . we must not suppose that propositions are linguistic signs or utterances, not that they are all expressible in any one language, nor even that there are only a countable infinity of them. We

> might take the notion of a proposition as primitive and suppose that propositions are self-subsistent objects; but we need not do so. We might try to construct them logically out of some other feature of the (actual) world.[36]

William Lycan also holds possible worlds to be sets of intensional objects. 'Thus, I would fall in either with Adams and Plantinga and construct worlds directly out of propositions or with Castaneda and Parsons and construct possible objects out of properties and then group the objects into worlds on the basis of their stipulated interrelations.'[37]

Andrew Roper, another noted linguistic ersatzist, in consideration of innumerable difficulties associated with the notion of propositions or of intensions generally, avoids reference to propositions. He, in presenting a detailed and systematic account of how quantification over possible worlds is to be reinterpreted as quantification over sets of linguistic entities, shuns reference to propositions. On the pragmatic consideration that the development of a satisfactory theory of propositions is still an unfinished task, Roper chooses sentences rather than propositions as the basic elements of maximal consistent sets of sentences called MCSS by him. The whole of Roper's reductive enterprise consists in showing that each sentence in a possible worlds semantics which quantifies over possible worlds can be replaced by sentences which quantify over maximal consistent sets of sentences.

In Roper we find a reinterpretation of the Kripkean semantics of possible worlds. In his model structure $< G, K, R >$, as we know, Kripke suggests that K be the set of all possible worlds, G the real world and R the relation of relative possibility. According to Roper, the model structure $< G, K, R >$ is to be understood in the following way: K is a non-empty set of maximal consistent set of sentences or propositions, or in short, MCSS of sentences; G is an element of K, G is that MCS (maximal consistent set) all sentences in which

[36] Robert Adam, 1979, 'Theories of Actuality', op. cit., p. 207.

[37] William Lycan, 1979, 'The Trouble with Possible Worlds', in *The Possible and the Actual*, ed. Michael Loux, p. 312.

are interpreted as true by that model, R is the converse of modal compatibility. According to Roper an MCS H_i is said to be modally compatible with an MCS H_j, i.e. H_jRH_1 if and only if for every sentence ψ, such that $\Box\psi \in H_j$, $\Box\psi \in H_i$. Thus, Roper provides an account of modal compatibility; but his definition of R in the modal structure $< G, K, R >$ is in terms of converse of modal compatibility. What is surprising in his account of this semantics is that he does not explain how the notion of converse of modal compatibility is to be understood. It cannot be denied that this notion of converse of modal compatibility is a technical term which is in need of further clarification.

Certain pragmatic considerations prompt Roper to take sentences rather than propositions as the basic elements of MCSS, but he considers sentences to be non-spatio-temporal entities. Roper does not leave any room for misunderstanding as to the nature of sentences in his system. For him, sentences are to be understood as sentence types rather than as token inscriptions or utterances. There are two reasons why he thinks this should be done. First, he feels, the notion of a type sentence is less obscure than that of a proposition. Second, there may be many sentences which are consistent and hence there is nothing to prevent those sentences from being elements of some MCSS; but we would not be able to include those sentences as elements of any MCSS because they have never been uttered or written by any one, and consequently do not have any tokens. If we take sentences to be non-spatio-temporal types, rather than sentence tokens, all sentences which are consistent could be included as elements in some MCSS.

It is clear that this view about possible worlds is closely related to Carnap's well-known proposal to identify possible worlds with state descriptions,[38] where a state description is defined as set of sentences (of some given language) which contains, for every atomic sentence, either that sentence or its negation, but not both, and no other sentences than these.

---

[38] Rudolf Carnap, 1947, *Meaning and Necessity*, Chicago: University of Chicago Press, p. 9.

Thus, broadly speaking, we find that linguistic ersatzism takes two lines: in one group, taking the first line, belong those philosophers who follow *in toto* the Carnapian strategy of identifying possible worlds with certain sets of sentences. For these philosophers possible worlds are sets of sentence tokens as individual vocables uttered by human beings or individual marks written on paper. One of the advantages of this view is that it is able to theorize with certain universally acceptable entities. But there is one great problem with this view. Lewis in his *Counterfactuals* refers to this as the cardinality argument, the problem that results from considerations of the cardinality of the class of possible worlds, against linguistic ersatzism. This particular version of the cardinality argument wants to draw our attention to the fact that the sets of sentences would always fall short of possible worlds with which they are sought to be identified. It may be difficult even to convey all the details of the actual world since there may not be enough sentences to express all that is required. Supposing we want to say about each *number* that it exists. Now, so far as numbers are concerned there are uncountably many of them, for, at least, there is an uncountable infinity of real numbers; and, so, if we want to say about each of these numbers that it exists, we shall require uncountably many sentences each of them specifying that a particular number exists. But the problem is that there are not enough sentences, for there are only countably many sentence tokens, each finite in length. Hence it is clear that sets of sentences in the sense of sentence tokens cannot express all the facts that we are required to express about the actual world. Thus, it is argued, the reductive enterprise is bound to fail as there are more possible worlds than there could be the linguistic entities. Thus, the cardinality argument tries to establish that our language cannot exhaust all the possibilities, hence sets of linguistic constructions cannot be supposed to be isomorphic with possible worlds.

How to combat this charge of cardinality? There are some linguistic ersatzers who do not identify possible worlds with any actual linguistic constructions. For them sets of sentence types are to be identified with possible worlds. Now, this group of linguistic ersatzers would not face this problem of cardinality. Hence one way to avoid this charge of cardinality is to appeal to sentence types rather than sentence tokens. But this version of linguistic ersatzism has its own difficulties.

However, I do not think that this charge of cardinality is so serious as it appears to be. Though Lewis, from the days of his *Counterfactuals*, has been harping on this charge, in *Plurality of Worlds* he concedes, 'cardinality problems do not threaten linguistic ersatzism, though they teach us how to go about it'.[39] No doubt, there are certain assumptions on the basis of which this cardinality argument has been developed.

We must find out what the main assumptions are that support this cardinality argument and we should decide how far these assumptions are beyond doubt. To quote Lewis:

> If we take "language" at all literally, so that sentences are finite strings over a finite alphabet, there are not enough sets of sentences to go round'.[40]

A question arises here regarding taking a language literally. That means, we can understand language literally as distinct from non-literal acceptance of language. From Lewis's account this can be presumed that by literal understanding it means the common way of or conventional understanding of language. Generally, by language it is meant natural language or, in an extended sense of the term, anything like a natural language. Now, natural languages are finite. But there cannot be any hard and fast rule that an ersatzer should confine himself to this sense of language.

In fact, Lewis too in his later writings realized that an ersatzer need not confine himself to this narrow sense of language. Language can be understood to stand for such a system of structure, signs and marks that can be parsed or interpreted. Not

---

39 David Lewis, 1986, *On the Plurality of Worlds*, p. 144.

40 Ibid.

once the notion of language is delinked from the notion of natural language, there is no compulsion to conceive this language infinite. We can have an *infinite* language, either because it has an infinite number of words, or because we introduce an infinite number of connectives to connect a finite number of words, or because we permit an infinite number of applications of a finite number of connectives on a finite number of words.

Phillip Bricker revives the cardinality argument against reductionism in a more guarded way and goes a step further than Lewis. According to him, 'the difficulty is this: no actual language could have the descriptive resources needed to represent all the ways things might have been'.[41]

For Bricker the cardinality problem arises not because the possible worlds always outrun the actual in number but because the possible outruns the actual in kind. That there are too many possibilia to be covered by linguistic entities was no longer supposed to present any problem. Bricker apprehends a threat to the prospect of any successful reductive enterprise on account of the deficiency of the descriptive apparatus of any language whatsoever. Faithfulness, non-circularity and naturalness — these are the three conditions, as mentioned by Bricker, are to be satisfied for any successful reduction of talks about possible worlds to talks about linguistic entities. First, the faithfulness condition requires that all such reductive attempts should preserve the truth and structure of the possible worlds theory. Hence one should be in a position to supply linguistic entities for distinct possible worlds. This would safeguard the linguistic entities from falling short of possible worlds. Second, the procedure of assigning linguistic entities to distinct possible worlds should be non-circular. Three, Bricker mentions naturalness as another condition. This demands that for the replacement of possible worlds by linguistic entities to be complete such replacement should be in terms of those linguistic constructions which can serve as a complete description

[41] Phillip Bricker, 1987, 'Reducing Possible Worlds to Language', *Philosophical Studies*, 52: 331.

of possible worlds. If a linguistic construction is true in the world which it is supposed to replace, or in the world which are not discernible from this world, but in no other worlds, then only it can be said to have given a complete description.

Every language has a logical part and a non-logical or descriptive part. Of the conditions mentioned by Bricker, the faithfulness condition is not difficult to satisfy. The reductionists can 'cook-up set-theoretic constructions out of the expressions of *L*'.[42] In this context, *L* stands for a sub-language of a natural language as used by actual people. That means if there is any deficiency in the logical part of the language that can be thus redressed. But the descriptive inadequacy that is found in each language cannot be removed by stipulating certain linguistic entities with the help of set-theory. In order to retain the naturalness condition of reduction what is required is that each linguistic construction should be able to describe the possible world completely. The non-logical or descriptive apparatus of a language cannot be thus improved or increased to meet the naturalness requirement. No attempt at linguistic reduction on possible worlds can succeed, for providing names for any and every non-actual entity is beyond the reach of 'the descriptive apparatus of the language'.[43] Hence the cardinality argument stands.

However, some linguistic ersatzers may not attach much importance to the cardinality argument. For they may feel that the source of the problem lies in identifying possible worlds with set of linguistic constructions. But even among the linguistic ersatzers there are some differences of opinion as to the entities that are to be identified with possible worlds. Those who have embraced the view that possible worlds are to be identified with sets of sentence types or propositions are no less reductionists. Those who try to avert the cardinality argument may somehow succeed against the simple version of the argument proposed by Lewis. But their approach to possible worlds at least apparently

---

[42] Phillip Bricker, 1987, op. cit., p. 349.

[43] Ibid., p. 331.

succumbs equally to the version presented by Bricker. However, the validity of Bricker's argument depends upon the three conditions he lays down, but the laying down of these conditions itself presupposes the validity of possibilism. Hence his attempt to revive cardinality argument may not stand in the long run.

Lewis too says that his common sense revolts against accepting our actual concrete world, and, consequently, a possible world as of well, to be nothing other than a set of sentence types or set of sentence tokens. This is so because he looks upon the actual world and all other possible worlds to be on a par. For Lewis, as he remembers, possible worlds are all real worlds like the actual world of ours. On Lewis's view the difference between an actual world and possible worlds does not lie in kind. Here the underlying assumption is that what is concrete and real cannot be identified with sets of linguistic marks. Now, the difficulty with Lewis is that he looks at the matter from this biased point of view. Hence, he finds it difficult to grasp the notion of possible worlds as set by sentences or propositions. Lewis begins with a preconceived notion about possible worlds, and any suggestion going against this notion seems to be absurd to him. To quote from the *Counterfactuals*:

> Since I cannot believe that I and all my surroundings are a set of sentences (though I have no argument that they are not), I cannot believe that other worlds are sets of sentences either.[44]

There are, however, some other arguments of Lewis which need much more careful consideration. As we have already seen, a linguistic ersatzer claims that a set of maximal consistent sets of sentences is a possible world. But how to give an account of consistency? Lewis observes that one of the ways of explaining the meaning of 'possible' is in terms of 'consistency'; thus, roughly, 'possibly *A*' is paraphrased as '*A* is consistent'. Again, it may be observed that the proposition '*A* is consistent' is ambiguous for consistency might be understood either syntactically or

[44] David Lewis, 1973, *Counterfactuals*, Oxford: Basil Blackwell, p. 86.

semantically. Understood syntactically or proof-theoretically, a set τ of formulas of a deductive system *X* is a consistent set *Y* if and only if for no formula *A* of *X* it is the case that both *A* is a theorem of τ in *Y* and ~ *A* is a theorem of τ in *Y*. But Kurt Gödel's first incompleteness theorem shows that any deductive system of arithmetic, if syntactically consistent, is incomplete; i.e. it will not include all arithmetical truths among its theorems. In other words, there is no way of axiomatizing arithmetic that is at once consistent and complete. Gödel has shown that some true formulas of arithmetic are not formally deducible within it. Taking the cue from this Gödelian theorem, Lewis wants to show that if we stick to this notion of consistency then we will fail to obtain all the sentences that we need for getting sets that would completely represent all the possible worlds. On the other hand, if we insist on obtaining all the sentences for completely representing possible worlds then we will have to sacrifice consistency itself. Hence when 'possibly *A*' is paraphrased as '*A* is consistent', this much is clear that the syntactic notion of consistency is of no help in clarifying our modal notions.

Lewis, therefore, turns to consider how far the semantic notion of consistency can serve our purpose. Understood semantically, the proposition, '*A* is consistent' (which is supposed to be a paraphrase of 'possibly *A*') may mean either

(a) that *A* is not necessarily false, or

(b) that *A* comes out true on some assignment of extensions to its non-logical vocabulary, or

(c) that *A* comes out true on some possible assignments of extensions to its non-logical vocabulary.

Now, in (a), where '*A* is consistent' is explained as '*A* is not necessarily false', and also in (c), where '*A* is consistent' is explained as 'A comes out true on some *possible* assignment of extensions to its non-logical vocabulary', we explain consistency in *modal* terms. Hence Lewis brings in the charge of circularity against such explanations. In the second case (b), Lewis relies on a Tarski-like notion of satisfiability to spell out the meaning of consistency.

But Lewis argues that if 'possibly *A*' is explained as '*A* comes out true on some assignments of extensions to its non-logical vocabulary' then such a proposition is false. The sentence 'some pigs are sheep' is satisfiable by assigning overlapping extensions to the two terms, but it is surely not possible true.

From all these considerations Lewis comes to the conclusion that the notion of consistency, depending on which the linguistic ersatzers carry out their reductive enterprise, swings between circularity and falsehood, and, hence, the whole of reductive enterprise is bound to fail. The point that Lewis wants to establish since the days of his book on counterfactuals is that modality has to be taken as a primitive notion. And, he adds, modality can be so taken, if we accept the thesis of modal realism. To avoid both circularity and falsehood one must take modality to be primitive.

The friends of the reductive thesis, however, do not so easily give in to the charges levelled by Lewis. Frank Jackson, who does not deny that the reappearance of an analysandum in an analysis is a defect, maintains, nevertheless, that sometimes such circularity in analysis or explanation may be helpful in resolving ontological issues. For example, if it is said that virtue is rare, one may suppose that there is a property called 'virtue' as there are tables, chairs and other material objects. This proposition can, and should be, paraphrased as 'virtuous people are rare'. But such a paraphrasing is obviously circular. It does not add anything to our understanding of virtue. But in one way this paraphrasing, though circular, is of immense importance. For it is at least not committed to the existence of an entity called 'virtue'. Thus, Jackson argues, circularity here is no barrier to our grasping of the notion of consistency.

Different modal systems provide us with different senses of necessity. But Haack thinks that, Lewis, while framing the charges of circularity and falsehood against various accounts of consistency, seems to have taken a 'monolithic view of logical necessity'.[45]

---

[45] Susan Haack, 1977, 'Lewis's Ontological Slum', *The Review of Metaphysics*, issue no. 119, March, XXX(3): 415.

Frankly speaking, I also do not feel that this circularity objection is unassailable. This much can be said that a reductionist should not in theory be at a loss to find a non-circular explanation of modality. Furthermore, Lewis is under the impression that to accept modality as primitive is also to accept full-blooded possible worlds as primitive. But it is difficult to see what logical link there is between the two. The primary aim of any reductive enterprise, as I understand the move, is to show that ontic commitment to possible worlds is not required. But on the question whether modality is to be accepted as primitive or derived the reductionists are divided.

According to Lewis, the need for primitive modality comes also via implicit representation. But what is this implicit representation as distinguished from explicit representation? According to Richard Jeffrey, we have noted, a possible world is a complete and consistent novel. And he speaks in a way which carries the impression that he takes these novels to describe the possible worlds. Taking the cue from Jeffrey's account, Lewis maintains that 'the ersatz worlds represent by saying'.[46] Subsequently, he draws a distinction between two kinds of representation. One he calls explicit representation and the other implicit representation. In the case of implicit representation, the idea is that not a single sentence but some sentences taken together represent a possible world. The way in which Lewis develops the argument in favour of primitive modality shows that he has not budged an inch from his realistic standpoint. To say that a set of sentences *represents* a possible world is to admit that there are possible worlds over and above the linguistic entities that are supposed to represent those possible worlds. Really, the reductionist need not commit himself to the view that linguistic constructions *represent* possible worlds.

It appears to me that the same fallacy has been committed by Bricker while enumerating certain minimal conditions that the reduction must satisfy. He maintains that faithfulness of translation

---

[46] David Lewis, 1986, *On the Plurality of Worlds*, p. 142.

is one such condition. To quote Bricker:

> If a reduction provides a truth and structure-preserving translation of possible worlds theory, then I will call the translation faithful, and say that the reduction satisfied the *faithfulness* condition.[47]

I cannot but repeat once more that this demand for faithfulness could be justified only if it could be shown that to accept modality as primitive is to admit a primitive notion of possible world to one's ontology. But that is not so. There is no logic in supposing that the reductionists are attempting some sort of translation by tagging one linguistic entity to each possible world which is out there to serve as its representative.

Adams, who is a great exponent of the reductive enterprise, however, admits that the notion of maximal consistent sets of propositions may be shown to be incoherent on the basis of one of Cantor's theorems. Now, according to his theorem of Cantor 'the power set of a set has a greater cardinal number than the set itself'.[48]

According to Adams and others, a maximal consistent set of propositions (or sentences) is a possible world. Finding a maximal consistent set of propositions, we may identify it with a possible world; and again finding another maximal consistent set of propositions we may identify it with another possible world. But the problem is that corresponding to each maximal consistent set of propositions there is a power set, which has a greater cardinality than this set, but that is also a maximal consistent set. So if we want to identify possible worlds with a maximal consistent set then we must not identify it with the maximal consistent set of

---

[47] Phillip Bricker, 1987, 'Reducing Possible Worlds to Language', *Philosophical Studies*, 52: 334.

[48] See Geoffrey, 1971, *Hunter's Metalogic*, Macmillan & Co.

Let A be the set {1, 2, 3}. Then the power set of A (i.e. the set of all subsets of a set A) will be the set ({1, 2, 3}, {1, 2}, {1, 3}, {2, 3}, {1}, {2}, {3}, ϕ)

Hence we see that there is no 1–1-correspondence between A and its power set.

propositions but with the power set of that maximal consistent set of propositions which is also a maximal consistent set. But the problem is that the power set of that (power set of a set) will have a greater cardinality. With which set to identify possible worlds? If this goes on ad infinitum no identification is possible between a maximal set of propositions and possible worlds. It seems to me, however, that this argument rests on a basic misconception.

A set of propositions and a set of sets of propositions are not the same thing. In the case of the first set, certain *propositions* are members of this set; but in the case of the second, certain sets are its members. If a linguistic reductionist decides to identify a possible world with a maximal consistent set of propositions, then no indecision should arise as to with which set he is to identify his possible world. It does not matter that the power set of the original set of propositions has a greater cardinality.

No doubt, there are some definite advantages of the doctrine of linguistic ersatzism. The semantics or maximal consistent set of sentences or propositions provides us with greater ontological economy. Of course, Lewis too has also given a definition of parsimony which suits his ontology of possible worlds. Further, the notion of sets, and types of sentences, are quite familiar and their identity and individuation conditions are quite clear.

The notion of actuality presents a perplexing dilemma to one who attempts to explain actuality in terms of difference between our world and other possible worlds. But Adams argues that the doctrine of linguistic ersatzism steers clear of any such dilemma. Why do we say that our world is the actual world?

Lewis, as we have already seen, has given an indexical analysis of actuality, according to which the actuality of our world depends on our relation with this world. We, as inhabitants of this world, call it 'this world'; so this is an actual world for us. But to the inhabitants of another possible world who call their place of habitation 'this world' is *their* actual world. Thus, in the indexical analysis, the actuality of the actual world is a relative notion. Adams calls this indexical analysis of actuality counter-intuitive.

For when we say something to be actual as distinguished from the possible we are under the impression that what is said to be actual is real. But if we adhere to the indexical theory of actuality we will have to maintain that the difference between Benazir Bhutto and Cinderella is just a matter of relation to us.

On the other hand, the simple property theory of actuality, whose origin may be traced back to Descartes, asserts that actuality is a property which the actual world possesses absolutely. But if it is maintained that the actual world is absolutely actual then actuality is no longer contingent.

Hence it is clear that in the indexical theory of actuality, we are led to hold:

I. For every possible world, *w*, the proposition that *w* is actual is true in *w*, and false in every other possible world. As the actuality is a world-relative property in this theory, so no distinction can be drawn between our world as 'actually actual' and other worlds only as 'possibly actual'. But, in the simple property theory, we are led to hold just this.

II. There is a world *w*, such that the proposition that *w* is actual is true in every possible world.

Now, the notion of absolute actuality makes it difficult to understand the sense in which all other worlds are even possible. For to say of something that it is possible is to assume that it could have been actual.

Adams, however, wants to abandon both of these alternatives. He is against admitting actuality as a world-relative property. Nor is he willing to accept that the world which is actual is necessarily actual. Adams calls his own theory an actualist theory of actuality. The actualist theory wholly differs from the indexical theory of actuality, as well as from the simple property theory, because its peculiar approach to actuality. It does not begin with a system of possible worlds and looks upon the actual world as a member of a greater system of possible worlds. In the view of the actualists there are possible worlds; but these possible worlds are not regarded as primitive. To him, as we have already discussed, the maximal consistent sets or propositions are primitive. The claim that our world is actual (i.e that all the elements of a maximal consistent set are true) can be made outside the system of maximal consistent set of sentences and is thus not be relative to the maximal consistent set. Although every maximal consistent set is possibly 'actual' the actual maximal consistent set is distinguished from the others in that it alone has elements all of which are true.

III

Now, these are some of the views about the nature of the possible worlds. However, I must acknowledge that it has not been possible to examine or even mention all the alternative views offered or suggested by different philosophers. Also, here, I have mainly dealt with some of the major views about the nature of the possible worlds. Modalism, as I conceive it, stands for the view that modality is primitive. By contrast to modalism, we have non-modalism, the view that denounces primitive modality. But it would be wrong to infer from this that I do not consider non-modal actualism to be one of the viable alternative views about the nature of the possible world. The belief that possible-world account of the meaning of modality is adequately led me to undertake the task of expelling worries that are connected with the notion of possible world. A metaphysically interesting analysis of the nature of possible worlds should explore the hook up between modality and possibility. But at the same time this has occurred to me that the decision to treat modality as primitive should not be tied up with the notion of possible worlds as primitive. In this context, primitiveness, as I understand, stands for nonderivativeness. I join issue with those who try to subject modal notions to further analysis to unearth their physicalistic basis. There is a significant sense in which modality is to be accepted as primitive. Plurality of possible worlds provides insight into our modal notions. With this assertion, I think, I am coming close to the jargon that possible worlds are aids to imagination. No doubt possible worlds are devices put forward by the possible world semanticists to explain the notions of possibility, necessity, etc. In themselves these possible worlds are not primordial real entities. Possibilism with regard to possible worlds is hard to digest. It is not a metaphysically tenable position. The actualist denial of the view that possible worlds are other real alternative worlds seems reasonable to me. But the actualists, who house possible worlds within the actual world cannot deny the responsibility of answering the charge of contradiction that may be levelled against them. This objection, however, is not formidable. The source of this misconception is not far to seek. The actualists begin with the supposition that the possible worlds are not real entities. That is, on actualist hypothesis, the possible worlds are not existent. But in their zeal to accommodate possibilia within the actual world, they assert that possible worlds are in the actual world. Thus, they are taken to claim that possibilia which are not existent are existent, a contradiction.

A careful consideration of the matter, however, reveals that there is no contradiction. The notion of existence is ambivalent and confusion between the two notions of existence is responsible for the charge of contradiction. We should maintain a distinction between two senses of existence. The existence of the actual world, which is existence in the first sense is different from the existence of the possible worlds, which is existence in the second. I want to draw attention to the fact that it is existence in the first sense which is basic, fundamental. The possible worlds exist, but they exist in a derivative sense, their existence belongs to a second order. If placed in a scale of successive order, the actual world would occupy the first order, followed by the possible worlds occupying the second order.

The actualists however, as we have already discussed, are found to present divergent views as to the nature of the possible world. The actualists are unanimous on the point that possible worlds are not other concrete worlds on a par with the actual world. In defending possible worlds, I side with those actualists who are conceptualists in their attitude. To me possible worlds are a kind of conceptual entities. They are not entities that belong to the Platonic realm. Possible worlds may be interpreted as concepts, i.e. as things conceived by some mind or other. They exist, but their existence is relative to a certain mind. My position with regard to possible worlds is very close to that of Rescher, who remarks:

> Their [possible worlds] existence is confined to the intensional order — as the correlative objects of actual or potential thoughts.[49]

The things that are intensional entities do exist in their own way; and that justified my placing of possible worlds in the second order of existence. Speaking of orders may create a confusion in some minds. It would be a mistake to equate this second order of existence with the realm of subsistence as preached by some philosophers. To clarify the matter further we may depend on the distinction between *objectivity* and *reality*, as has been suggested by Rescher. Reality may be taken to have a wider denotation. Reality encompasses the actual world and all the possible worlds. The notion of objectivity, on the other hand, has a link with the notion of mind-independent existence. Only those things are said to be objective whose existence is in no way dependent on human minds. Of course, that does not mean that because something is objective we cannot think, imagine or talk about it. The actual world is also an object of thought. But possibilia are wholly and fully objects of our mental acts. Apart from being conceived or thought of, they cease to exist.

---

49 Nicholas, Rescher, 1975, *A Theory of Possibility*, pp. 199-200.

4

A Transcendental Argument for Essentialism

THE predominant anti-essentialist trend in some of the present-day philosophical discourse may carry the impression that essentialism, being bereft of sound arguments, is dead. Essentialism as the doctrine that proclaims that objects have essence is one of the oldest doctrines that have come up for discussion since the Aristotelian time. In recent times issues relating to essentialism have received a great deal of attention from contemporary philosophers, linguists and modal logicians. Since W.V. Quine's scathing attack[1] on essentialism, it has become all the more urgent to consider whether essentialism as a philosophical viewpoint is innocuous or pernicious. The exact characterization of essentialism is quite challenging as its scope extends over many branches of study and multifarious discourses. Essentialism has been variously interpreted and there is no unanimity even among the proponents of the doctrine about what are essences as distinguished from non-essences or contingents. To speak of essential property in terms of individual essence is to suppose that each particular has a characteristic property or properties which are exclusively possessed by it and nothing else could possess those characteristics. A belief in individual essence rules out the possibility of simultaneous existence of two objects which share the same individual essence. The claim that each object has its own individuating essence does away with the very possibility of sharing the same individual essence by different objects. In some literature we come across the notion of internal principle of

[1] W.V.O. Quine, 1963, 'Reference and Modality', pp. 139-59.

distinction, which seems to be more or less akin to the notion of individual essence. The word, 'haecceity'[2] is taken to stand for individual essence or essence of an individual thing. Haecceities are supposed to be a collection of unanalysable properties. There are some who have taken the notion of property in a very restricted technical sense, and thus have left no room, however, for the admission of individual essence. The supporting argument runs as follows: since a property must be applicable to more than one object, and, if the property in question, does not apply to more than one object then it is not to be regarded as a property at all. Others talk of general essence in defining or explaining essentialism. Natural kind properties or the properties that define a kind are conceived as essence. Those who talk about general essence can easily accommodate two or more objects as sharing the same essence. What passes for the Aristotelian essentialism is of this type for according to this view the properties that are essential to an object are not individuating properties but kind properties. Thus understood, the essential property may be defined as follows: a property P is an essential property of an object x, if x could not exist and lack P. Language offers us various interchangeable words for general essence like 'universal', 'property', 'quality', 'type', 'kind', 'sort' and some others. It is interesting to note that D.M. Armstrong maintains a distinction between universals and properties.[3] Armstrong thinks that universals are there to provide grounds for the objective resemblance and causal power of things. Properties are numerous and undiscriminating and do not provide explanation for resemblance or causal power of things. Almost all properties are causally irrelevant. This may be conceded, however, that this view of Armstrong does not receive unanimous support from all quarters.

In most discussions on essentialism, the emphasis has been put on the connection between essential properties and modal

---

[2] The word '*haecceity*' is a term available since the time of medieval philosophy and was coined by Duns Scotus.

[3] 'Predicates and Universals' in *A Theory of Universals*, vol. II, p. 9.

properties. With the advent of quantified modal logic the debate on essentialism came to the forefront with renewed interest and vigour.[4] Quantification into a modal context is possible only if necessity is de re. But there cannot be any de re necessity unless a thing can be said to possess a property necessarily. To say that a thing possesses a property necessarily or essentially, as we have already seen, is to be involved in essentialism. This is one of the ways in which essentialism is involved in the case of quantified modal logic. The charge of essentialism may be framed against quantified modal logic from some other related consideration. One way to make de re modality intelligible is by providing a semantics of possible worlds. The semantical representation of modal logics[5] as suggested by Saul Kripke and his followers gives rise to fascinating questions about trans-world identity of an object across different possible worlds, accessible to the actual world. For Kripke himself the problem of trans-world identity was a pseudo problem,[6] but for others who considered it to be a genuine problem, one of the suggested ways for the resolution of the problem was by appealing to the notion of essence. This, we may say, is the second way in which essentialism relates to quantified modal logic.

Let us try to explain how the charge of essentialism does arise in the case of quantified modal logic.[7] To say, '$(\exists x)$ (x is necessarily greater than 7)' is to suppose x, i.e. 9 has necessary greaterness than 7 independently of any particular mode of characterization. When we say that an object x is such that, whether we describe it as this or that, it is necessarily possessed of a particular property,

---

4 For a detailed discussion on the issue, see 'How Is $(\exists x)$ (x Is Necessarily Greater than 7) Possible?', *Journal of Indian Council of Philosophical Research*, IV(2), 1987.

5 'Semantical Considerations on Modal Logics', in *Acta Philosophica Fennica*, 1963, Proceedings of Colloquium on Modal and Many Valued Logics, pp. 83-94.

6 Kripke, 'Naming and Necessity', p. 273.

7 Indrani Sanyal, 1984, 'The De Re Modality and Essentialism', *Indian Philosophical Quarterly*, XI(3), July; this volume, pp. 65-73.

we say that this property is the essence of the object concerned. Let us suppose that 9 is an object which is necessarily possessed of the property of being greater than 7. Now, if it is necessarily possessed of the property of being greater than 7, whether we describe 9 as the number of planets or as the successor of the number 8, we can say that 9 is necessarily greater than 7, independently of any mode of characterization, or that 9 has some essence. Since it is an essence of 9, the object, to be necessarily greater than 7, we can substitute the term '9' by the term, 'number of planets' and in that case the application of the principle of existential generalization does not present any problem. If '$(\exists x)$ (x is necessarily greater than 7)' is true, then there is at least one object of which it is true that it is necessarily greater than 7. And if we admit that 9 has some essence, then 9 can be such an object whose name can be written in the place marked by 'x' in '. . . is necessarily greater than 7'.

Kripke presented models for the semantic treatment of modal logic by invoking possible worlds as heuristic devices to make the idea of modal concepts more vivid. What distinguishes modal logic, whatever is the type of it, from non-modal logic is the admission of modal operators like 'necessity' or 'possibility' in that logic. The truth conditions for different types of modal propositions cannot be the same; in the case of de dicto modal propositions, a necessary proposition and a possible proposition are different and their difference is reflected by their requirements for truth conditions. A necessary proposition is said to be true, if it is true in all possible worlds; and a possible proposition is true provided it is true in at least one of the possible worlds, even if that is not the actual world. In the case of a de dicto proposition and in the case of a de re proposition we have different truth-conditional requirements. A de dicto necessary proposition and a de re necessary proposition have different requirements for truth conditions. Given a proposition, 'necessarily x is P', we regard it as true, provided 'x is P' is true in the actual world and in all possible worlds accessible to the actual world. In the case of the proposition, '*x* is necessarily *P*', we call it true provided 'in this actual world and in all possible worlds wherever *x* exists, *x* has *P*'. The truth requirement as discussed here for de re propositions has triggered the problem of trans-world identity. For how do we say that *x* of this world is identical with *x* of another possible world unless we have some criterion for trans-world identity? The basic idea here is to track the object of this actual world as one and the same in other possible worlds wherever it exists. The problem would not have been serious if we could have identified at least one such property of an object that remains invariant across all possible worlds. The question, however, continues to pester, as to which property which can serve as the criterion for trans-world identity for it is quite conceivable that *x* of this world may acquire some new properties or may lose some older properties? This calls for postulation of some essence or essential properties for an object which would retain identity of the object across different possible worlds. Kripke though owns the responsibility for giving birth to this pseudo-problem, he makes it clear that in his semantical models these possible worlds are not to be taken as distant lands wherefrom through telescopes attempts are made to locate *x* of this actual world in another possible world to fix its criterion for trans-world identity. Kripke acknowledges that along with some others he himself has given a formal treatment of modal logic which has wrongly encouraged many to look upon the matter in this way. Kripke puts it categorically,

> A possible world is given by the descriptive conditions we associate with it. . . . Possible worlds are stipulated, not discovered by powerful telescopes.[8]

Kripke considers possible worlds as counterfactual situations.

Other than the domain of modal logic, we have some other areas where the doctrine of essentialism receives immense consideration. Many philosophers believe that necessity is something which has been constructed by human beings and are

[8] 'Naming and Necessity', p. 267.

not something in the world that we discover. Quine has no respect for any higher or more austere kind of necessity than Hume's regularities. For Bertrand Russell the notion of essence is a mere verbal convenience. A.J. Ayer very strongly rejects essentialism. According to him objects do not have necessary predicates except in virtue of the way we describe them. On the other hand, there are people from opposite camp who claim that scientific inquiries are made possible by necessities existing in objects rather than in us. Among some prominent thinkers there is a strong tendency to revive essentialism and not to junk the notion of necessity. Broadly speaking, three main arguments are available in the literature to retain or reinstate essentialism from the clutches of the staunchest critics. Aristotle's metaphysics may be cited as defending essentialism but his argument is totally different in kind from that of David Wiggins or of Kripke. These three philosophers provide us with three different arguments in favour of essentialism:[9] we may call, one as metaphysical argument from Aristotle, the second as a semantical argument from Kripke and the third as a transcendental argument from David Wiggins. So far the tenet of essentialism is concerned, neither Kripke nor Wiggins have anything to compete with one another.

II

I am not over-ambitiously attempting to cover all the major arguments and their nuances to counter the challenges posed against essentialism, but concentrating primarily on elaborating arguments derived from Wiggins from his *Sameness and Substance* and from the reiteration of same argument in some details from his later work, *Sameness and Substance Renewed* where he has claimed to work out, 'the essentialist consequences of the theory of individuation'. In this essay the major thrust is on explicating and analysing Wiggins's pro-essentialist arguments. This would also enable one to comprehend what is distinctive in Wiggins's approach. Second, Wiggins's proposal for recovering essence from the charge of

---

[9] *On Essentialist Claims*, 2002.

violating extensionality principle will be considered. Wiggins's struggle to defend essentialism has been quite obviously sustained on the basis of a transcendental argument though it has never been explicitly mentioned by Wiggins himself. As in a typical transcendental argument, the necessity of a conclusion is asserted as an explanation from the observance or acceptance of the actuality, hence the possibility as well, of some phenomena, so does here the argument pattern of Wiggins proceed. In its generality, the strategy of Wiggins consists in elaborating certain necessary conditions as providing an explanation for some actual experiential occurrences for their being as those have been. All these details will be addressed in course of subsequent elaborations.

Wiggins shares the anxiety of the proponents of the extensionality principle and their anguish for the failure of quantification in a discourse dealing with essence. The strategy adopted by him to overthrow the objection raised by some logicians and philosophers regarding the failure of substitutivity principle and miscarriage of quantification will be discussed subsequently. The problems relating to possible worlds[10] seemed to him quite obnoxious and his ingenuity lies in proclaiming essence minus possible worlds, one of its generally supposed correlates. The task of enumeration of the principles was very seriously considered by Wiggins for he believed that this would guide his 'dialectical of that to which we are committed by our simplest thoughts about continuants and our simplest individuative practices.'[11] To speak in a very plain and simple language, Wiggins is attempting analysis of the cognitive act of individuation. His defence for essentialism, which has been characterized as individuative essentialism and also as 'mild' or 'modest' form of essentialism, thus we shall see, depends on three closely interconnected and very important observations: one is about the very pattern of the common individuative practices; second is

---

10 A detailed discussion is available in Indrani Sanyal, 1990, 'Modality and Possible Worlds', pp. 193-242.

11 *Sameness and Substance*, p. 104.

about the principle that supports and explains it; and the third is regarding the meaningfulness of logic of such de re constructions as discoverable through individuative practices. Wiggins has indeed initiated to found practices indicative of individuation and persistence through change in the logic of identity and the absolute conception of identity.

Wiggins draws our attention to certain cognitive concepts like conceiving and individuating, their interrelations and subsequent metaphysical consequences. To the question as to why should one embrace essentialism, the answer that is derived from Wiggins, may be summarized as follows: to conceive anything of *x*, or to counterfactually conceive anything of *x*, *x* has to be individuated; to individuate *x* is to provide an answer to the question, 'what is *x*?'; to answer what *x* is, is to say that *x* is necessarily so-and-so; this is to embrace a kind of essentialism. The essentialism as espoused by Wiggins is a consequence of the very manner of our epistemic activity of conceiving that makes it possible to account for a connection between the man and the world. The discussion about the cognitive act of individuation necessitates an answer to the question regarding what it is that performs the task of individuating. According to Wiggins:

> That which individuates . . . is in the first instance, a thinker. (Derivatively, but only derivatively, one may find oneself saying that a substantive or predicate individuates).[12]

The basic idea seems to be that for a thinker to conceive of any object *x* as something is to conceive of *x* as qualified by a property say, *P*. Literally speaking, by conceiving is meant referring to a thing as something. Broadly speaking, two ways have been discerned for any act of conceiving to be possible befitting human beings; these two types of conceiving can be characterized in the following ways:

1. *x* can be *P* if and only if it is possible to conceive of *x* that it is *P*.

---

[12] Indrani Sanyal, *On Essentialist Claims*, p. 104.

2. *x* must be *P* if and only if it is not possible to conceive of *x* that *x* is not *P*.

To put these expressions in other words, is to say, in the first case, it is being said that conception of *x* presupposes '*x* is possibly *P*'; and in the second case, '*x* is necessarily *P*'. In the language of modern logical techniques these expressions such as '*x* is possibly *p*' or '*x* is necessarily *p*' are called de re modal assertions, where not only properties are asserted of objects but also the manner or mode in which these properties belong to the object are also included in the assertions. To make counterfactual statements is to assert something of a particular which it is not, in fact. We take a round ball and may start thinking of that ball, as if it were not round. We take a green mango and may counterfactually think of it as being blue. In order to think counterfactually the object of conception has to be present or given to us. And in that case we will have to admit that there is a limit to our counterfactual conception. Or, we can say that counterfactual conceiving is conditional, provided the thing is present, then only such conceiving is possible. The property on account of which the thing is that very thing, its essence, thus has to be admitted. This suggests a close link, though may be in a hierarchical order, between the act of conceiving and what are called individuative practices. We can see that the idea of conceiving is rather a broader idea within which falls the act of individuation. To individuate *x* is to conceive of *x* as necessarily *P*. Thus individuative practices may be characterized as conceiving of something as necessarily falling under a concept. In the writings of Wiggins one should not fail to observe how subtly the connection between the act of conceiving and the individuative practices has been highlighted. Given the individuative practices as determinate, to individuate *x* is to individuate *x* as this or that such. This is often nicknamed as this such conception of individuation, which is the main argument running through *Sameness and Substance*.

> To single *x* out is to isolate *x* in experience; to determine or fix upon *x* in particular by drawing its spatio-temporal boundaries

> and distinguishing it in its environment from other things of like and unlike kinds (at this, that and the other times during its life history).[13]

Now let us try to bring out the main idea running behind this argument. It has already been pointed out that the act of individuation is primarily thinker-dependent and derivatively substantive predicate dependent. Why do to individuate x, x is to be understood as necessarily falling under a sortal concept? He assumes a close link between the individuative practices and contrary-to-fact conceiving about the same object. To make contrary-to-fact conditionals we entertain diverse things about an individual. To speculate diverse things about an individual there must be some feature f, such that no matter what else he is, he can be picked up as this f. This f stands for the most general sortal specification about the individual. Generally, some natural kind terms and artefacts are taken to play the roles of sortals and substantial predicates. Thus, we find here is a requirement for some specialized sort of predicate and the things regarding which this specification has been sought are three-dimensional material particular continuants. Wiggins says:

> By the elucidation of identity that I advocate, . . . will first have to say, what are the terms of identity. He will have to explain that *a* is a continuant which . . . and *b* is a continuant which . . . , and then expand each specification separately in a way sufficient to make determinate (with the help of the word) which continuant *a* is and which one *b* is, and what each is.[14]

Wiggins has proposed an explicit analysis of the necessary and sufficient conditions for any act of conceiving to take place. In the first place, any sort of conceiving to be possible there must be some objective empirical starting. That means something has to be given to our experience centering which the act of conceiving takes place. We cannot form any conception whatsoever, of purely

---

13 *Sameness and Substance Renewed*, p. 6.

14 *Sameness and Substance*, p. 51.

possible substances. The imagination of purely possible substances, if equated with objects that God will never create, is absolutely untenable. Wiggins reminds us of a passage from Ayer[15] which runs as follows:

> We can significantly ask what properties it is necessary for something to possess in order to be of such and such kind.

His metaphysics has left no room for the projection and assumption of any domain of *possibilia* — of mere possible entities. This is to emphasize that we cannot determine one entity just by making a long list of properties without saying what that thing is. 'We have to say that it is this or that such'.[16] More clearly articulated in *Sameness and Substance Renewed*, 'We have to say *x* is this such and such or that so and so'.[17] Just by picking any properties or complexes of properties, or by preparing a long list of properties with regard to any object we may fail to individuate the bearer of the property. This has been clearly stated by Wiggins:

> For any entity there are properties or complexes of properties such that nothing could count as conceiving of that entity as possessing them; likewise properties or complexes of properties such that nothing could count as conceiving of the entity as lacking them.[18]

Thus there are non-essential properties as distinguished from essential or necessary property of an individual.

In recent times among the protagonists of essentialism Kripke is undoubtedly the most remarkable one. However, since both Kripke and Wiggins speak favourably for essentialism, it would be quite impetuous to make much of Kripke–Wiggins similarity than their difference. Kripke's notion of essentialism heavily leans upon the notion of possible worlds, though Kripke did not forget

---

15 A.J. Ayer, *The Central Questions of Philosophy*, p. 197.

16 *Sameness and Substance*, p. 104.

17 *Sameness and Substance Renewed*, p. 109.

18 Ibid., p. 110.

to remind that for him possible worlds are rather tools for heuristic devices. Admittedly, however, Kripkean semantical treatment of modality had to call into use notions of possible worlds, whatever may be their extension or intension. On the other hand, Wiggins is wholly sceptic about the whole apparatus of possible worlds. It is one of his explicitly stated principles not to rely on the concept of possible worlds. The second principle that has been clearly formulated by Wiggins avoids and sort of dependence on the notion of possible worlds. He is strongly convinced that possible worlds are, as put by Kripke, 'heuristic devices'. One very significant aspect of Wiggins is that he takes the notion necessity or possibility much seriously. We shall see quite clearly though he had rejected any sort of reliance upon the concepts of *possibilia* and possible worlds, yet that does not weaken his acceptance of necessity and possibility de re. His treatment of modality de re is not to be read as another version of reductive approach to modality. In formulating his fourth principle, Wiggins also acknowledges his indebtedness to Ayer. Ayer's suggestion that 'we have to maintain some anchorage in reality if our references are to be successful'[19] struck Wiggins, only he substituted 'references' by 'conceiving'.

III

In the scheme proposed by Wiggins we find that the main thrust lies in upholding determinate individuative practices. One may have misgivings about the basic hypothesis and some reservations regarding the very nature of the individuative practices. Why the individuative practices are fancied to be like that and not something different? Wiggins makes a case for the individuative practices on a posteriori commonsensical grounds. None the less the individuative practices presuppose a theory about identity which is not to be understood merely in terms of community of properties. While seeking to answer the question what it is to individuate, we may clarify the connection between the

---

[19] *The Central Questions of Philosophy*, 1973, p. 197.

individuative practices and the theory of identity. According to the lexicography, the meaning of 'individual' is 'not divisible without loss of identity, subsisting as one', etc. Granting the minimal of this lexicographical meaning it may be suggested that to individuate means to give individuality to an entity as such and such or to individualize it as so-and-so entity: i.e. to be able to accomplish something as an indivisible entity. To individuate is to identify an individual as the very same individual and not as something other. The basic insight that underlies Wiggins's *Sameness and Substance* and which was given re-emphasize in his *Sameness and Substance Renewed* is that everything that exists is this such. Wiggins treads a middle course by offering a third alternative to the battling philosophers who are either strongly arguing for bare particulars or are proclaiming only realities of qualities or properties. For Wiggins neither thisness alone is primitive nor suchness is primitive; it is rather, so to say an alloy of this–such which is to be accepted as the primitive. Thus, the answer to this why-question has been provided by proposing a thesis of sortal dependency of identity. The thesis of sortal dependency of identity provides a kind of, transcendental argument to sustain common individuative practices which are determinate in nature. In general, this thesis of sortal dependency of identity maintains that being the same *a* as *b*, depends on the specification of a sort instantiated by both a and *b*. Wiggins says:

> By the elucidation of identity that I advocate, . . . will first have to say, what are the terms of the identity. He will have to explain that *a* is a continuant which . . . and *b* is a continuant which . . . and then expand each specification separately in a way sufficient to make determinate (with the help of the world) which continuant *a* is and which one *b* is, and what each is.[20]

This thesis laying its claim to sortal concept as flanking two terms of identity statements, makes the following claims:[21]

---

[20] *Sameness and Substance*, p. 51.

[21] Ibid., p. 48.

D: $a = b$ if and only if there exists a sortal concept f such that

1. a and b belong to a kind which is the extension of f,
2. a falls under f or that a is an f, is to say in other words, what a is; and
3. a is the same f as b; or, a coincides with b under f.

To figure out the main contention of Wiggins's thesis on identity, his notion of sortal concepts requires to be explained. Wiggins makes it clear that by a 'concept' he does not mean something that is in someone's mind or an ingredient in someone's thinking or categorization; but it is a way that things are or can be. Thus Wiggins says:

> The concept horse is not then an abstraction such as horsehood or horseness (whatever these are). It is something general, or better, universal: and to that extent it is philosophically contentious.[22]

Later he says:

> . . . the reference of a sortal predicate such as horse, i.e. what horse stands for, is the concept horse, the general thing horse.

The concept of a horse is then something general which exists, or is present in the world, and to which we can refer, and to which it is the role of certain predicates to refer. Wiggins says:

> But horse or mammal or carnivore are surely things that we need to speak of or quantify over in metaphysics and in science.[23]

Thus in Wiggins's view the notion of a concept is that of a sort or type.

The very meaning of sortal concepts as distinguished from mass concepts has received elaborate treatment in the writings of distinguished philosophers of language, linguists and logicians.[24]

---

22 *Sameness and Substance*, p. 10.

23 Ibid.

24 For more on the subject see *Mass Terms: Some Philosophical Problems*, ed. F.J. Pelletier, 1979.

In the literatures differing criteria have been proposed as variant as syntactic, semantic and pragmatic. For the present discussion, a very rough and ready understanding about what is meant by a sortal concept, I think, would suffice. In our day-to-day uses of language we often make a distinction between terms like 'man', 'animal' and bird' on the one hand and terms like 'water', 'iron' and gold' on the other hand taking the former group of terms as denoting compact-enduring things whereas the latter as denoting stuffs out of which enduring things are constituted. In the literature sortal terms are often referred to as count terms and mass terms are referred to as non-sortal terms, bulk terms, material names and so forth. G. Frege offers on the sortal and non-sortal distinction a very pointed statement: according to him, if we can ask 'how many *s*es are there in a space appropriate to it', then *s* is a sortal term, but if we cannot count 'how many *m*s are there in a space appropriate to it' then *m* is a non-sortal term. The countability principle is derived from Frege who in his *Foundations of Arithmetic*[25] gives certain clue for distinguishing a count term from a mass term on the basis of this criterion. From Frege's observations two focal points emerge about the nature of general terms: some terms are such that these terms isolate in a definite manner whatever fall under them and they do not permit any arbitray division of them into parts and can be a unite relative to a finite number; whereas the some other general terms are such that no finite number can belong to a thing falling under them and are so-called non-sortal terms or mass terms. Grammatically speaking, generally sortal terms use numerals and quantifiers like 'many', 'few' in the plural forms and 'a', 'an' in the singular forms. With regard to mass terms like 'gold', 'water' and 'silver' all we say is 'much gold' or 'more water', and words like 'much', 'more' are called amassives, and so it will be quite suitable to say that mass terms are characterized by amassives instead of numerals and quantifiers. However, in many instances these two criteria are in vain and philosophers of language import pragmatic criterion to bail them

25 Frege, Gotlobe, 1950, Blackwell, Oxford, p. 62.

out of difficulties.[26] Further even within the fold of sortal terms, the very relevant distinction is between natural kind terms and artefact terms. Wiggins is quite unambiguous in his comment:

> Among the best candidates to play the roles of sortal and substantial predicates . . . are natural kind words.[27]

However, ordinary artefact words like 'clock', 'chisel', 'drinking vessel', pen' and 'table' are also included under 'the other sortal predicates' and it is needless to add that artefact identity had posed some serious difficulties for Wiggins also.[28] Wiggins we shall see gradually had perception of a very inseparable relation between 'what is it questions' and a genuinely sortal concept. His categorical remark that 'a genuinely sortal predicate must stand for a concept that implicitly or explicitly determines identity, persistence and existence conditions for members of its extension'.[29] The thesis of sortal dependency of identity (D) as proposed by Wiggins advocates that any explanation of identity has as its prerequisite a presumption about the kind of continuant substantive thing that *a* and *b* are. According to this view, if carefully pursued, the elucidation of identity $a = b$ entails that there is an *f* such that *a* is identical with *b* as the same substantive continuant *f*, but it does not entail any specification regarding what that sortal concept is. This view does not demand from the knower or the believer that in knowing or believing that *a* is *b*, one is to have knowledge about the sortal concept underlying *a*'s identity with *b*. One who claims that *a* is *b*, claims thereby by implication that *a* is the same something as *b*, without making any commitment as to what that sortal concept is. Wiggins's discovery that the 'most important and most single feature of sortal predicates

---

26 'Mass Expressions', F.J. Pelletier, pp. 327-407. See also Aparajita Mukhopadhyay's MPhil dissertation (1992-93) entitled 'Problems of Mass Terms' done under my supervision dealt elaborately with syntax, semantics and pragmatics of mass terms.

27 *Sameness and Substance*, p. 77.

28 'Problems of Artifact Identity', in *Sameness and Substance*, pp. 90-101.

29 *Sameness and Substance*, p. 62.

is that they are used not only to say what things are but also to cover identity statements in the "*x* is the same *f* as *y*" form — *a* form that is available in every natural language. . . .'[30]

The third clause of the D-thesis introduces the idea of coincidence, which encourages spatial interpretation. In his attempt to explain D-thesis, Wiggins brings to the forefront the notion of a sortal, and so of a substance, in particular a material substance. In his impressive and excellent book, *Identity and Spatio-temporal Continuity*, Wiggins is looking for an answer what it is for a material thing to maintain its identity through time? Strawson's suggestion, 'one of the requirements for the identity of a material thing is that its existence, as being continuous in time, should be continuous in space' seems to have influenced Wiggins also.

A schema may be proposed[31] to account for this thesis of sortal dependency which is as follows:

> $(x)(y)$ (x coincides under sortal concept f with y just if 'x falls under f' says what x is and 'x coincides under f with y' implies that for all θ, $(\theta x = \theta y)$.

The analysis of identity statements as provided by the thesis of sortal dependency of identity overrides any such view that ascribes any semantic indeterminacy to identity.[32] The belief regarding incompleteness of identity stated plainly in the form $a = b$, provoked Peter Geach to posit relativity thesis of identity. According to Geach, to say that $a = b$, is a vague expression of half-formed thought having no significance unless we say the 'same *f* as' where *f* represents some substantival general term or sortal concept. Since the days of Geach's *Reference and Generality* published in 1962, the thesis of relative identity is considerably gaining ground as one of the viable alternatives to the classical conception of identity, the chief proponent of which is Frege. The classical identity theorist is an absolutist. For Frege the notion of identity belongs to the

30 *Sameness and Substance*, pp. 58-59.

31 Ibid., p. 53.

32 Ibid., p. 90.

realm of logic. Geach also begins with the common assumption that the notion of identity is a logical notion. In logic, especially that is due to Frege, identity is treated as one of the logical constants. But it is essentially different from other logical constants in that it is not a sentence-forming operator; on the other hand, it is considered as a relational expression for forming atomic sentences. The thesis of relative identity as proposed by Geach[33] depends on two assumptions:

1. Identity is a kind of relation; and
2. identity is a kind of relative relation.

These two assumptions of Geach bring him into conflict with:

a. The pro-Wittgensteinian thinkers who deny that identity is a relation.
b. The pro-Fregean thinkers who deny that identity is a relative relation.

Wiggins is a full-fledged absolutist in spite of entertaining similar 'same what' demand in the analysis of identity statements and supplements the requirement by positing a sortal concept. It is clear that for Wiggins understanding of any identity statement by relating to a sortal concept is not to redress the incompleteness of the plain, $a = b$. To many critics and commentators and even to Quine, it seemed that the thesis of sortal dependency of identity and the thesis of relative identity are very much interdependent. This sort of assimilation of two completely distinct theories rests on certain grave misconceptions about the exact implications of the two theories.[34]

Now we may turn straightforwardly into the detailed exposition of the thesis of sortal dependency (D) and its various sub-theses.[35] This discussion would also enable us to have a better

---

33 For a fuller treatment of the subject, see Indrani Sanyal, 1998, 'Ideology versus Ontology'.

34 *Sameness and Substance*, p. 17.

35 This has been discussed in the present author's *On Essentialist Claims* (2002).

comprehension of this reserved but insistent brand of essentialism embraced in *Sameness and Substance* and later retold in *Sameness and Substance Renewed.*

Wiggins has presented many subsidiary formulations of this thesis to avoid one difficulty or another that may arise with regard to this thesis. Wiggins does not specifically state merits or demerits of each of these formulations, but there is some order implicit in his presentations. Now let us turn to his presentations:

D(i): $(x)(t)[(x \text{ exists at } t)\ (Eg)(g(x) \text{ at } t)]$.

To put the above formulation in words: for all objects x, for all times t at which a continuant a exists there is a sortal g under which a falls at t. In this formulation, the symbol x stands for continuants that have three dimensions, g stands for individuative concepts that divide their reference and t stands for time. This is a quite ordinary and a plain reading of the thesis of sortal dependency of identity. This unrefined reading gives the impression that a continuant is to be traced under a sortal concept. But among sortal concepts various types of classifications are admissible. It is quite possible that some sortal concepts are applicable to an individual throughout its existence; whereas some sortal concepts are not so. Thus, a need is felt for drawing a distinction between sortal concepts that present-tensedly apply to an individual x, and those which apply at every moment throughout the existence of x; this first type of sortals is temporarily restricted sortals hence are called phased sortals. As the expression, 'phase' implies stages in the development or existence of an object at a period of time, it is not difficult to guess that these sortals are applicable to objects in some phases or stages of their existence at a time. Hence to say, just this that there is a sortal under which the object falls at one time or another, is to make rather an inadequate statement.

One of the objectives for bringing an entity under a sortal is to provide an answer to the question, 'what is x'? However, any and every type of sortal cannot provide answer to 'what is x'.

Those sortals which are temporarily restricted in their application to the objects are considered to be deficient in providing an answer to the question, 'what is x?' A hierarchy of sortals may quite be envisaged making room for supplementation of phased or restricted sortals by more comprehensive and unrestricted sortals. This does not imply any serious antagonism between a restricted phased sortal and an unrestricted comprehensive sortal. He has rightly pointed out that there are many sortal predicates like, 'boy', 'cub' and 'graus' (Greek word for an old woman) whose status as sortal predicates is not quite manifest either syntactically or etymologically. In some cases the status of phased sortals is to be discovered empirically, e.g. 'tadpole' and 'caterpillar'. In the end, though, all phased sortal concepts are either latently or manifestly restrictions of underlying more general sortal concepts. In this present formulation of (D) what is lacking is the clear-cut and unambiguous pointer to the relevant sortal type. In this D(i) case in the absence of any clear-cut commitment as to the nature of the sortal, it remains a big question whether x falls under that sortal throughout the whole period of its existence. 'It does not guarantee the availability of one concept with application for all times.'[36] This led to the formulation of a stronger principle to replace the earlier one:

D(ii) : $(x)(Eg)(t)[(x \text{ exists at } t)\ (g(x) \text{ at } t)]$.

In this formulation it is made more precise by saying that there is a sortal concept g such that for all x, x have that sortal predicate for all time of their existence.

Thus the inadequacy of the first formulation has been sought to be redressed by this formulation as it claims to provide answer to what is it questions. The phased sortals are not to be treated as genuine sortals for the requirements for being genuine sortals are lacking in terms of their capacity for determining identity, persistence and existence, conditions for members of its extension. Some may ask whether it is possible to deduce D(i) or D(ii) from

---

36 *Sameness and Substance Renewed*, p. 64.

certain premises? If one presses too hard for any logical support for ontology of three-dimensional continuants which have spatial parts but no temporal parts and endure through time, it is very difficult to provide any positive response. Wiggins acknowledges his incapability to prove D(i) and D(ii) deductively as following from certain premises. Does it mean that the failure to prove D(i) and D(ii) will lead to the rejection of the substance assumption? Now what does one gain or lose if one has to give up the substance assumption? Wiggins's starting point is the fact that our commonly adopted individuative practices are determinate. He starts from the actual empirical context of a situated speaker's perspective engaged in the act of 'singling out' or 'picking up' a particular distinguishing it from other things like it or unlike it. Wiggins does not search for a priori arguments in support of his claim. Wiggins has made it quite clear that 'logic alone cannot force us into any particular ontology'.[37] Wiggins is committed to the substance ontology but he has no tools to prove his theory. The ontology of three-dimensional continuants which have spatial parts but no temporal parts and which endure through time is not logically an unacceptable position. If we have to give up the substance assumption then we shall have to give up many of our existing beliefs which we consider fundamental to our actual individuative practices.

Three important observations emerge from the above discussion:

1. Wiggins does not claim to have proved or derived by the process of logical deduction, D(i) or D(ii) from certain indubitable premise or premises.
2. The ontology of the substance which is the supporting pillar behind D(i) or D(ii) is not a logically untenable position.
3. The rejection of the substance ontology would lead us to give up many of our existing beliefs which are fundamental to actual individuative practices.

---

[37] *Sameness and Substance*, p. 62.

The D(ii) formulation, however, is inadequate to cover some problematic situations. Some forthright challenging questions ensue: How far can we extend the extension of a continuant to account for its existence as the same continuant? Where do we put an end to the extension of that continuant as being changed into something different? Wiggins refers to a story from Genesis about Lot and Lot's wife who were told by the Lord not to look behind but Lot's wife looked back and became a pillar of salt. This story is meaningful but does it not counter D(ii)? Because what will be the covering concept here? The other alternative left is to suggest that there is a substantive sortal concept appropriate to cover the identity between Lot's wife at the beginning when she was told by the Lord not to look behind and Lot's wife afterwards when she looked back and was turned into a 40-ft pillar of salt still observed near the Dead Sea. The important question that crops up is whether to retain D(ii) or to reject D(ii)? The retention of D(ii) as already discussed, requires for all continuants there be some sortal predicate which is applicable to it throughout its whole realm of continuous existence. The rejection of D(ii) would imply the rejection of the thesis of sortal-relative identity and eschewing one of the foundational arguments for the endorsement of the determinate individuative practices. The other option is to be faithful to D(ii) just 'by inventing arbitrarily concept woman-pillar, which a thing satisfies by being first a woman and then a pillar of salt'.[38] But this alternative also has not been acceptable to Wiggins and the main reason for his objection is that this stand would permit arbitrary invention of sortal concepts at will and then the question regarding the survival of any substantive continuant till t and its subsequent perish at a later time t_2 would be 'trivialized completely'.[39] The individual caprice for inventing sortal predicates would thus shatter the determinacy of the individuative practices. This particular example is really thought-provoking as challenge to the thesis of sortal

38 *Sameness and Substance Renewed*, p. 65.

39 Ibid.

identity. Wiggins does not succumb to this challenge, but rather the imperativeness of the situation leads him to further dialectical probe. As an Aristotelian in many respects, especially as a recognized Aristotelian in being champion of the substance ontology of this-such substantive continuants, Wiggins discovered a suitable way out of this impasse by taking a cue from the Aristotelian distinction between a thing's changing and its being replaced. The whole discussion here rotates round the proper understanding of sortal predication by taking it seriously and demarcating it from the mimicry of sortal predication. For Wiggins, the present counter-example to D(ii) thesis does not hold good for he does not accept the identity between Lot's wife and the subsequent 40-ft pillar of the salt.

We have already touched upon the viewpoint of Geach according to whom all identity statements are incomplete and these statements need to be completed by a sortal predicate. But in spite of his acceptance of a version of sortal relative identity thesis, Geach is a committed relativist and his doctrine is known as the relative identity theory. Thus we find that some striking points of similarity and dissimilarity are really conspicuous between Geach and Wiggins. Thus both Geach and Wiggins advocate supplementation of identity statements by a sortal substantive predicate as a covering concept, though reasons for such requisition are not the same. The Geachian interpretation of identity thesis led to the reconsideration of the question as to whether all the sortal predicates that apply to a thing can be used to cover identity claims. Wiggins in fact tried to demonstrate that the doctrine of relative identity *R* does not comply with Leibniz's law and shows the incompatibility of the properties of reflexivity and congruence of identity with the relative identity. Thus in his view the thesis *R* is false and from this Wiggins draws a principle that according to which all sortal predicates that apply to a thing at all must be concordant with respect to predicates that provide for identity conditions for the thing. Wiggins while explaining the notion of concordance between two predicates says:

> I suppose, the best explanation and characterization of this concordance is that all true sortal attributions to a given thing are restrictions of one substance-concept (or are restrictions of a set of substance concepts that are individuatively concordant). . . .[40]

In this connection a distinction is to be kept in mind between a predicate that are such that they apply at every moment of an entity's lifespan — e.g. 'man', 'horse', 'tree' — and predicates which are not so applicable throughout the whole lifespan of an entity's existence. Thus the predicate 'boy' does not apply to any entity throughout its lifespan. The assertion of Wiggins as per requirement of D(ii) thesis that an individual must satisfy at least one substance concept has been misunderstood. Wiggins does not say that an individual can be subsumed under one substance concept, nor does he make any such claim. His candid remark, 'no argument is known to me for the conclusion that an individual can answer to only one substance concept'; rather we find him to admit that his account of substance concept allows an individual to fall under several or many substance concepts. The denial of relativity thesis would entail an individual as capable of satisfying several concepts, of which it is required that these concepts should fulfil the requirement for the satisfaction of the persistence condition of the individual. These substance concepts should be sortally concordant. D(ii) would thus exclude the possibility that an entity *a* be both *f* and *g*, both being substance concepts and be the same *f* as *b* but not the same *g* as *b*. Thus he puts the restriction on the relativity identity requirement.

Wiggins in course of theorization has always tried to retain his link with the actual empirical situations where such practices take place. In practice we find that the degree of determinacy to questions as to whether at a given point of time *t* an object *a* still exists. This finding regarding the determinate individuative practices may be looked upon as derivatives of his thesis of concordance. In his *Sameness and Substance*, while acknowledging

---

[40] *Sameness and Substance Renewed*, p. 67.

the seriousness of the example of Lot's wife he is very much against trivialization of sortal predication, he is in favour of projecting in this case of Lot's wife a 'real and substantival discontinuity'.[41] To quote from Wiggins, 'what I think that shows is that we cannot say that this pillar is the same as the wife of Lot'.[42] A sceptic of D(ii) will grumble that there is no cannot to be had here. He had introduced a complementary principle for D(ii) known as the principle of sortal continuity 'to distinguish as sharply in principle as we do in practice distinguish between the persistence of a thing through change and its replacement by some quite other thing'.[43] The principle of sortal continuity runs as follows:

> If an entity x survives from t to t_1, then there is some articulation of the time between t and t_1 into periods $P_1, P_2, \ldots P_n$ such that, for every period P_i, $(Ef)\ (f(x)$ throughout the adjacent period P_i $+/-)$.[44]

Wiggins also tries to be more specific about predicates that are to be accepted for serious sortal predication. His suggestion is to maintain a distinction between genuine sortal predicates from the apparent sortal predicates and within the fold of apparent sortal predicates he accommodates purely generic predicates like 'animal', 'machine' and 'artefact'. He also suggests purely determinables such as 'space-occupier', 'entity' 'substance' to be demarcated from sortal determination. Wiggins's suggestion is theoretically acceptable though it has to overcome many more hurdles when actually put to use. He introduces some more sub-theses with a view to make more specific the nature of the sort variable *f*.

> D(iii): *a* is identical with *b* if and only if there is some concept *f* such that (1) *f* is a substance concept under which an object that is an f can be singled out, traced and distinguished from other *f*

---

[41] *Sameness and Substance*, p. 61.

[42] Ibid., p. 61.

[43] Ibid.

[44] Ibid., pp. 61-62.

> entities and other entities; (2) *a* coincides under *f* with *b*; (3) 'coincides under *f*' stands for congruence relation, i.e. all pairs <*x*, *y*> that are members of the relation that satisfy the Leibnizian schema $\theta x = \theta y$.[45]

One of the main observations here is that the community of properties is not to be taken for identity; rather community of properties is the consequence of identity. This sub-thesis once again reiterates Wiggins's commitment to the Leibnizian schema. One of his weapons to combat Geachian thesis of relative identity is his reliance on Leibniz's law. In this connection, we may refer to Wiggins's remark: 'provided we have leibniz'z law then, and provided that "is the same *f* as" is as Leibnizian as "=", we can disprove any purported instance of *R*.'[46] Wiggins does not flounder when it comes to routing the thesis of relative identity along with all its paraphernalia of an ontology of relative existents. This viewpoint of Wiggins has already been reflected when he was formulating his D thesis.

> D(iv): *f* is a substance concept only if *f* determines (with or without the help of further empirical information about the class of *f*s) what can and cannot befall an *x* in the extension of *f*, and what changes *x* tolerates without there ceasing to exist such a thing as *x*; and only if *f* determines (with or without the help of further empirical information about the class of *f*s) the relative importance or unimportance to the survival of *x* of various cases of changes befalling its complaints (e.g., how close they may bring *x* to actual extinction).[47]

> D(v): *f* is a substance concept only if *f* determines either a principle of activity, a principle of functioning or a principle of operation for members of its extension.[48]

We speak of activity of material things and extend this concept to cover fulfilment of function with regard to organs and artefacts.

45 *Sameness and Substance*, p. 68.

46 Ibid., p. 20.

47 Ibid., pp. 68-69.

48 Ibid., p. 70.

The substance concept *f*, Wiggins is speaking about, is broadly restricted either to natural kinds or artefacts, regarding both of which there are lots of unresolved doubts and questions. How to define a natural kind concept is really a problematic issue. The proponents of natural kinds propound that every natural thing throughout its actual existence satisfies some sortal concept which says what that thing is. Natural kinds are considered as real constituents of the world and are believed to be exemplified under the physical laws of the actual world. Thus Wiggins also joins the group who are anti-constructivists in rejecting the view that there is no objective distinction between natural kinds and others. Aristotle in the first chapter of Book Two of Physics[49] has drawn our attention to some important distinction between a natural kind and an artefact. Among the natural kinds are included different animals, their organs, stuffs, etc. and their naturalness has been accounted for in terms of their own inherent principle of change and of remaining the unchanged.

> Things which exist by nature . . . such as animals and the organs of the plants and elementary stuff . . . have in them a principle of change or rest . . . the nature of a thing being the source or cause of non-accidental change or rest in anything it (the nature) belongs. . . .[50]

With regard to these natural substances we can reckon with their changes in respect of place, quantity, as in their growth and decay, and quality. The absence of any self-generated change in respect of place, quality or quantity may be proposed as the criterion for the artefacts. However, what is true about the artefact as a non-natural composite whole is not true about the constituents of the artefacts for these are natural elements. As an artefact happens to be composed of natural elements, it has to be conceded that it does have the principle of change within itself as inhering in its constituent natural elements. Taking any instance of artefact such as pen, pencil, chair, train, building and computer, this can be

---

49 Aristotle, *Physics*, Book I, chaps. 7-9; Book II, chaps. 1-3.

50 Aristotle, Physics, Book II, chap. 1.

testified. Echoing the Leibnizian idea[51] that the activity is the essence of substance, it is not very difficult to account for the substantiality of natural kinds. But in the case of artefacts, it may become difficult to determine their substantiality. What is the principle of activity for a chair or for a tiny pin? The principle of activity may be given a wider interpretation to incorporate within it the principle of serving certain function or other. Thus the persistence condition for an artefact is satisfied if a certain parcel of matter structured in a certain fashion is instrumental to serving some purpose. From Wiggins's D(v) we learn *f* is a substance concept only if *f* satisfies either a principle of activity or a principle of functioning or a principle of operation for members of its extension. Roughly speaking, generally on the basis of the function that is being performed, the nature and classification of artefacts are based. A quick glance at any dictionary may confirm the observation. The *Oxford Advanced Learner's Dictionary* provides the functional description of the artefact clip as a small metal or plastic object used for holding things, together. Another artefact, say compass, is defined in the same dictionary as an instrument for finding direction with a needle that always points to the north. Thus, artefacts are not explained on the basis of resemblance or on the basis of any scientific or nomological principles. Artefacts are classified on the basis of functional descriptions which are in no way dependent on theoretically hypothesized specific inner constitution of the artefact. Unlike natural kinds which provide framework for any scientific theory building, artefacts generally lack nomological import. However, I do not enter into the problem of artefact identity, for, because its immense importance and various philosophical dimensions are themselves topics for separate discussions.[52]

---

[51] 'I also maintain that substances cannot be conceived in their essence as bare or without activity, that activity is of the essence of substance as such' — Leibniz, 1969, *Philosophical Papers and Letters*, tr. L.E. Loemaker, Dordrecht: Reidel.

[52] Indrani Sanyal, 2002, 'Artifact Identity and Essence'.

Let us turn to other sub-theses as follows:

> D(vi): If *f* is a substance concept for *a* then coincidence under *f* is determinate enough to exclude this situation: *a* is traced under *f* and counts as coinciding with *b* under *f*, and *a* is traced under *f* and counts as coinciding with *c* under *f*, while nevertheless *b* does not coincide under *f* with *c*.[53]

This formulation prevents any form of relativity with regard to identity. Identity relation is transitive in its formal logical aspect and this is reinforced by this formulation. A relation is said to be transitive if $a = b$, $b = c$, then $a = c$. In the case of D-thesis the transitive relation is to be reformulated as follows: if *a* is the same *f* as *b*, *b* is the same *f* as *c* then *a* is the same *f* as *c*.

> D(vii): There are no essentially disjunctive substance concepts (*f* or *g*) coincidence under which might allow *a* to be the same (*f* or G) as *b*, and the same (*f* or *g*) as some *c* that was distinct under every covering from *b*.[54]

This is to establish, that the so-called thesis of relative identity is not acceptable. This formulation discourages in taking any disjunctive property in general to be a sortal concept. This does not mean all disjunctive sortals are problematic. Sometimes, however, it will be seen that there are disjunctive sortals and that are quite innocuous. For example, animal or man is an innocuous sortal concept as one is subordinate to the other and the corresponding conjunctive property, e.g. both animal and man are a satisfiable sortal.

> D(viii): If *f* is a substance concept for *a* then, however, indefinitely, and unforeseeably the chain of *a*'s *f* coincidents *a*, *a**, *a***, . . . extends, whatever is truly or falsely applicable to one member of the chain must be truly or falsely applicable to every member of the chain whatever. But then all *f*s must belong to one category.
>
> D(ix): *f* is a sortal concept only if there always exists the theoretical possibility of a definite and finite answer to the

[53] *Sameness and Substance*, p. 71.

[54] Ibid., p. 72.

question, 'How many *f*s are there in region *r* at time *t*?[55]

This is the famous countability criterion that is generally associated with sortal concepts. Generally, what are taken as concepts of material substances satisfy the criterion of countability but Wiggins does not consider it to be a necessary condition for it.

D(x): Only *x* and *y* rule.[56]

Wiggins characterizes this rule as 'a dialectical rule for the adjudication of persistence and coincidence claims founded in the nature of identity relation'.[57] This particular formulation was suggested by Wiggins to tackle the problem of artefact identity especially with regard to the problem of Theseus's ship, viz. what it is to account for the sameness of a sort with itself — whether it is its unity of form or unity of matter something else? An answer to this question draws a dividing line between the upholders of only *x* and *y* rule and the upholders of the best candidate theory. By the addition of 'only *x* and *y* rule' 'the requirement that what makes the identity of *a* and *b* should be independent of objects distinct from *a* and *b*'.[58] was introduced. According to the only *x* and *y* rule, it is plausible: if *y* at time t_2 is *x* at t_1 in virtue of standing in some relationship *R* to *x* at t_1, then there could not be another additional thing at t_2 also standing along with *y* in *R* to *x* at t_1. If there were also another additional thing *z* at t_2 then neither it nor *y* would be identical to *x*. If that *z* could exist, even it actually does not , then *y* at t_2 is not identical with *x* at t_1 . . . at least in virtue of standing in the relationship *R*. Wiggins does not support the best candidate theory of identity and his statement is worthy of notice.

> What we need if identity is what we want to elucidate is a criterion which will stipulate that for a relation *R* to be constitutive of identity of *a* and *b*, *a*'s having *R* to *b* must be such

[55] *Sameness and Substance*, p. 72.

[56] Ibid., p. 233.

[57] *Sameness and Substance Renewed*, p. 96.

[58] *Sameness and Substance*, p. 233.

> that objects distinct from *a* or *b* are irrelevant to whether *a* has *R* to *b*.[59]

On this principle and its rival of best candidate theory, many discussions are available but at present, I do not enter into the details.

Thus by formulating the D thesis and its ten subsidiary theses, Wiggins finally arrives at his individuative essentialism. What we see clearly emerges from the above discussion is that an individuating concept at the very threshold of conceiving or individuative practices has a de re necessity governing its application, depending on the speakers of a language and the world. This may be characterized as a posteriori necessity, as opposed a priori necessity, one grounded in language independently of experience. Wiggins's view of these concepts in this way opposed both to the anti-conceptualists' view, on which these individuating concepts are wholly derived from objects independently of our ways of talking about them and the anti-realists' view on which these concepts are wholly conventional. The conceptual realism of Wiggins advocates an absolute identity theory and annuls the vague identity theory and vague objects. The belief an identity statement is indeterminate in truth value (neither true nor false) where the indeterminacy is due to vagueness has never been entertained.

IV

From the account of Wiggins we learn that his kind of essentialism is 'individuative essentialism' and it also happens to be 'the modest form of essentialism'. We have already found some clue for his nicknaming it as individuative essentialism. He has never explicitly stated as to why does he call his kind of essentialism as a modest kind of essentialism, but the answer is not very difficult to find. His claim for modesty in the kind of essentialism espoused by him consists in establishing contra Quine that the conflict between essence and extension is not a perennial problem. One of Quine's

---

[59] *Sameness and Substance*, p. 96.

worries was that since three grades of modal involvement of modal operators in sentences either as semantical predicate, or as statement operator or as sentence operator exhaust all instances of their uses and these all cause hindrances to quantification, the principle of extensionality does not accord with the essentialist claims. If essentialist claims boastfully excludes Quinean jargon, 'to be is to be the value of a variable', then that would not be acceptable to Wiggins at least.

The interesting point is that the content of essentialism as obtained from Wiggins does not differ much from the orthodox or Kripkean viewpoint in respect of truth values of the de re claims like, 'Hesperus is necessarily Phosphorus' or 'Socrates is necessarily a man'. But the strategy that has been developed by Wiggins in support of these de re claims is markedly different from that of Kripke. Wiggins develops a strategy called a predicate modifier approach to modality backed by sufficient logical intricacies and shows that this kind of construction, involves necessity outside Quine's three grades of modal involvement. One advantage claimed in favour of this construction is that 'must' is here to govern not the sentence but the predicate and this kind of presentation and this kind of presentation of modality does not blur the old distinction between the de re and the de dicto. We would like to discuss in detail this logical construction that suffices to dispel the illusion of those who think that necessity is linguistic and second, it avoids all the difficulty about the referential opacity of a term occurring in a modal context.

According to the predicate modifier conception of modality, the modal concepts of 'necessarily' and 'possibly' are treated as the modifier of a predicate. He maintains that this sort of predicate modifier role of modal concepts is exhibited by ordinary English language. This is not to be supposed a technical innovation divorced from the actual English locutions. Wiggins acknowledges that he got the idea of treating 'necessarily' as a predicate modifier from Geach, with the publication of his *Reference and Generality*. Wiggins's main intention lies in giving a construction of predicate operator, 'Nec', which is a symbol for de re must or necessarily. Wiggins uses the signs 'Nec' and 'Poss'. Now let us follow the steps followed by Wiggins to form the expression to which 'Nec' or 'Poss' is to apply.

1. In the first place, one should begin with some open sentences such as 'x is a man' or, 'if x is a man then x has genetic make-up G' or 'x is identical with y'.
2. To bind the free variable or free variables in the open sentence with an abstraction operator, lambda (λ). Thus we have the following abstracts resulted from the above operation.

   $(\lambda x)[\text{Man}]$

   $(\lambda x)(\text{Man } x \text{ G}x]$

   $(\lambda x)\ (\lambda y)\ [x = y]$

The above-mentioned abstracts are to be read as: 'the property which any x has just if x is a man', 'the property that any x has just, if x is a man then x has genetic make up G', 'the relation in which x and y stand, just in case x is y'. We can form judgements with regard to an entity or sequence of entities that satisfy some property or relation mentioned above as follows:

Caesar has (λx) [Man x].

Everything has the property $(\lambda x)\ [M(x)G(x)]$.

<The evening star and the morning star> have $(\lambda x)\ (\lambda y)\ [x = y]$

The same judgements, Wiggins shows, can be expressed in another alternative way. This is a method of juxtaposition.

1. $(\lambda x)[\text{Man } x]$, <Caesar>
2. $(z)((\lambda x)[M(x)G(x)], \langle z \rangle)$
3. $(\lambda x)\ (\lambda y)\ [x = y]$, <the morning star, the evening star>.

This procedure for forming sentences with abstracts can be carried to work with 'Nec' or 'Poss', i.e. modal operators are playing the role of predicate modifiers. They are required to work on the abstracts which are predicates, leaving the subject term outside the scope of modality thus preventing any sort of controversy.

Hence we have,

$[\text{Nec}(\lambda x)[Mx]], <\text{Caesar}>$

$(z)([\text{Nec}(\lambda x)[M(x)G(x)]], <z>$

$[\text{Nec}\ (\lambda x)(\lambda y)[x = y]\ <\text{the evening star, the morning star}>$

Thus these statements, say that Caesar is such that he *necessarily* has the attribute of being a man or Caesar is such that it is *necessary* for him to be a man. A man is *necessarily* a man if a man has the genetic make-up G. The evening star and the morning star *necessarily* have the relation which any x and y have if and only if they are identical. In these construction of modality Caesar, z, the evening star and the morning star are no more within the scope of modal operator 'necessary' and their positions are manifestly transparent. Wiggins remarks in the 'The De Re', 'Must', 'and from this characterization we shall have it as a proper consequence, not as a stipulation, that de re necessity has a transparent subject place'. Wiggins claims this kind of construction to fall outside Quine's three grades of modal involvement of modal operators in sentences.

Wiggins refers to Quine and admits that the strategy for presenting de re necessity has no more credentials than those of Quine's relational senses of saying and believing. Though Quine is among the chief opponents but Wiggins has also some debt to him.

This approach saves Wiggins from the Quinean accusation regarding the failure of quantification in a de re necessity and possibility context. This would sustain his claim for enabling de re necessity, quantification and essentialism go hand in hand. To enforce his viewpoint that there need not be any antagonism between essence and extensionality principle Wiggins also refers to the instance of set theory. The shorter section, 'Conceivability, Theory and Essence' of *Sameness and Substance*, receives further extension in *Sameness and Substance Renewed*, where the author refers to the domain of set theory where in spite of absolute reign of extensionality principle, the notion of essence has also been accommodated. From the very beginning of our discussion we have seen Wiggins frequently claims to espouse a modest form of essentialism, his claim vindicating a modest form of essentialism rests on showing that the concept of essence is not antagonistic to that of extensionality. His effort lies in projecting that essence and extensionality can match with one another. He suggests a formula, which is taken to convey that even though an object might have belonged to different sets, any set that contains an object contains it necessarily. This is an expression of a de re claim maintaining that if β is a class containing *x* and *y*, then β could not have lacked *x*. Thus, it is supposed that the connection between being a member of a set and the identity of a set is a constitutive connection. Wiggins in this context draws a distinction between instances which exemplify constitutive connection and instances which are not. He says that there is no constitutive between being this or that property and any actual extension, or between being this or that man and some actual particular position in space–time. Let us conceive of the set α containing {Eiffel Tower, Crystal Palace}. Can the set α, be α and lack Eiffel Tower or Crystal Palace? Suppose one begins by describing the set α containing Eiffel Tower and Crystal Palace in a different way as the pair set whose members are in Z's opinion the most remarkable works of the nineteenth-century engineering in the capital cities, London and Paris. The proposal for substituting with an alternative definition has come from those who are sceptic about any essential connection between membership and identity of a set. But this is no rejoinder to the claim that the very set we are concerned with could lack Eiffel Tower, one must envisage that set as lacking Eiffel Tower. Once we tried to do this, the question would be what it was. We could succeed in envisaging as lacking the Eiffel Tower.

In my *On Essentialist Claims* while elaborating and analysing three major arguments in favour of essentialism, I have nicknamed Wiggins' argument as epistemological to distinguish it from that of Aristotle which I called metaphysical and that of Kripke as semantical. Because Wiggins's approach has been characterized as epistemological from this it is not to be assumed that his approach to essentialism is to be viewed as conceptualistic or conventional. To impose upon Wiggins a conventional reading of essentialism is really a matter of concern. To look upon his sort of essentialism as conventional is to derogate it to the level of subjective construction. Wiggins himself said in so many words that his sort of essentialism is not the result of subjective construction. Like Van Frassen, Wiggins does not say that all necessity is verbal. Philosophers proceeding in the line of Van Frassen would say that 'necessarily x is α' is not different from 'it is necessary that x is α'. Thus in this view, the human power of conceiving determines essence since what a thinker can envisage or conceive of x, determines the essence of x. Wiggins' essentialism is a remarkable combination of both realism and conceptualism. Wiggins himself has relentlessly argued for his brand of metaphysics wherein real essences of concrete things are in a sense made to depend on the human power of conceiving. Wiggins did not circumscribe to the supposition that objects to be independently existents should not be described in terms of subject-related properties. Wiggins shows his staunch realistic commitment by his admission of objectivity and independence of essence. But at the same time he does not desist from admitting his inability to describe the world independently of any conceptual scheme. As a conceptual realist, Wiggins argues that surely the human power of conceiving must depend on the conceptual scheme, which again in its turn is conditioned by time, culture and interest of the conceiver. Wiggins sounds Kant-like, when he says that from the concept pattern in our conceptual scheme we can only say what kinds of objects are in our experience, and not what kinds of objects are beyond our experience. No doubt, we do not require Kant or Wiggins to remind us that as compared to the whole cosmos how insignificant and limited human beings are. But this is unable to warrant the truth of the statement that because something is so-and-so in the way it is conceived by human beings, it cannot be so-and-so as an independently existing reality. It is an error to suppose that realism and conceptualism are absolutely antagonistic. While characterizing Wiggins's kind of essentialism, it has been quite clearly established that essentialist claims arise at the very threshold of cognitive act of individuating. Wiggins himself also characterizes his standpoint as individuative essentialism. But none of these offers ground for contending that essences are human constructs. The essentialism that we derive from Wiggins is through the trajectory of epistemology. This approach of Wiggins led me to characterize his defensive argument in favour of essentialism as epistemological argument. The espousal of epistemological argument on the part of Wiggins is not to be viewed as a mark of weakness in logic. Nor should anyone obliterate the difference between an epistemological argument and a psychological one. This is not psychological or private, for the conceptual scheme that is being employed by the conceiver is not idiosyncratic, but universal.

5

Sen's Views on Reference and Quantification and Their Implications in a Modal Context

ONE of the chief pursuits of Pranab Kumar Sen as an analytic philosopher is to get illumination about the workings of our language.[1] One of the questions that worries Sen is how to account for the mechanism of our verbal communication. Reference, no doubt, is one of the very important components of verbal communication. The mechanism of language enables us to refer to objects, to single objects and to objects in general. To speak of reference, predication must come in naturally. In the case of a normal adult human's verbal communication (if not explicitly, at least implicitly) reference and predication go together. With the development of quantification logic, the question as to the exact relation between reference and quantification has also become important. Sen in his different papers dealt with these topics quite extensively.[2] In this essay, I would like to discuss some of Sen's views on matters relating to reference, predication and quantification with special reference to a modal context. My main objective is to focus upon some of the insights of Sen to combat

---

1 P.K. Sen, 'Reference, Modality and Predication', in *Reference and Truth*, p. 57.

2 '. . . it can be added to what has been said that it tries to remedy a deficiency from which the literature on the subject of reference suffers, namely, a lack of enough attention paid to the fact that there is a great variety of ways in which reference can be made (Gareth Evans has done a great deal in his *The Variety of Reference* to remedy this deficiency). But there are many things that remain to be done.' In Preface to Sen's *Reference and Truth*, p. xii.

the Quinean challenge against quantification into a modal context. For a considerable period of time, the Quinean stricture against quantified modal logic had continued rather unabated. Scattered solutions were offered from different quarters but no complete rejoinder to Quine was forthcoming. Ruth Barcan Marcus, A.F. Smullyan, Jaakko Hintikka, David Kaplan, and some others gradually were preparing the ground for the reclamation of modality by removing antithetical attitude towards modal logic from one point of view or other. A summing up of Sen's views on the subject may take the form of a complete counter-argument to Quinean objection.

Before I enter into a detailed explication of Sen's views I would just like to enumerate some of his inspiring insights. In the first place, Sen's argument that the occurrence of a singular term in any context whatever not be necessarily referentially opaque, is worth considering.

Second, Sen has suggested that the supposed link between existential generalization and substitution is a myth.

Third, in this connection Sen has also drawn our attention to one important thing, i.e. as to the interplay of the different kinds of use of singular terms and the various kinds of predication that we can make. Adequacy of this view may be considered in a modal context as well.

Fourth, his lucid account of the logical techniques of substitutional quantification brightens up the prospect for quantified modal logic.

In this essay I would like to elaborate some of these insights in the next two sections.

II

Quine's antithetical attitude towards quantified modal logic rests on a number of questionable assumptions. In the first place, according to Quine, the position of a singular term in a modal context is referentially opaque, since there is a failure of the law of substitution. Thus, Quine argues, though the terms, '9' and 'the number of planets' are co-designative, the term 'the number of planets' cannot be substituted for the term '9' in the sentence '9 is necessarily greater than 7'. For it is false to maintain: 'The number of planets is necessarily greater than 7'; it is a mere contingent matter of fact that the number of planets happens to be 9.

Second, since Quine accepts a close link between substitution and existential generalization, he maintains that quantification into a modal context is not possible either. For, if, by the application of the principle of existential generalization we get the sentence, '($\exists x$) (x is necessarily greater than 7)', the question may arise as to what this x is. According to Quine there is no such object at all, i.e. an object any of whose names could be written in place of 'x' in the open sentence, 'x is necessarily greater than 7'; 9, for example, is not such an object. If it were, we could replace '9' by its co-referential term, 'the number of planets' in that position. But we cannot do that.[3]

Third, he takes the objectual interpretation of quantification to be the only legitimate interpretation of quantification. Sen, however, controverts these assumptions of Quine. In this section, I would like to consider mainly Sen's position as controverting the first two assumptions, as mentioned above, of Quine.

Let us begin by making a comparative study of the following two charts:

I. Quine's way of classifying reference of a singular term

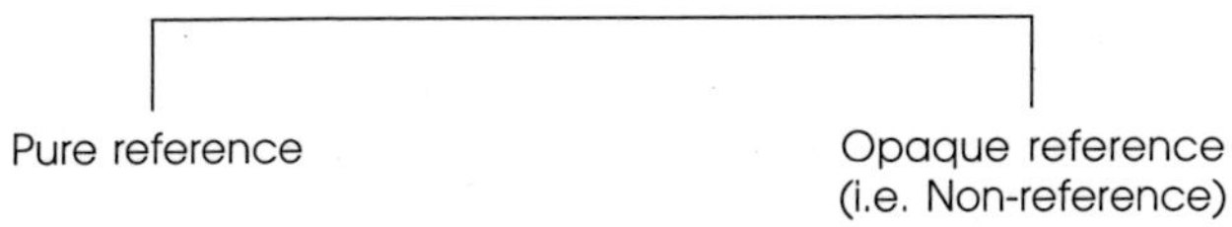

[3] Quine on 'Reference and Modality' in *From A Logical Point of View.*

II. Sen's way of classifying reference of a singular term[4]

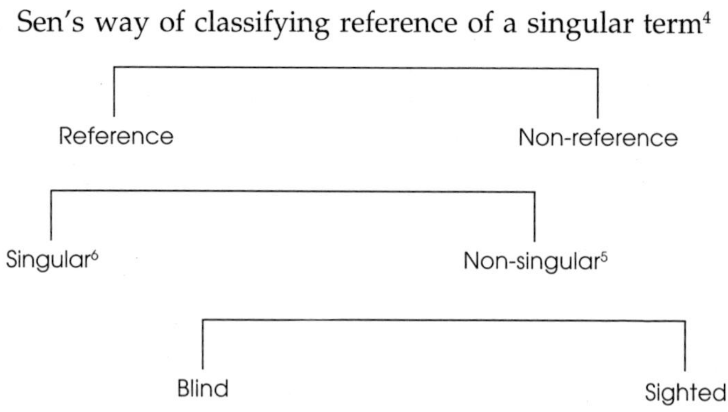

Superficially considered, a glance at the two above-mentioned charts may lead some to think that Sen is just introducing certain further classification with regard to the concept of reference. Actually, a terse synthesis of relevant literature helped Sen to arrive at a substantially new position by extending the extension or scope of reference of a singular term. This has a great impact in a modal context. From all that we have said about Quine, it is clear that Quine seeks to determine reference of a singular term by considering the position in which it occurs in a sentence. But Sen's discussion about the nature and types of reference was launched from an altogether different perspective from that of Quine. To understand Sen's position let us turn to his views.

Reference to objects, to single objects and to objects in general are supposed to be of two sorts. Generally, proper names, definite descriptions are said to be singular terms and they make singular reference. Sen admits that a singular term may *make* non-singular reference as well. Thus, the ground on which Sen draws a distinction very succinctly between singular reference and non-

---

[4] I have presented the views of Quine and Sen diagrammatically to pinpoint the exact difference between these two approaches. For Sen's views refer to 'Non-singular Reference'.

[5] Sen opposes the view that all reference is singular; see his 'Non-singular Reference'.

[6] Singular reference is always 'sighted' as opposed to 'blind'. A purely referential use makes singular reference.

singular reference is not just by considering the syntax of the linguistic expressions. He defines singular reference as reference to one single, definite particular object, it is the object which the speaker may have *in mind*. Non-singular reference on the other hand, may be *made* by the use of a singular term as well. Sen shows Russell was wrong in supposing that the definite descriptions do not have any referring function. According to Sen, definite descriptions are used to make reference to some unique individual but not to some definite singular individual. Thus, in the example, 'Smith's murderer is insane' one refers to an unique individual, whoever that individual may be, who is the murderer of Smith. In this connection it should not be overlooked that Sen draws a subtle distinction between uniqueness and singularity. Of course, in this case he got the cue from Donnellan's distinction between referential use and attributive use. Sen is not slow to realize the actual implications of Donnellan's distinction, that like the referential use, this attributive use has existential import as well. When a singular term is *used* referentially it has a direct reference. And when a singular term is *used* attributively, Sen would say it has non-singular reference. Hence the case of non-singular reference should not be supposed to be the case of no reference at all.

Furthermore, Sen introduces a fine distinction even within the attributive uses of a singular term. The attributive use of a singular term may be done in two different ways. Consequently non-singular reference again may be said to be of two sorts. A blind *reference* of a singular term occurs when an attributive *use* is blind; and a sighted reference of a singular term occurs when an attributive *use* is sighted. The nature of use determines the type of reference, hence the two are closely connected. But in no case should use of a singular term and the type of reference be confused to be one and the same thing. In fact, this idea is very clearly implied in Sen's writings, but he does not maintain it so clearly in this case. He uses terms 'blind' and 'sighted' simultaneously to stand either for uses of a singular term or for types of reference of a singular term. In this instance he deviates from his earlier practices where he employs different terms to designate uses of a singular term and types of reference made thereby.

Now, in the example, 'Smith's murderer is insane'[7] when used attributively, the attribute of being 'Smith's murderer' is essential. In the case of attributive use, what we want to imply is that whoever has murdered Smith, a man or a woman, by virtue of being Smith's murderer is insane. But here, we cannot substitute 'Mary's brother' for 'Smith's murderer' though these terms may be coreferential. For here, our point is not to say 'Mary's brother, whoever is he, by virtue of being Mary's brother is insane'. So in this case substitution fails; but this is not the case where existential generalization fails as well. By applying existential generalization we can infer, $(\exists x)$ (x is insane).

Sen characterizes this kind of attributive use of the singular term as generating *blind* reference, for the speaker knows that Smith has a unique murderer, but he does not know who that murderer is.

However, at this point some difficulty may arise. Now, in order to delink existential generalization and substitution, what is required is that the two should not go together. One of the ways of such delinking procedure is to show that where substitution fails existential generalization is still possible. The point is that the question as to the failure of substitution is relevant only where substitution is possible. But in this example, 'Smith's murderer' has no coreferential term, the speaker is not in possession of any description whatsoever of 'Smith's murderer', hence the question as to the failure of substitution does not arise at all.

Apprehending this sort of objection Sen brings into consideration another variety of attributive use, where the singular term may be said to have '*sighted*' reference. In this case also substitution fails, but not because the speaker is not in possession of any description whatsoever. The speaker may know that the man is Mary's brother, or that he lives in a certain house, etc.; still

[7] Here Sen utilizes the example of Donnellan to explain his position.

substitution fails. But we can infer by existential generalization, '($\exists x$) (x is insane)'.

But what relevance has this for a modal context?[8] This really opens the way to delinking existential generalizations from substitution. Once we see that the failure of substitutivity does not necessarily imply failure of reference, it is not too difficult to see that it does not imply failure of existential generalization either. This lesson may be carried to modal contexts as well. In the light of what we have said so far, we see that merely from the failure of the principle of substitutivity, it does not follow that the context is referentially opaque; for from Sen's analysis it follows that substitution is possible provided the singular terms occupying the subject position have a pure reference to the object. Hence from the failure of the substitution of coreferential terms we may conclude that a modal context is such that a singular term does not have a pure reference to the object. But from Sen's analysis it is quite evident that it is totally unjustified to jump from this to the conclusion that if a singular term in a sentence is not purely referential it cannot be referential at all.

So it seems that the whole controversy as to the possibility of quantification into a modal context reduces to the issue as to whether a singular term in a modal context is referential or non-referential. According to Quine a singular term in a modal context is referentially opaque, whereas according to Sen, a singular term in a modal context may be referential. Really, the perspective from which Sen handled the problem is different from that of Quine. Quine was considering the *position* for a singular term in classifying types of reference, whereas from the same motive Sen was considering *use* of a singular term. For Quine it was a logical or a semantical question which can be settled on purely semantical considerations just by considering the position of a linguistic expression in a sentence. Sen, on the other hand, analyses the reference of a singular term in relation to the use of that particular expression. What Sen wants to emphasize is that it is not correct

8 *Reference, Modality and Predication*, p. 67.

to suppose that a term can be referential independently of its use. For a term does name and occur referentially, only when it is used to name or used to refer purely. Sen under the influence of Donnellan was not slow to realize the role of pragmatics in determining reference of an expression. Sen does not totally controvert Quine, but rather tries to find out why do we say that the position or an occurrence of a singular term is referential or referentially opaque. According to Sen, this is because of the use to which a singular term is put. In itself in the term, 'Smith's murderer' or '9' there is nothing that can make it referential or not. One must take into consideration the role of the speaker, who uses the term in a particular manner. In fact, there is a long-drawn controversy in the philosophy of language as to a distinction between language *per se* — the language competence in the abstract and the use that is made of that competence by speakers and hearers. Thus, there is a definite reason to suppose that Sen, deals with pragmatics. Reference, according to Sen, is something which is performed rather than something that exists in the expression concerned. P.F. Strawson also argues that referring is something that speakers, rather than expressions do. Sen, in other words, does not disregard the role of force in analysing the notion of reference. The study of language in relation to the users of the language was not neglected by Sen. Thus we see that quantification in a modal context can be salvaged in either of two ways; if the position or occurrence of a singular term is referential, or if the use of a singular term is referential. Sen endorses Donnellan's distinction between (a) purely referential use of a singular term, and (b) attributive use of a singular term and thus has come to the conclusion that one and the same linguistic expression in the same sentence can be used in either of the two ways. This is pragmatic ambiguity. Sen utilizes this concept of pragmatic ambiguity to fix the reference of a descriptive phrase.

Sen, however, does not explore the possibility of pragmatic ambiguity with regard to proper names or other singular terms other than descriptions. The expression 'attributive' is not fully suggestive of its role: this expression, it appears, has certain limitations. By saying that use of a singular term is attributive, one may not be able to convey all that he wants to suggest. But what do we actually want to convey when we say that a term is used attributively? To quote from Sen,

> An attributive use does not tolerate any inappropriateness of the description. It is of the very essence of this use that it refers to whatever object satisfies that description.[9]

Here what I feel is that certain terminological modification is desirable. Sen himself in conversation some years back suggested the expression 'broadly referential'.[10] This expression is far more suggestive than Donnellan's expression 'attributive'. Since Sen wants to explore the ambiguity of a referential expression, from that consideration also the expression 'broadly referential' is closer to the idea than the expression 'attributive'. What will be the attributive use of a proper name? Can there be an attributive use of 'Smith' in the sentence 'Smith is insane'? Then should we say that the attribute of being Smith is important here? Most of the people will be in difficulty in determining the property of being Smith. Sen, however, does not say anything about proper names and their different uses. Michael Devitt in his paper, 'Singular Terms' suggested more or less a similar distinction between two sorts of uses of proper names. Following Devitt we may state the distinction between two uses of proper names in the following way: the individual (or object) to which I want to refer may be such an individual (or object) which I have in mind in using the proper name; or it can be an individual (or object) which I do not have in mind in using the name.

I do not think Sen has anything to disagree with Devitt.

III

A reconstrual of the substitutional interpretation of quantification by Sen may be considered to be another important breakthrough

---

9 Sen's Non-singular Reference', p. 41.

10 See Sen's Non-singular Reference', p. 39.

out of the impasse created by Quine.[11] Since Marcus pioneered the move for an interpretation of quantification substitutionally,[12] serious debates have arisen as to the exact nature and implications of substitutional quantification. To explicate the nature of substitutional quantification, broadly speaking, logicians adopt either of the two stands:

1. There are some who consider the substitutional interpretation of quantification to be absolutely different from the objectual interpretation of quantification. They may be called the absolutists.
2. On the other hand, there are some who may be called non-absolutists in the sense of not admitting any absolute difference between substitutional quantification and objectual quantification. Even among the so-called non-absolutists one may observe different shades of opinion.
   (a) There are some non-absolutists who maintain that substitutional quantification is ultimately reducible to objectual quantification. They are said to be reductionists in thus eliminating substitutional quantification in favour of objectual quantification.

---

[11] Quine however does not find the substitutional interpretation of quantification acceptable at all. For Quine's view refer to 'Reply to Professor Marcus', in *The Ways of Paradox and Other Essays*, Harvard University Press, 1976, pp. 182-83.

Also Indrani Sanyal's 'How is $(\exists x)$ (x is necessarily greater than 7) Possible?', *Journal of Indian Council of Philosophical Research*, IV: 1-33.

Of course, Sen does not discuss how the substitutional interpretation of quantification is a boon for quantified modal logic. But his views about the nature of substitutional quantification may remove some of the prejudices against substitutional quantification and may increase its credibility. Now if substitutional quantification is acceptable and if this kind of construal of quantification is possible in a modal context in particular then the impasse created by Quine against QML may vanish, at least partially.

[12] Ruth B. Marcus, 1962, 'Interpreting Quantification', *Inquiry*, 5: 252-59 and 1972, 'Quantification and Ontology', *Nous*, September, VI(3): 240-49.

(b) The other group does not assume that the only adequate analysis of substitutional quantification is a reductionistic one.

However, even among the non-absolutist non-reductionists there are differences in detail as to their views about the exact nature of substitutional quantification. Pranab Kumar Sen in this regard is definitely a non-absolutist, for he does not have any hesitation in maintaining that objectual quantification and substitutional quantification do not stand against one another in absolute opposition. But the next question to ask is, is Sen a reductionist as well? In this section my main objective is to find a right answer to this question. What I can guess is that Sen's being a reductionist would have a very demoralizing effect on the defenders of quantified modal logic. He himself, also being an ardent supporter of quantified modal logic, should not like to be clubbed together with the reductionists. According to John Wallace and Leslie Tharp, whose views are usually known as, 'Wallace–Tharp thesis', since objectual interpretation of quantification and substitutional quantification are not two different types of quantification, substitutional quantification can be reduced to objectual or referential quantification. Sen does not belong to this group. Another important non-absolutist is Saul Kripke. Kripke thinks that substitutional quantification can be combined with objectual quantification in a system. Neither can we tag Sen in this regard with Kripke. Sen agrees with Wallace, Tharp and Kripke in maintaining that substitutional quantification and objectual quantification are not two rival theories of quantification.

Now, I would like to turn to Sen's way of explaining non-absolute difference between objectual quantification and substitutional quantification without being a reductionist.

The assertion that there is no absolute difference between substitutional quantification and objectual quantification does not commit one to the view that there is no difference whatsoever between substitutional quantification and objectual quantification.

No doubt, substitutional quantification being a kind of quantification, an objectual quantification must have something in common with it. If quantification is defined, as it is *defined* by P.K. Sen,[13] as a way of obtaining sentence from a sentential function, then substitutional quantification can as well share this characterization. But then wherein lies the speciality of substitutional quantification? Sen has rightly emphasized the difference when he says that substitutional quantification is different from the objectual quantification so far as procedures are concerned whereby a sentence is obtained from a sentential function. This idea might have been implicitly present in the views of the substitutionalist or objectualist. Sen's endeavour consists in making explicit this idea. If we consider some examples then the point will be clear. Suppose there is a sentential function '*x* is human'. In the case of objectual quantification either by adding a universal quantifier or by adding an existential quantifier we may infer,

1. for all *x*, *x* is human.
2. for some *x*, *x* is human.

On the other hand, in the case of substitutional quantification, we obtain sentences from a sentential function by describing it in terms of its true substitution instances. Thus from the sentential function, '*x* is human', we may infer:

1. All substitution instances of '*x* is human' are true sentences.
2. Some substitution instances of '*x* is human' are true sentences. When we are saying that all substitution instances are true or some substitution instances are true of a sentential function, there are actual substitutional instances, all of which are true, or some of which are true. How do we get these substitution instances? These are obtained simply by replacing the variable occurring in that sentential function by a name. Thus, if in terms of all of those true substitution instances of the sentential function is described we get the sentence, 'All substitution instances of the sentential function

[13] Sen on 'Variables and Quantification', p. 67.

"*x* is human" (or *Fx*) are true'. When some of the substitution instances are true, we get the sentence, 'Some substitution instances of "*x* is human" (or *Fx*) are true'.

Thus, from what has already been said two important points emerge:

(a) In the case of objectual quantification as Sen puts it the sentential function is being used to get a sentence.

(b) In the case of substitutional quantification, on the other hand, by mentioning the sentential function we characterize it in terms of its true substitution instances. Thus, the underlying logic of adopting substitutional quantification has been brought out very clearly by Sen.[14]

Undoubtedly, the substitutional interpretation of quantification has a wider field of application. In fact, there is a kind of mixed response with regard to the substitutional quantification. One of the advantages claimed in favour of substitutional quantification is that it does not have any ontological commitment regarding existence. Quine's dictum, 'To be is to be the value of a variable'[15] ceases to have any application in the case of substitutional quantification. But what we are considering to be the advantage of substitutional quantification has often been supposed to be a serious disadvantage of it. For it has been objected by many that substitutional quantification has no link with reality, therefore by thus interpreting quantification we are concerned with mere linguistic entities. In Tarskian semantic theory of truth, the concept of satisfaction plays a crucial role. Here the property of being true has been explained in terms of a relation between language and something else. Hence the question arises as to substitutional quantification as defining truth without satisfaction. This problem of truth and satisfaction has been tackled by Wallace–Tharp in one way, Kripke in another way and Sen in yet another way. Sen tries to tackle the problem of truth and satisfaction by

---

[14] Sen on 'Variables and Quantification', p. 77.

[15] Quine's 'Designation and Existence' in *Readings in Philosophical Analysis*.

giving an extra-linguistic reading of substitutional quantification.[16] But this does not mean that Sen wants to obliterate the distinction between substitutional quantification and objectual quantification, for basically they are two different techniques of obtaining sentences with different implications. If by adopting substitutional quantification we are restricted only to linguistic entities then it is surely a futile exercise to interpret quantification substitutionally.

Sen as a spokesman of substitutional quantification tries to answer these objections. In the first place, Sen argues that it is a misconception if one maintains this sort of objection against substitutional quantification. For all the sentences that we obtain by substitutional quantification are the result of characterization of sentential function in terms of all or some *true* substitution instances. In order to characterize a sentential function in terms of its true substitution instances one must have some idea as to whether the resulting substitution instances are true or not. The moment we talk about the truth and falsity of substitution instances, we are not delinked from reality. Hence, we cannot maintain that substitutional quantification has no link with reality. If we were confined to linguistic entity only, the question of truth and falsity cannot arise at all. Therefore, it is a mistaken view which maintains that substitutional quantification is devoid of reference to reality.

There is another alternative way to answer this charge against substitutional quantification. Ruth Barcan Marcus has shown that substitutional quantification in its turn may be understood in two different ways:

1. It is possible that substitution is taken in a purely linguistic or syntactical manner. The previous discussion of substitutional quantification proceeded in the above direction.
2. But it is also possible, as Marcus points out, that substitution be understood in terms of such ontological categories as

[16] Sen's 'Variables and Quantification', esp. sect. II.

individuals, properties, etc. within the framework of substitutional quantification.

P.K. Sen elaborates the technical details of the substitutional quantification in its second sense. The sentence, 'There is some substitution instance of the sentential function "*x* is human" which is a true sentence' may also be expressed in an equivalent form as:

> There is a name such that when the name is written in place of the variable *x* in the sentential function "*x* is human" the result is a true sentence.

In this case, we can further understand substitution instances in terms of some ontological categories so that it is not totally devoid of any reference to object. This is as follows:

> There is an individual (or at least one individual) such that, when the name of that individual is written in place of the variable *x* in the sentential function "*x* is human", the result is a sentence which is true.

If one admits only objectual quantification then from the sentential function, 'Socrates F' no sentence can be obtained by quantification. But when quantification is interpreted substitutionally there is no difficulty in obtaining a sentence from a sentential function 'Socrates *F*'. For what we require here is that there be at least one substitution instance of the open sentence, 'Socrates *F*'. Now, to say that 'there is some substitution instance of the sentential function "Socrates *F*" which is true' is to say that 'there is a predicate such that when it is written in place of the place-marker "*F*", the result is a sentence which is true'.

This linguistic version of the sentential function, 'Socrates *F*' may also be matched by a non-linguistic version as follows:

> There is a property (or at least one property) such that when a predicate expressing that property is written in place of the place-marker *F* in the sentence frame "Socrates *F*" the result is a true sentence.

Similary Sen shows how substitutional quantification can cover as well the case of the sentential function 'if S then S′. Given this sentence-frame by substitutional quantification expressed linguistically we obtain the following sentence:

(a) 'The result of writing any sentence in place of the place-marker *S* in the sentence-frame "if *S* then *S*" is a sentence which is true.' This may be matched by the following extra-linguistic version as follows:

(b) 'Every fact is such that, when a sentence by which we can state the fact is written in place of the place-marker *S* in the sentence frame "if *S* then *S*" the result is sentence which is true.'

At this point an important question arises: are these two versions — one linguistic and the other extra-linguistic — of substitutional quantification equivalent? The author himself seems to be in doubt about their equivalence. To argue for the thesis that substitutional quantification can always be understood both in terms of linguistic entities and non-linguistic entities as well one will have to establish equivalence between these two versions in each of the cases considered so far. Thus in the case of '*x* is human' one must be in a position to establish:

1. For every name there is an individual, and for every individual there is a name.

   In the case of 'Socrates *F*' one must be in a position to establish:

2. For every property there is a predicate, and for every predicate there is a property.

   Similary for the case 'if *S* then *S*' this has to be established that:

3. For every fact (or state of affairs) there is a sentence, and for every sentence there is a state of affairs.

Here Sen's success depends on establishing interesting correlations between the main lexical categories and types of semantic representations. Thus, if some revealing ways are found in which linguistic items like names, predicates and sentences can be matched semantically with non-linguistic items like individuals, properties and states of affairs, then this may provide justification for Sen's thesis. For all individuals, even though there are no names, that can be provided by artificially constructed names. But can we say that for every name there is an individual? Are there individuals to be denoted by the expression 'sky flower' or 'Pegasus'?

Similarly, for contradictory sentences what are facts? These questions are philosophically intriguing.

Sen also at this point hesitates to reinforce such correlations between linguistic and non-linguistic entities.

But can we not maintain that the kind of justification that Sen is searching for is empirical in nature? It may or may not be the syntactic delineation that is available in a natural language matches with interesting semantical distinctions. Can we not hope for a language where syntax is 'tailor-made' for semantics so that syntactic delineations and semantic distinctions never fail to be correlated with each other?

The main thrust in giving an extra-linguistic version is to cross the confines of linguistic entities. So, why in this case should it not be sufficient to show that in each of the cases considered, linguistic version in each case implies an extra-linguistic version? However, still the problems remain to show that for every name there is an individual, for every predicate there is a property, for every sentence there is a state of affairs, etc. The talk of implication does not lessen the difficulty much.

Sen no doubt presents an interesting alternative by his interpretation of substitutional quantification. The substitutional quantification and objectual quantification are *not absolutely* different from one another. But substitutional quantification and objectual quantification are two *different* techniques for inferring sentences from sentential functions. Further, substitutional quantification cannot be explained away in terms of objectual quantification. In this connection Sen maintains a strong anti-reductionist stand. But he admits even in the case of substitutional quantification, ordinarily offered in terms of linguistic entities, an account may be provided in terms of non-linguistic entities as well; this is how I sum up Sen's view on substitutional quantification. His account is illuminating and interesting. However, since some of the consequential issues of this reading of quantification are still unsettled, these are sufficient to encourage exploration in several divergent directions.

But this is clear that the acceptance of the substitutional interpretation of quantification paves the way for quantifying into a modal context. Quine, as we already know, prefers objectual interpretation of quantification. When Quine argues that a modal context is referentially opaque, so quantification is not possible, he means by quantification only objectual quantification. But when quantification is interpreted substitutionally we need not maintain any distinction between positions of a singular term that are referentially transparent and that are referentially opaque. For, if quantification is substitutionally interpreted we can have existential generalization with respect to a word even if it does not designate any object. What is more important for our present purpose is that if we interpret quantification substitutionally we can easily apply it to a modal context as well.

6

Pragmatic Ambiguity

IT is very difficult to state the main tenets of analytic philosophy as it represents heterogeneous views of different shades and temperaments. Conjectures of speculative metaphysicians about issues relating to life, death, reality, etc. are all matters of disdain for analytic philosophers. One thing, however, that keeps all analytic philosophers together is their greatest concern for language. Reverberating with scientific spirit and zeal analytic philosophers think that to understand the structure of our language by a careful study of its elements and their interrelations is a key to the solution or the dissolution of many of the philosophical problems. Looking at language it is not at all difficult to discover that one of the greatest mechanisms of language is reference, or the word–world hook-up whereby the words and the world are connected. The discussion about the problems of reference occupies an important place in the analytic tradition of philosophy. In this connection, one of the profound philosophical questions in which Pranab Kumar Sen is particularly interested as to whether all reference is singular? Russell's theory of definite description which is generally viewed as providing a model for analysis eventually ends up in declaring that the descriptive phrases have no reference whatsoever. In Russell's view the same is true about what are ordinarily called proper names since these are all truncated descriptions. Hence the task of genuine reference rests on logically proper names, 'this' or 'that' indexicals, yielding only one kind of reference which is singular. The belief that all reference is singular is nicknamed by Sen as a Russellian tradition. Now, as Upal Dutta Gupta has already pointed out, Sen challenges this tradition and tries to argue for non-singular reference. What led Sen to argue for non-singular reference as well?

An anecdote of history of the year 1966 is to be recalled when Keith Donnellan published his paper, 'Reference and Definite Description'. Sen's idea of non-singular reference as acknowledged by Sen himself in his 'Non-singular Reference' owes much to Donnellan's distinction between the referential use of a description and the attributive use of a description. I need not here once again elaborate the distinction since that task has already been effectively done by Upal in his paper, 'Some Referential Expressions'. However, to bring out the very basis of this distinction I cannot resist quoting a few lines from Donnellan. According to Donnellan,

> A speaker who uses a definite description referentially in an assertion, on the other hand, uses the description to enable his audience to pick out whom or what he is talking about and states something, about the person or thing.

Reading between the lines of this passage we see clearly that when a definite description is said to be used attributively, the attribute of being so-and-so is very important. Hence this use of a definite description is said to be the attributive use. To put the matter differently, in its attributive use, the attribute that is expressed by the definite description is essential for what is being said about the individual referred to by the definite description. On the other hand, when a definite description is used referentially, the chief concern is to pick out someone or something. As in this second use of the definite description the referring is of primary concern, so this use is termed 'referential'. In this case it is enough if the description succeeds in picking out the person or the object. The attribute of being so-and-so is used only for referring to or picking out the object of reference. The very basis of drawing this distinction between the referential use and the attributive use depends on the intention of the speaker concerned who makes use of these expressions in uttering or writing sentences containing these expressions. This concern for the study of language in relation to the users of language, which Sen shared with Donnellan, has been greatly either overlooked or neglected by many logicians and philosophers of language. Sen introduced furthermore sub-divisions within the attributive use of a definite description as a blind attributive use and a sighted attributive use. How to account for this distinction in use of a definite description? We have already seen that in the case of an attributive use, the attributive of being so-and-so is very important for the speaker to pick up an individual or a particular of some sort. However, the particular that satisfies the description may be some definite particular which the speaker has in mind or some other or any one of the many particulars that satisfy the description. In the second instance Sen would say the attributive use of the description is blind for it is involved with a kind of generality and here the reference of the expression is non-singular. This shows Sen's first point of disagreement with Russell in whose view all reference is singular. Again Sen has shown that when an expression is used purely referentially such use cannot be shown to be associated with any kind of generality. But by insisting on purely referential use of a descriptive phrase Sen, on a second ground, joins issue with Russell. Thus we see that both in the case of the referential use of the definite description and its attributive use, there is a presupposition that something or someone fits the description. We see that one and the same description in the same sentence can be used in either of two ways. How does it happen? The grammatical structure of the sentence contains no syntactical ambiguities. Nor do the sentences containing definite descriptions are ambiguous in meaning. These sentences are diagnosed to have pragmatic ambiguity, which follows from the speaker's intention. This context of utterance, however, is no part of the meaning of an expression. But this helps to fix the reference. So while discussing the problem of reference, we cannot neglect the context of utterance of the sentence in which the description occurs. The question may arise as to whether we can also mark the distinction between two sorts of use of proper names as is done by Donnellan in the case of definite descriptions. Michael Devitt in his paper 'Singular Terms' develops the causal theory of proper names to bring out this distinction more vividly. However, how far this distinction is tenable in the case of proper names is a matter of doubt. But that does not in any way invalidate or lessen the importance of this distinction elsewhere.

This has already been arguably established that to allow this sort of distinction in use with regard to referential expressions is to admit the role of the context in which the statement is made. Here one must not be unaware that the presuppositions that are required by the context in which a descriptive phrase is used purely referentially is different from the context in which the descriptive phrase is used attributively. The same sentence with the same descriptive phrase as the subject carries with it different presuppositions accordingly as the subject term is understood either as purely referentially or as attributively. A news headline reads as follows: 'the daughter of water landed at Calcutta's airport'. Now how to interpret the phrase 'the daughter of water'? If the statement is given the referential reading, then it is presupposed that Bula Chowdhury does exist. On the other hand, if we take the statement as conveying an attributive use of the descriptive phrase 'the daughter of water', then the presupposition is that there is one and only one girl who is the daughter of water.

From this difference in the presuppositions required by the context of two different uses of a descriptive phrase, we may also note that if the description fails to apply then we have different consequences. When a description is being used referentially but the description does not apply uniquely, then in that case there is at least no reference failure. The speaker may still succeed in referring to the object to which he intends to refer. But in the case of an attributive use of a description the attribute of being so and so is essential in picking up the referent that is being talked about by the speaker. So in that case if the description does not apply uniquely to any person or object, then no reference has been made at all. If there is no one who fits the description, viz. the daughter of water, then the description fails. In the case of a referential use of a descriptive phrase if there is no one person who is presupposed to fit the description, then there is a reference failure. In this case even if the description fits someone, that cannot be regarded as a success in reference. To sum up, this can be said that in the case of the referential use of an expression what is presupposed is very much important but in the case of the attributive use what is true that is much more important.

It is very important to unearth the insight that lies behind the admission of this distinction between the two uses of referential expressions. It will not be a blind guesswork to suppose that Sen believes that all that matters to language are not mere syntax and semantics but pragmatics as well. We have syntax of language that deals with grammatical structure of signs and its correlations; we have semantics of language that deals with the relations between the signs or words and the non-linguistic things denoted by the words. But another important aspect of language is pragmatics which is concerned with acts of language use. The strong positivistic bias of the majority of the analytic philosophers often stood in their way of assigning any importance to the speaker, the person concerned who makes the utterance to mean something in the world. Ludwig Wittgenstein initiated a great dichotomy in the philosophy of language by his Tractarian standpoint of earlier phase and his later views as expressed through *Philosophical Investigations*. The Tractarian model of language grants independent status to each completely analysed elementary statements. Wittgenstein of this period optimistically says:

> If all true elementary propositions are given, the result is a complete description of the world. — 4.26

Thus the theory of picturing that the early Wittgensteinian tradition gifted us entails that every meaningful language must of necessity be complete. This is the calculus model of language wherein the language is viewed as a system of words or sentences abstracted from its use to look for the essence of meaning. But Wittgenstein in his *Philosophical Investigations* overcomes the Augustinian temptation and directs us to imagine a concrete instance of people using language in the course of their everyday lives. Augustine's over-simplified account of language is replaced to make room for the richness and complexity of the phenomenon of language when seen language as functioning. This stand of Wittgenstein is the precursor of the view that sees language in terms of techniques that speakers employ within their active everyday lives. Sen in his approach is more akin to later Wittgenstein as he understands that when language is functioning within the active, practical lives of the speakers it is quite possible that different expressions play different roles.

The recognition of the phenomena of pragmatics and pragmatic ambiguity thereof had enormous consequences in various aspects of philosophical logic. Against the strong adversaries like Quine and others the very possibility of quantified modal logic has been defended by utilizing the fact of pragmatic ambiguity in a modal context. Quine rejects the possibility of quantified modal logic, for in his opinion, it is sheer non-sense to try to extend quantification to the logic like that of Lewis. For Quine the main point is that de re modality even if it is possible, leads to certain philosophically baffling consequences. In outline his argument is as follows: it is not possible to quantify over expressions occupying referentially opaque positions, i.e. positions which do not allow expressions to refer to anything. So modal contexts which are also referentially opaque, do not permit quantification. Quine supposed that there is a close connection between the existential generalization and the principle of substitutivity of co-designative singular terms. The existential generalization is possible in a context only if substitution *salva varitate* is possible in it. In fact, as we see that it is one of the premises of Quine's central argument for rejecting quantified modal logic. So, according to Quine, it is impossible to have existential generalization with respect to a term occurring in a sentence such that the truth value of the sentence is liable to alter if we replace that term by a coreferential term. Thus the idea that the existential generalization and substitution go hand in hand dominates Quine's ideas throughout.

Ordinarily we find, of course, that existential generalization and the principle of substitutivity go hand in hand. But that is not the whole truth about the supposed link between the existential generalization and the principle of substitutivity. Quine's main thesis is that the position for a singular term occurring in a modal context is referentially opaque and so no quantification is possible with respect to that term in that context. To put it in other words, here Quine is concerned with the question of the possibility of quantification with respect to a term occurring in the subject position in a modal context. So it is clear that here our concern is with the behaviour of singular terms in modal contexts.

Quine did not entertain the possibility of any pragmatic ambiguity and his failure to realize any differences in the role of singular terms in their referring functions leave just two options open before him with regard to a singular term in a subject position, viz. either

(a) referentially transparent; or

(b) referentially opaque.

On the other hand, the recognition of the pragmatic ambiguity and consequential upon which is the admission of a distinction between the referential use of a description and an attribute use brightened up the prospect for a delinking of the supposed mythical tie between the existential generalization and the principle of substitutivity. Thus, it can be shown that there are instances where existential generalization is possible, in spite of the fact that substitution of co-referential terms is not. This point can be established by making use of the ambiguity lurking in the referential use of the singular terms. Let us consider the following sentence: '9 is necessarily greater than 7'. Quine argues that in this instance inter-substitution of the two co-referential terms '9' and 'the number of planets' is not possible for such a substitution yields falsity. Since substitution is not possible in a modal context, Quine concludes that a modal context is referentially opaque. In the light of what we have said so far we see that merely from the failure of the principle of substitutivity, it does not follow that the context is referentially opaque. Substitution is possible provided the singular term occupying the subject position has a pure reference to the object. In other words, when a singular term has a purely referential function in a sentence, substitution of it by its co-referential terms is permissible. Hence from the failure of the substitution of co-referential term we may conclude that a modal context is such that a singular term does not have a pure reference to the object in this context. But it is totally unjustified to jump from this to the conclusion that because an occurrence of a singular term in a sentence is not purely referential, it cannot be referential at all. Such a conclusion would have been valid if there were only two possibilities, i.e. either a context is purely referential or it is referentially opaque. Language considered abstractly as divorced from the active practical life of the speakers and contexts thus distorts the proper perspective. We can see that with respect to the context of occurrence for a singular term our choice is not restricted to two; with the recognition of pragmatics as a feature of language possibilities widened up to three:

1. the purely referential use of a singular term,
2. the attributive use of a singular term (here the singular term does not cease to be referential in its role), and
3. the non-referential or opaque position of a singular term.

It is clear that the sentence, '9 is necessarily greater than 7' is such that the singular term '9' does not make a pure reference to the object. Since the occurrence of '9' in the proposition is not purely referential,

1. we can take the context of occurrence of '9' to be opaque, or
2. we can take this context to be broadly referential.

In this case the term '9' has a broadly referential use for it does refer to the number 9. But the term is not used purely to refer to the object, but does some other function; it indicates or suggests, though not actually states, why or how 9 is greater than 7. That is why, if we obtain by substitution the proposition 'the number of planets is necessarily greater than 7', the substitution fails if the definite description is taken to be broadly referential; or, to put it in the language of Donnellan, if the description has an attributive use. In the attributive use of the definite description, the sentence would mean that the number of planets as the number of planets is necessarily greater than 7. That is, the attribute of being the number of planets would be all important. The speaker would have no particular number in mind. What he would be saying in this: whatever is the number of planets, it is necessarily greater than 7. So naturally, substitution fails, in fact, it is clear that we cannot begin with either of the two proposition '9 is necessarily greater than 7', and 'the number of planets is necessarily greater than 7' when the singular terms occurring in those propositions are taken to be broadly referential to show that substitution is possible.

But we do not find any problem in these instances about existential generalization. We can well apply the rule of existential generalization. The assertion that a condition is satisfied by some named individuals implies the assertion that the condition is satisfied by at least one individual. So when a singular term is said to be broadly referential, it does not fail to refer, there is no reference failure. '9' refers to an object, and so does 'the number of planets', though not purely. We can put the matter as follows: assertion of necessary greaterness than 7 is true of at least one object. This amounts to saying, '($\exists x$) (x is necessarily greater than 7)' is neither meaningless nor false. Therefore, we see that the so-called de re modal sentences are possible.

However, it should not be supposed from the above discussion that in a modal context though existential generalization is possible, the principle of substitutivity fails. What we have shown is that when a singular term occurring in a modal context is taken to have a broadly referential use, substitution is not possible, though existential generalization is. At the same time we hinted at the ambiguity of the 'referential use' of a singular term. In fact, if a singular term occurring in a modal context is used purely referentially, then we can have both substitution and existential generalization. When the term 'the number of planets' is used purely referentially, then we can have both substitution and existential generalization. When the term 'the number of planets' is used purely referentially, it refers to the number which happens to be the number of planets. In this case, the attribute of being the number of planets is wholly irrelevant. It does not matter much whether we refer to that number as the number of planets or as 9. Therefore, substitution of '9' and its coreferential terms 'the number of planets' does not present any problem. And here existential generalization is also possible. That is, '($\exists x$) (x is necessarily greater than 7)' is not meaningless or false. For, certainly there is some object, i.e. the number that happens to be the number of planets.

For Sen it might not have been at all difficult to make room for pragmatics, for Indian philosophers speak of *tātparya*, i.e. intention of the speaker (i.e. *vaktur icchā*) in accounting for our understanding of a sentence meaning. This notion of *tātparya* is indeed a very technical expression and about it in different texts various issues have been discussed. In Sen's writing there is a very clear hint for recognizing pragmatic ambiguity, but he himself does not provide any detailed explanatary account of this feature of language. A section of analytic philosophers has always looked upon the move to recognize the speaker's role in the understanding of language with great apathy. As analytic philosophy is born out of a revolt against the spirit of transcendental philosophy it has some fear and suspicion towards granting any importance to the subject, for from there a revival of belief in self, soul-like transcendental entities may not be a far cry. However, what is encouraging is that this sort of rigour is not maintained throughout the whole period of analytic philosophy. During this transition phase of the analytic philosophy the role of pragmatics is well acknowledged in deciphering the problems of reference. Sen in his effort to emphasize the distinction between two sorts of referential uses of descriptive phrases lets us see language not as a mere *tertium quid* between subject and object.

7

The Logical Space

ONE of the very important concepts in *Tractatus Logico-Philosophicus* (*TLP* or *Tractatus* hereafter), is the concept of logical space. In the whole of *Tractatus*, the expression 'logical space' is not one among the expressions that has been frequently mentioned in the text. In the whole of *Tractatus* the expression 'logical space' occurs very infrequently. Let us recapitulate some of the obvious Tractarian propositions where the expression 'logical space' is found to occur:

> 1.13 The facts in logical space are the world.[1]
>
> 2.013 Each thing, as it were, in a space of possible states of affairs. This space I can imagine empty, but I cannot imagine the thing without the space.[2]
>
> 2.11 A picture presents a situation in logical space, the existence and non-existence of states of affairs.[3]
>
> 3.4 A proposition determines a place in logical space. The existence of this logical is guaranteed by the mere existence of the constituents — by the existence of the proposition with a sense.
>
> 3.411 In geometry and logic alike a place is a possibility: something can exist in it.
>
> 3.42 A proposition can determine only one place in logical space: nevertheless the whole of logical space must already be given by it.[4]

---

1. *TLP*, 1981, tr. Pears and McGuinness, p. 5.
2. Ibid., p. 6.
3. Ibid., p. 8.
4. Ibid., p. 18

But from the infrequent occurrence of the expression logical space, there is no ground for belittling the implication of this concept in the *Tractatus*, or for supposing that the concept of logical space is not so relevant in the context of the whole text. The main objective of this article is rather, to bring out the captivating philosophical role of the idea of logical space in *TLP*. Philosophy of Wittgenstein is often characterized as logical atomism; according to the common perception, Wittgenstein is an atomist and that is how he is usually introduced in a discussion. But Wittgenstein himself has never called his viewpoint as atomism. Whenever, the subject of logical atomism, especially in connection with the modern Western philosophy, comes to the fore, the name of Bertrand Russell can hardly be overlooked. In Russell's *Logic and Knowledge*,[5] logical atomism has been described as the view, according to which:

> You can get down in theory, if not in practice, to ultimate simples out of which the world is built, and that those simples have a kind of reality not belonging to anything else.

The logical atomism in some form or other is also available in the writings of other distinguished modern philosophers. In this regard, we find that Wittgenstein has also been to some extent, rightly, labelled as a logical atomist. Some interpreters have claimed that both logical atomism and metaphysical atomism are simultaneously present in *Tractatus*. Wittgenstein on the basis of some a priori arguments establishes the existence of simple indivisible objects, but for Russell, certain epistemological consideration based on his 'principle of reducibility to acquaintance' was the criterion for picking up the ultimate simples. But for Wittgenstein, it was never an epistemological enterprise in the *Tractatus*, hence its objects were never sought to be fixed by any epistemological means whatsoever. In the *Tractatus*, Wittgenstein, however, spoke about two sorts of ultimate simples; 'atomic facts' and 'objects'. The atomic facts are ultimate units in the sense that these facts are not further reducible to any other

[5] Russell, 1956, *Logic and Knowledge: Essays 1901-1950*, ed. Robert C. Marsh, London, p. 270.

facts. In his view, ultimately there are simple objects, which are not reducible to any other objects. In *A Hundred Years of Philosophy*, John Passmore had admitted the difficulty either in assessing the influence of Russell upon Wittgenstein in the formation of his idea about logical atomism, or in evaluating Wittgenstein's contribution towards Russell's understanding of logical atomism. However, from this logical atomistic perspective of the *Tractatus*, it is not difficult to guess about its analytic trend. The twentieth century in the history of Western philosophy is the period of analytic philosophy, when philosophers became overwhelmingly engaged with logic, language and thought to discover the key to metaphysical problems either through the process of dissolution or resolution. Wittgenstein is, indeed, one of the pioneers of the modern analytic philosophy which had its origin at the banks of Cam and thence spread to many countries of the world. This aspect of Wittgenstein's *Tractatus* has received considerable attention from different interpreters of his Tractarian position.

However apart from this analytic and divisive aspect of the *Tractatus*, it seems to me the synthetic and holistic perspective of the *Tractatus* is no less important. The holistic viewpoint of *Tractatus*, if properly researched, may turn out to be its more important strand. It would not be an impertinent claim to maintain that within the very core of the *Tractatus*, the idea of the indecomposable, irreducible, completeness is quite persistent. The scope of the *Tractatus* left no provision for discussing whether such 'completeness' is to be accounted for by reference to any metaphysical jargons or theories. If one keeps himself confined to the Tractarian realm, he has no privilege to enter into any metaphysical debates. Wittgenstein's viewpoint of the *Tractatus* has been rightly characterized in the following way, by Russell in his Introduction to the *Tractatus*:

> Every philosophical proposition is bad grammar, and the best that we can hope to achieve by philosophical discussion is to lead people to see that philosophical discussion is a mistake.[6]

---

[6] *TLP*, Introduction by Bertrand Russell, p. X.

The elucidation and explanation of Wittgenstein's idea of logical space may throw some light on the claim that the idea of a synthetic whole is none the less important in the *Tractatus*. Therefore, the primary consideration for writing this essay is to make the idea of the logical space perspicacious.

Wittgenstein as the precursor of the twentieth-century analytic philosophy initiated a linguistic turn in the domain of philosophy. The theory of meaning was central to his enquiry and he was not interested to provide explanation of any directly intuited ontology. Wittgenstein's starting point is the belief that every proposition has a clear and definite sense; and along with this, he believed in the proposition's relation to the world. According to him, language is a collection of propositions that pictures states of affairs; this led him to admit a sort of analogy between propositions and pictures. To substantiate his claim, Wittgenstein maintained that the world consists of totality of facts which are nothing but possible and actualized combination of simple objects. This view about the world he derived on the basis of his belief about language, as a system of elementary propositions, constructed out of concatenation of names, that it is a picture and its being picture account for its representational capacity. He thought:

> There must be something identical in a picture and what it depicts, to enable the one to be a picture of the other at all.[7]

This led him to admit names, the ultimate units of language, to hook simple objects, which are admittedly, the indestructible constituents of states of affair.

The Tractarian Philosophy of Language

In the *Tractatus*, Wittgenstein was guided by some basic beliefs about language. In the first place, he thought that all languages have some common essence, that is a universal aspect, whether that is Bengali, English, German or Persian. He also, diagnosed that the root cause of all philosophical problems is basically

---

[7] *TLP*, p. 9.

language. Wittgenstein along with many like-minded philosophers, recommended a different approach for philosophy, through the catchy slogan:

> All philosophy is a 'critique of language'.[8]

He condemned language for being responsible for generating all sorts of misunderstanding and vagueness in philosophy. The surface grammar of language is often held to be deceptive, because of which wrong or inappropriate and inexact messages are conveyed about the meaning. Hence through the analysis of language, all philosophical illness was supposed to be eradicated and cleared up. Wittgenstein of the *Philosophical Investigations* phase describes the objective of investigation of the earlier Wittgenstein as follows:

> Such an investigation sheds light on our problem by clearing misunderstandings away. . . . Some of them can be removed by substituting one form of expression for another; this may be called an 'analysis' of our forms of expression, for the process is sometimes like one of taking a thing apart.[9]

Later Wittgenstein sounds little bit sarcastic when commenting on his Tractarian position, but what he says is not the misrepresentation of his Tractarian position. He continues:

> But now it may come to look as if there were something like a final analysis of our forms of language, and so a single completely resolved form of every expression. That is, as if our usual forms of expression were, essentially, unanalysed; as if there were something hidden in them that had to be brought to light. When this is done the expression is completely clarified and our problem solved.
>
> It can also be put like this: we eliminate misunderstandings by making our expressions more exact: but now it may look as if we were moving towards a particular state, a state of complete exactness; and as if this were the real goal of our investigation.[10]

---

8 *TLP*, 4.0031, p. 19

9 *Philosophical Investigations*, sect. 90, p. 43.

10 Ibid., sect. 91, p. 43.

> This finds expression in questions as to the essence of language, of propositions, of thought. — For if we too in these investigations are trying to understand the essence of language — its function, its structure — yet this is not what those questions have in view. For they see in the essence, not something that already lies open to view and that becomes surveyable by a rearrangement, but something that lies beneath the surface. Something that lies within, which we see when we look into the thing, and which an analysis dig out.[11]

Thus, just by dropping out 'as if' clauses from the above passages a clear-cut statement of the notion of analysis, as adopted by the analytic philosophic tradition, particularly by Wittgenstein himself, is obtained. It would not be beside the point to remark this is what Wittgenstein strongly believed to be the sense and procedure of analysis during this phase of his philosophy. Wittgenstein thus introduced a linguistic orientation to the notion of analysis. He asserted that philosophy is not a body of doctrine, philosophy has nothing to say, philosophy is an activity, not a theory, directed towards logical clarification of thought. He maintains, 'Philosophy is not one of the natural sciences.'[12] It was believed that the process of analysis does not go on ad infinitum, but has a point of termination where analysis completes. The language defined in a calculus model with a system of expressions, interrelated by definitions and a set of formation and transformation rules predominated the Tractarian conception of language. The conclusiveness of analysis marks the completion of analysis, hence the stage of complete analysis supposedly provides an arrangement of logically independent elementary propositions which are truth-functionally combined to obtain compound propositions. Such elementary propositions are composed of only names. This standpoint of the *Tractatus* immensely influenced the new empiricism and positivism of the Vienna Circle and it was explicitly reflected in their manifesto.[13]

---

[11] *Philosophical Investigations*, sect. 92, p. 43.

[12] *TLP*, 4.111.

[13] 'The Impact of the Tractatus', in Hacker 1996.

This is the background from which we need to proceed to comprehend his notion of logical space. In the quoted passages from the *Tractatus*, we find two sorts of approaches in respect of the concept of logical space; in one case logical space is being understood as a metaphysical concept and in the other, the logical space is being dealt with as a logical concept.

Objects, Possibility of Combination of Objects, Logical Space

In the sentence, 1.13 of *Tractatus*, we first come across the expression, 'logical space' wherein it has been stated that the totality of existing combination of objects, which is world, is in logical space. It may seem that in this case, the notion of logical space has been introduced in the analogy of a huge container. No doubt, this is an important question as to how does that Wittgenstein understand the relation between the world and the logical space. Can it be said that the world is in logical space as the linens are in a trunk, or coins are in a money bag, or water is in a jug?

Tractatus begins with the discussion about the nature of the world. Apparently, it may seem that there is not much difference between the approach of Wittgenstein and that of other traditional metaphysicians like Aristotle, Descartes, Spinoza and others. Wittgenstein has made it clear that according to him, the world is the totality of facts and not of objects. In his view, each object contains certain possibilities because of which each object combines with another object to form a state of affairs. But not any object can combine with any object whatsoever. If an object lacks the possibility of combining with another object, it will never be able to form a combination with that object. Each object is essentially a possible constituent of a state of affair. Wittgenstein has introduced the expression 'logical form' to signify the essence of an object or its very possibility to be a constituent of a state or states of affair. All objects are simple, but the resultant combinations of objects are complex. Objects are different from one another, because of inherent possibility of each object, for any object cannot enter into a combination with another object. These objects provide the unalterable form of the world. He writes, 'Objects are just what constitute this unalterable form'.[14] Being combined with one another, objects fashion combination of objects wherein these objects are held together by one another, like links of a chain. All combinations of objects which are called states of affairs are possible states of affairs, but among these states of affairs some, over and above being possible, are also actual states of affair. According to Wittgenstein totality of facts, in other words, totality of all actualized states of affairs is the world. But logical space includes totality of all states of affairs, which have been actualized and are mere possibilities. Thus all the combinations of objects which are possible and have been actualized and those which are possible but have not been actualized together are in the logical space. Since it has been claimed that it is the nature of each object to be the possible constituent of a combination of objects, so each object may be said to be a member of a possible combination of objects. In fact, it is superfluous to add the adjective 'possible' to qualify a combination of objects for unless the potentiality to combine was not in the objects that have combined, the combination would not have taken place.

To be visually perceptible, a figure has to be either blue or red or of some colour whatsoever. There is no compulsion that the figure has to be red or blue. But what is necessary that the figure must have some colour or other, and not any particular colour as such. Likewise, it may be quite appropriate to say with respect to an object that it is necessary for an object to be a constituent of a possible combination of objects, but no necessity has been imposed upon an object for being an actual constituent of a combination of objects. It is a mere contingency that an object is a constituent of an, say *ab* state of affairs and not of an *ac* state of affairs, though it is its essence to be a possible constituent of both *ab* and *ac* states of affair. Henceforth from our discussion, what we learn about objects, possible combination of objects and

---

[14] *TLP*, 2.023, p. 7.

logical space are as follows: (1) objects are constituents of any possible combination of objects; and (2) all possible combinations of objects are placed, though difficult to specify in which sense, in logical space. One may like to proceed further and maintain by utilizing the law of transitivity, that objects are in logical space. Here it is needless to add that the notion of inclusivity or containment in logical space has been understood very ambiguously. In a rough and common sense of containment, a medium-sized pot may contain a small-sized pot of the same shape and proportion within it, again another larger-sized pot may contain the medium-sized pot of the shape and proportion within it and so on. But in the context of logical space, it is scarcely warrantable to interpret the concept of containment in that rough-and-ready sense of the term.

Objects and Logical Space

How should we interpret the relation between the objects and logical space? We have already referred to *TLP* 2.013, wherein the essence of an object has been explained by saying that each object is in a space of possible states of affairs. It is possible to imagine empty space but it is not possible to imagine objects or combination of objects as devoid of logical space. Wittgenstein's way of expressing, here, naturally reminds Kant's second argument with respect to the metaphysical exposition of the concept space, wherein he tries to establish that space is a priori because it is a necessary idea. Kant argues that although we can imagine the absence of all objects in space, we cannot imagine the absence of space itself. Thus he was proving that the idea of space is a necessary idea. The analogy between Wittgenstein and Kant may be drawn in this regard. For Wittgenstein also it may be maintained, the idea of logical space is an a priori idea towards his metaphysics of objects, and this is not to be considered as a too far-fetched observation.

Objects, according to Wittgenstein, are never imaginable as bereft of their essence. Essences are not comparable to one's clothes, hats or ornaments-like objects which can be taken off and separated from the person who possesses these items. These passages clearly reveal Wittgenstein as a staunch, committed essentialist. The essence or the core nature of objects, understood in the sense of their potentiality or possibility, is inseparably tied with their being. It is difficult to imagine a logical space, without any items contained in it, but Wittgenstein puts more emphasis on the opposite way of thinking; in his opinion, if one tries to imagine objects as devoid of logical space, i.e. the totality of all possible combinations, then such imagination would lend itself to absurdity. Objects are impregnated with all possibilities of combining and if we think in terms of extension or spreading out of the totality of the possible combination of objects, the totality has no being as stripped off from these objects. This is the interesting aspect of Wittgenstein's *Tractatus*, where his atomistic bias has been overpowered by his holistic insight.

World and Logical Space

One's imagination may be ignited by the thought of another world, superior in many respects to this world, a far more extended super-world. But to hurriedly attribute this sort of tag upon Wittgenstein's conception of logical space is not warrantable. The logical space, spoken of by Wittgenstein, does not stand for any super-world, which amalgamates this full-blooded empirical world of ours, along with tens, hundreds, thousands, hundred thousands, thousand thousands and so on countless possible worlds. Erik Stenius's explanation[15] of logical space as a space of possible states of affairs, seeks to relate the notion of logical space with that of possible worlds. According to Stenius, since logical space is a space of possible states of affairs, and states of affairs devise a world as a whole, logical space may be defined as a space of all 'possible worlds'.

The idea of logical space may call for some idea of extension or stretchability, then it has to be maintained, without any doubt, that the extension of logical space is the same as that of the actual

[15] Tractatus, 1960, p. 52.

world. If compared from the parameter of extension, in Wittgenstein's *Tractatus*, totality of actualized states of affairs, which is world, is also coextensiveness with logical space. Neither the actual world nor the logical space can be said to be either too wide or too narrow in comparison to one another, if extensionally considered. The world is given to us as the totality of facts, i.e. as the totality of states of affairs which have been realized, in other words, as the totality of actualized combinations of objects. But objects which are constitutive of such realized states of affairs also are ingrained with unrealized but possible states of affairs. Hence all those unrealized possibilities of state of affairs are also implanted in objects that make up the substance of the world. Finally, we are led to hold that if totality of all the possibilities, both realized possibility and unrealized possibility of combination of objects, is logical space, then that logical space is nowhere outside this world of ours. Thus, to put the matter straightforwardly, logical space is the world. The world as it has been, how in the actual world, one object has combined with another object, these are all contingencies. The world could have been altogether different from what it has actually been. Wittgenstein is particularly cautious in drawing a distinction between the contingency and an accident, and he would absolutely turn down any plea for considering the world as accidental. His explanation of 'accident' is as follows:

> it would seem to be a sort of accident, if it turned out that a situation would fit a thing that could already exist entirely on its own.[16]

But in his scheme, that sort of a thing has not been entertained. Things, that are considered as objects, are supposed to be both independent and dependent of combinations of objects. This dual aspect of dependence and independence with respect to an object has been clearly stated; in one respect an object, a logical simple does not need to occur in any particular state of affair, in that

---

[16] *TLP*, 2.0121, p. 5.

sense the object may be said to enjoy its independence. But the dependent aspect of the object to states of affairs is accounted for by the principle that it must be possible for the object to occur in states of affair. He made it clear that in his model there is no room for accidents. He does not believe in the thesis that something that happened or occurred is just a matter of accident. To quote from his *Tractatus*:

> In logic nothing is accidental; if a thing can occur in a state of affairs, the possibility of the state of affairs must be written into the thing itself.[17]

Those who are in favour of accepting the occurrence of an event to be accidental, think that something has happened though it did not have the possibility to happen. Thus, it amounts to holding that what was impossible to occur or happen has come into being. But this sort of argumentation has been banished from the domain of logic. The totality of the logical space, according to Wittgenstein, defines the essentials of the world. The unalterable logical form of the world is the logical space.

Possible Worlds

Now the question may be raised as to the metaphysical status of this logical space? In recent times after Saul Kripke, the notion of possible world has become quite popular among many logicians, philosophers of logic and philosophers of language. Among the philosophers, there is no unanimity about the nature and connotation of possible worlds. In the writings of Wittgenstein there is no reference to the notion of possible worlds as such. But we may bring the idea closer to the notion of possible worlds to find whether there are any similarities between the two. Among the philosophers who were committed to possible worlds, David Lewis is one who believes that possible worlds are just like our actual world: real and substantial.

There are enumerable possible worlds, of which our world is

---

[17] *TLP*, 2.012, p. 5.

one. Each possible world is like a planet situated in a far-off space. Each of this possible world is a description of the enumerable multiple ways in which the world would have been. The possibility of each world is different from that of the other. Of these enumerable possible worlds, which is to be considered as the actual world, depends upon the speaker. The speaker *A*, when refers to a particular world indexically as 'this' world, then in relation to that speaker *A*, the world is said to be the actual world. Again with respect to another speaker, say *B*, as per this speaker's indexical reference to another possible world as 'this' world, makes that world an actual world relative to that speaker. There are strong arguments against the view of Lewis, and he has been accused of needless multiplication of entities. There are some thinkers who interpret the Witgensteinian concept of possible worlds as realistic, for they think that he supported realism to account for the nature of the world. With a view to account for the metaphysics of logical space, that Wittgenstein adopts a realistic stand is quite beyond doubt. If it is assumed that for Wittgenstein, the notion of möglichkeit, i.e. possibility, is real, and the notion of logical space is not just a piece for romanticization, then obviously the question will arise as to the nature of realism implied by the notion of logical space.

The Logical Space and Logic

Wittgenstein, as we have already pointed out, was a philosopher of language in the tradition of analytic philosophy. He had arrived to his metaphysical thesis about the world through his programme of analysis. Wittgenstein admitted that there is a close relation between the world and the language. Wittgenstein believed that the logical form and the form of the world are isomorphic. We have already discussed that according to Wittgenstein the form of logical space and the form of the world are identical. If it is maintained that Wittgenstein's idea of logical space has been derived from language, then it may carry the impression that the form of the world has been derived from the language. Under that circumstance, how far Wittgenstein's view about the world can be considered to be realistic is a question. Hence to give an answer to the question whether Wittgenstein is a realist or an idealist, we need to have some idea about the nature of the relation between the logical space and language. This would also require an understanding of what has been maintained by Wittgenstein as logic. In his *Tractatus*, i.e. Treatise on Logic, Wittgenstein was looking for the foundation of logic. In his later writing he has pointed out that logic is a sort of a priori arrangement of possibilities — this arrangement of possibility is a feature common both to the case of the world and language. The arrangement of possibility though it is presumed to be a priori, it is vindicated through all actualized combinations. Wittgenstein has compared the clarity and unambiguity of logic with the clarity of the purest crystal. For Wittgenstein of this Tractarian period, to discuss about the nature of logic is but to discuss about the nature language as such. In the Tractarian period, Wittgenstein was searching for the isomorphism of the logical form of all languages, or to be more accurate, of all possible languages.

Logic and the World

While discussing about logic, Wittgenstein had commented that 'logic is a great mirror'.[18] Hence it would be correct to say that the world is mirrored in logic but the world does not mirror logic. The interpreters of Wittgenstein, however, differ as how to interpret the views of Wittgenstein about the nature of the relation between logic and the world. According to some, Wittgenstein, while explaining the relation between the world and language, has given primacy to the world. Those who maintained this view argue that unless world were not taken as primitive, Wittgenstein would not have been able to account for the relation between the world and language, because according to him logic to be capable of representing the world as a mirror, the prior existence of world has to be admitted. Hence, it seems logical to admit that whatever is described or represented by logic or at least capable of being

[18] *TLP*, 5.511, p. 49 and 6.13, p. 65.

represented or described because the world corresponds to such representations or descriptions. But there are interpreters who would straightforwardly reject this sort of reading of the *Tractatus*. They focus on the very objective of the *Tractatus*. In the *Tractatus*, the verily announced objective of Wittgenstein was to find out the hidden logic of language through analysis, for he believed the form of proposition is the form of reality. He was quite sure that what the world is, may be stated in an a priori way just by deciphering the logic of language. In his Tractarian scheme, language is a picture of the world and in virtue of being the picture of the world, since according to him:

> 2.2 A picture has logico-pictorial form in common with what it depicts.

there has to be reality, for a picture depicts reality. In this way of presenting Wittgenstein, logic is taken to be primitive. Among those who have interpreted Wittgenstein as giving primacy to logic have gone to the extent of denying any realistic account of the world. Now, there is no doubt, Wittgenstein's use of the mirror analogy has given rise to different interpretations. But actually what led him to use this particular mirror analogy to account for the nature of the relation between the world and logic need to be threadbare analysed. The main intention of Wittgenstein was to put emphasis on the isomorphism between logical form and the form of the world. His objective was to establish that the limit of the world and the limit of the logic are the same. The question as to whether logic is primary or the world is primary did not seem to have any deterrent effect upon his project.

A Proper Proposition

We require to say something about the nature of propositions with which logic is concerned. According to Wittgenstein, among what are accepted as propositions in language, all are not to be regarded as proper propositions. He maintains that there are some so-called propositions, which are not proper propositions, although. Wittgenstein has proposed some criteria for determining what is a proposition and what is a pseudo-proposition. Propositions which give description of the reality are the propositions which represent the reality. According to Wittgenstein, these are only commendable as propositions. This sort of propositions are contingent propositions, which can be either true or false. But necessary propositions, which are either necessarily true propositions or necessarily false propositions, are not regarded as proper propositions.

Necessarily True Propositions and Necessarily False Propositions

Wittgenstein, while discussing about necessarily true propositions or necessarily false propositions, is not completely deviating from their standard uses. During the period of the *Tractatus*, Wittgenstein was very much influenced by the paradigm of *Principia Mathematica*[19] of the truth-functional logic particularly. According to the very basics of truth-functional logic, truth value of a compound proposition is dependent on the truth value of its constituent elementary propositions. In the case of a necessarily true proposition, which is also called a tautologous proposition, the truth value of a compound tautologous proposition would come out to be true in all cases of truth-value assignment in the final column of the truth value, irrespective of the truth value of its constituent elementary propositions. Similarly in the case of a necessarily false proposition, the truth value for all instances will be *F* in the final column of the truth value irrespective of the truth value of its constituent elementary propositions. Such propositions in the terminology of logic are said to be self-contradictory propositions. According to Wittgenstein neither tautologous propositions nor self-contradictory propositions are admissible within the fold of proper propositions for these propositions do not represent any situation of the world. These propositions cannot represent any existing or non-existing combinations of objects. According to Wittgenstein, these propositions as they do not

---

[19] Russell and Whitehead, 1910-13.

represent anything are not to be regarded as pictures. 'What a picture represents is its sense', according to the 2.221 and since neither tautology nor contradictory propositions represent anything, these propositions, according to Wittgenstein, are without sense. In 4.4611, Wittgenstein has asserted:

> Tautologies and contradictions are not, however, non-sensical.

Naturally, how these two sorts of quite apparently similar qualifications, viz. 'without sense' and 'non-sense', one is affirmatively attributed to tautologies and contradictions and the other is denied of tautologies and contradictions? Hence the question is, as to how to draw the distinction between 'without sense' and 'non-sense' becomes important. In the *Tractatus* the expressions such as 'without sense' and 'non-sense' are never to be treated as synonymous expressions for to Wittgenstein the distinction between a proposition 'without sense' from a proposition which is 'non-sense' was very much relevant.

Without Sense and Non-sense

There is a sense in which we may maintain a distinction between these two phrases, viz. 'without sense' and 'non-sense'. In any language whatsoever, whether natural or artificial, there are certain rules that account for well-formed formulae of that language. Those rules are known as syntactical rules in modern terminology, and these syntactical rules are peculiar to each and every language. The expression 'logical syntax' occurs in 3.325a where it is used by Wittgenstein as synonymous with 'logical grammar', and also subsequently in propositions 3.327, 3.333, 3.334, 3.344 and 6.124. Here we are not required to explore all that has been said by Wittgenstein about *logical* syntax except the following: in the first place, his use of the expression logical in the compound expression *logical* syntax in italics, indicates that he prefers to distinguish *logical* syntax from the ordinary grammatical syntax. The reason for which is not far to seek for during this phase he was determined to unearth ideal sign language with a well-formed ideography to cure philosophy from confusions created by ordinary language.

Second, it is noteworthy, his notion of *logical* syntax as stated in his 'Logical Form', is as follows:

> By syntax in this general sense of the word, I mean the rules which tell us in which connexions only a word gives sense, thus excluding non-sensical pseudo-propositions.[20]

We may also allude to the Tractarian proposition, 3.33, wherein it has been stated:

> In logical syntax the meaning of a sign should never play a role. It must be possible to establish logical syntax without mentioning the *meaning* of a sign: *only* the description of expressions may be presupposed.

What clearly transpires from the above discussion is that no formulae are acceptable as well-formed formulae of a language, if it violates these syntactical rules. Under those circumstances, formula violating formation rules are excluded from the domain of well-formed formulae of that language. Those formulae that are not according to the formation rules of a language are considered to be non-sense in that language. In this way, we may account for the notion of non-sense. The propositions which are tautology or contradictions are not opposing grammar of truth-functional logic. Wittgenstein also cannot say that tautology or contradictory propositions violate logical syntax of propositional logic. Hence, Wittgenstein maintains that tautology or contradictory propositions are not senseless. But questions may be raised what are the features of these propositions? Negatively speaking, it may be said that tautology or contradictory propositions are not descriptive propositions, these propositions do not describe anything. If a proposition does not describe anything, it is said to be without sense. In the *Tractatus,* a proposition which does not describe anything, but has some uses, is not senseless, rather such propositions are without sense. Thus we find according to that criterion, tautology and contradictory propositions are without sense.

---

[20] *Logical Form*, 1929, p. 162 in 'Some Remarks on Logical Form', *Proceedings of the Aristotelian Society* (Supplementary), vol. 9, pp. 162-71.

But the question remains: are these propositions without sense in the same manner? Wittgenstein, however, in the *Tractatus* has not given any suggestions as to whether tautology and contradictory propositions are without sense in the same manner. In his collection of later speeches, known as *Moore Notes*, some clarifications are available in this matter. When it is said that a tautological proposition does not describe anything, what actually has been tried to convey by saying so? Suppose, the tautological proposition, '$q \ v \sim q$' is conjoined with another contingent proposition say, 'p' and the resulting proposition is '$[(q \ v \sim q) \ . \ p]$'. In this case, the truth value of the compound proposition depends on the truth value of the contingent proposition p. Thus we get the proposition, $[(q \ v \sim q) \cdot p] = P$. Thus, what is clear from this explanation that a tautological proposition does not describe anything over and above that of what is being described by a contingent proposition. For that reason, a tautological proposition is said to be without sense.

The contradictory propositions are also said to be without sense, but that these propositions are without sense cannot be accounted for in the same manner. If a contingent proposition is conjoined with a contradictory proposition, it cannot be said that the truth value of the compound proposition depends on the truth value of the contingent proposition. Suppose there is a proposition of the form $[(q \ . -q \ ) \ . \ p)]$, then in that case the truth value of the proposition is equivalent to the truth value of the contradictory proposition and not to that of the contingent proposition p. Thus, by using the same criterion, it is not possible to establish that both the tautological proposition and contradictory proposition are without sense in the same manner. Thus, we find, it is not feasible to account for the meaning of the expression, 'without sense' in this way.

Propositions and Logical Space

The question arises as to how to draw the distinction between a proposition that is with sense and that is without sense? Let us try to understand what it is, according to Wittgenstein, for a proposition to be with sense. In this context, Wittgenstein's notion of logical space is very important. Each and every proposition, which has sense, has a definite place or extension in logical space. His picture theory of propositions depends on following such contentions:

> 2.202 A picture represents a possible situation in logical space.
>
> 2.221 What picture represents is its sense.
>
> 3.144a Situations can be described and not given names.

The main contention of Wittgenstein is that a proposition represents a situation in logical space, and that is the sense of the proposition; the sense is independent of truth value and sense can be described. According to Wittgenstein, all propositions are truth functions of elementary propositions. He says in 4.4:

> A proposition is an expression of agreement and disagreement with truth-possibilities of elementary propositions.

And this is further elucidated by the proposition, 4.41 as follows:

> Truth-possibilities of elementary propositions are the conditions of the truth and falsity of propositions.

Each point of logical space is what is called 'truth possibility' of elementary propositions. If there were only three elementary propositions, say p, q and r, one such point would correspond to the possibility $(p \cdot q \cdot r)$, another to the possibility $(p \cdot \neg q \cdot r)$ and there would be eight such truth possibilities. Max Black brings out that the notion of logical space, thus, becomes equivalent with the totality of elementary truth possibilities. Now, we need to comment upon the nature of elementary propositions in the *Tractatus*. The interpreters found it difficult to discuss about the nature of elementary propositions in the *Tractatus*. We have already got the idea that elementary propositions are contingent propositions, i.e. these may be either true or false. If an elementary proposition matches with an atomic fact, then elementary proposition is taken to be true; but if an elementary proposition, p is false, there is no corresponding situation in respect to which the proposition may be said to be verified. Thus, the question as to what falsifies *p* is really difficult to answer. The falsity of an elementary proposition can at all be verified by any positive fact? When an elementary proposition *p* is false, is it not falsified by something being not the case? Then again problems crop up for the *Tractatus,* for then the *Tractatus* would be required to make room for negative facts. This is one of the controversial issues in the *Tractatus* as to whether Wittgenstein has admitted negative facts or not. According to one of the standard readings of the *Tractatus,* Wittgenstein did not admit negative facts. Hence in this case, to account for the falsity of a contingent proposition, it would be a sort of imposition upon Wittgenstein to make him accept negative facts as its falsifying factor, but this would go against Wittgenstein's position. To avoid these problems, some have suggested how through some surreptitious ways the problem of negative facts may be tackled. A true elementary proposition may be verified by a single atomic fact, but this analogy cannot be carried further. A false proposition may be verified by the whole universe, for to verify this proposition, we need to verify the whole of reality to establish its truth value.[21]

Thus what space a proposition would occupy in a logical space is determined by the totality of its truth value assignment. A proposition whose truth value is true is included within the possible truth values of that proposition. According to Wittgenstein a proposition occupies that much space in logical space which it leaves open for actualized states of affairs to occupy. The domain of a contingent proposition is the same as the totality of all its possible truth value combinations. A proposition which is informative cannot be compatible with all of logical space. It shuns some space within logical space. If a proposition does not shun or reject some space of logical space that proposition cannot state anything. In the case of a tautological proposition the domain of its possible truth-value and the logical space are the same. That is why a tautological proposition is said to be devoid of descriptive

[21] Max Black, 1960, p. 214.

content for these tautological propositions that are compatible with all possible states of affairs. Propositions of logic are all tautologies, hence they do not state anything. Logical propositions do not shun any space in logical space.

Logical Propositions

The notion of tautology plays a central part in Wittgenstein's attempt to clarify the notion of logical truth. In this connection, we may recapitulate some of the following statements from the *Tractatus*:

> 6.1 The propositions of logic are tautologies.
>
> 6.11 Therefore the propositions of logic say nothing.
>
> 6.111 All theories that make a proposition of logic to appear to have content are false.

If we understand the very nature of tautologies then we can comprehend why did Wittgenstein said that these tautologies do not state anything but these are not non-sense. Tautologies occupy whole of logical space, hence they are not representing any portions of logical space as such. In that context, tautologies are not stating anything and have no descriptive content. So it cannot be said that logic gives description of the reality. From logic, we do not get any information about which particular combination of objects have been realized and which particular combinations of objects have not been realized. Thus logic has no link with the empirical. Propositions of logic are necessarily true propositions and their truth in no way depend upon anything that happens in the world. Thus the truth of tautologies is absolutely independent of empirical truth. But contingent propositions are very much dependent on reality, these propositions, are as if holding reality tightly. Contingent propositions are related to reality through their claims about the reality. The claims of contingent propositions about the reality are true or false as these agree or disagree with the realities. To say what have actually happened in reality is to shun the other possibilities of states of affair. But tautologies cover the whole of logical space and does not leave empty any portion of logical space. Hence logic cannot transcend the limits of all the possibilities.

Frege, Russell, Wittgenstein

Thus we find that in the *Tractatus*, the idea of logical truth is correlated with the idea of tautologies and the idea of tautologies presupposes the idea of truth-functional logic. In the *Tractatus*, Wittgenstein was investigating into the nature of logic and its foundation. His endeavour was not restricted to enquiring into the nature of logic, rather he established further that the foundation of logic tallies with the foundation of reality. There was no doubt that the deeper questions about logic and metaphysics were his objects of great worry. He became aware of these problems in various ways, by his reading literatures of Frege and Russell, by his regular dialogues and discussions with Russell during his Cambridge days and through his dialogues with G.E. Moore as well. In course of his discussion about the nature of logic, he has often criticized the views of Frege and Russell, but that does not mean he had absolutely dissociated himself from their influence in the formation of his idea about logic. In many important respects, Wittgenstein is found to share some of the Fregean and the Russellian convictions. In the first place, commitment to realism which is the common mark of Frege, Russell and Moore, is quite clearly present in Wittgenstein's metaphysics of the world. Second, the Augustinian conception of language that he has advocated in the *Tractatus*, he derived the basics of which from Frege and Russell. Third, Wittgenstein's conviction about the nature of relation between language and reality was very much influenced by the viewpoints of Frege and Russell. Fourth, Wittgenstein was very much influenced by bi-valued logics and their claim that the meaning of a proposition is restricted to either truth or falsity.

Nature of Logic

In delineating the nature of logic, we find Wittgenstein did not accept the viewpoints of Frege and Russell in all respects. In

Principia Mathematica, an attempt has been made to reduce whole of mathematics to logic. In other words, in *Principia Mathematica*, an attempt has been made to establish that from certain unanalysable truths of logic the whole of mathematics may be entailed. Russell believed that the logic that has been worked out by them is the perfect logical language through which the logical form and structure of states of affairs are mirrored. According to Frege, logical propositions are tautologous, and rules of logic are justified to be so by the logical source of language. These tautologous propositions are necessarily true propositions. If there is any doubt about the acceptability of a rule of logic, then it can be justified by reference to some other rules of logic. If, however, a logical rule cannot be derived from another logical rule, then according to Frege, logic cannot provide answer to such questions. Russell did not speak about tautologous nature of logical propositions with so much emphasis as has been spoken of by Frege. In his *Principia*, Russell-supposed propositions, which are accepted as elementary or basic propositions, have been accepted to be such without any further proof. Russell thought that the principle behind the acceptance of some tautologous propositions and rejection of other propositions can be stated with the help of an inductive argument as follows: whatever proposition has been accepted as a primary proposition or axiom, it is because, from it a large number of indubitable propositions may be derived. Tautologous propositions of logic are not provable and propositions which are beyond proofs are tautologous. Wittgenstein does not find any necessity for collating all tautological propositions in the form of a calculus, where some propositions are premises and some are conclusions. Frege and Russell, none of them has been able to discover the real nature of logical propositions. Frege and Russell, both of them, had accepted that logical propositions have content. According to Frege, a logical proposition describes how abstract objects are related with one another; according to Russell, logical propositions describe the relation among the most general objects of the world. Thus, both Frege and Russell thought that logical propositions have sense. Herein Wittgenstein differs both from Russell and Frege for he does not accept that logical propositions have sense.

Wittgenstein is of the opinion that from the account of Frege and Russell, we cannot derive right idea about the nature of logical propositions. According to Frege and Russell, logical propositions are generalizations of tautologous propositions. Wittgenstein does not approve the way of understanding logical propositions as generalized propositions. Wittgenstein does not maintain that the characteristic of a logical proposition is not that it is true about everybody. In this connection his argument is quite simple. According to him, a logical proposition may not be a universal proposition, for a name may occur in a tautological proposition, and that is not a universal proposition. Thus, there are lots of difference between Wittgenstein and both Russell and Frege. However, they all agree that logical propositions are independent of objects.

According to Wittgenstein, if we can get hold of all the elementary propositions, then we can give a complete description of the world. From the elementary propositions, we are able to derive all the compound propositions. Thus we will be able to get all the possible propositions. The process of deriving compound propositions from the elementary propositions are called by Wittgenstein operation. (The operation is what has to be done to the one proposition in order to make the other out of it. 5.23.) If *p* is an elementary proposition, it has the possibility of being either true or false, for Wittgenstein believes in the principle of bivalence. In this case from the proposition *p*, by using truth operation, we may derive the following four propositions which are not elementary. The following diagram may be taken to represent the relation between an elementary proposition *p* and its truth function *f*(*p*):

p	$f_1(p)$	$f_2(p)$	$f_3(p)$	$f_4(p)$
T	*F*	*T*	*F*	*T*
F	*T*	*F*	*F*	*T*

According to 5.101 from elementary propositions p and q as truth function $f(p \cdot q)$ we derive sixteen propositions as follows:

p	q	$f_1(p, q)$	$f_2(p, q)$	$f_3(p, q)$	$f_4(p, q)$	$f_5(p, q)$	$f_6(p, q)$	$f_7(p, q)$	$f_8(p, q)$
T	T	T	F	T	T	T	F	F	F
T	F	T	T	F	T	T	F	T	T
F	T	T	T	T	F	T	T	F	T
F	F	T	T	T	T	F	T	T	F

p	q	$f_9(p, q)$	$f_{10}(p, q)$	$f_{11}(p, q)$	$f_{12}(p, q)$	$f_{13}(p, q)$	$f_{14}(p, q)$	$f_{15}(p, q)$	$f_{16}(p, q)$
T	T	T	T	T	F	F	F	T	F
T	F	F	F	T	F	F	T	F	F
F	T	F	T	F	F	T	F	F	F
F	F	T	F	F	T	F	F	F	F

In similar ways, if there are three elementary propositions like p, q, r we may obtain as truth function $f(p, q, r)$ by the process of truth operation 256 propositions.

If we observe carefully, we will be able to grasp the originality of Wittgenstein's thought. The first row is the row meant for tautological propositions. This is how Wittgenstein has established the characteristics of tautological propositions. He does not say like Frege that necessary true propositions are self-evident or like Russell that necessary positions of logic are like axioms. Wittgenstein established tautological propositions as derivable from elementary propositions. It may seem that along with elementary propositions, if we had only logical constants we could have derived all propositions. But this sort of explanation will not be acceptable to Wittgenstein. If stated in that way, it may seem that logical constants add something more to the elementary propositions. According to Wittgenstein logical constants do not add anything more to the elementary propositions. According to Frege, logical constants are names of logical objects. Russell's view is also similar to this view, Russell also speaks about knowledge by acquaintance of logical objects and sometimes about logical definition of such objects. But Wittgenstein does not admit logical objects to have real existence. According to Wittgenstein, all logical constants are inter-definable, hence no logical objects are to be admitted as real. All logical constants are given with elementary propositions. As elementary propositions are contingent propositions, within these propositions are contained their possibility of being either true or false, and in their nature lies the possibility of being either asserted or falsified. The idea of negation has its origin from the idea of bivalence, from the bipolarity of truth and falsity. And two propositions can be true and from there the idea of conjunction has its origin. Thus from an elementary proposition, the idea of negative proposition originates, from idea of more than one elementary proposition, the idea of conjunction originates. If we proceed in that way, we may come to the negation of a conjunctive proposition. We know Morgan has formulated the negation of a conjunction, such as $\sim(p \cdot q) = \sim p \, v \sim q$. The logician Sheffer used the sign '/' , known as stroke sign as an independent sign and symbolized '$\sim (p \cdot q)$ as 'p/q'. Wittgenstein in fact followed Sheffer's way of symbolizing other logical connectives, like disjunction, implication in terms of stroke sign.

From the *Tractatus* we find that Wittgenstein's idea of logic is in many respects different from his other contemporary logicians. From Wittgenstein's perspective an enquiry into the nature of logic is really an enquiry into the nature of tautologous propositions. Logic is, in the real, actual world. The world, which is the totality of facts, contains within it the form of logic. The essence of the world consists of certain primitive possibilities, of these possibilities some have been actualized and some have not yet been actualized. The logical form is the same as the form of the possible combinations of simple objects. Thus in the *Tractatus* his logic binds the logical space. We have seen initially that the idea of logical space was presented as a metaphysical idea. Finally, we find that logical space embraces the logic of the *Tractatus*.

8

The Limits of Language and the Unlimited Beyond

In the Preface to the *Tractatus Logico-Philosophicus*, Ludwig Wittgenstein's remark, viz. 'The whole sense of the book might be summed up in the following words: what can be said at all can be said clearly, and what we cannot talk about we must consign to silence'[1] was a baffling one. The portrayers of Wittgenstein zealously engaged themselves to decipher Wittgenstein's vision, but foundered on different views. What really does Wittgenstein intend to convey by this statement? A credible reply to this question presupposes a clear and comprehensive understanding of the philosophical background wherein Wittgenstein was situated. Two major perceptions centre round the following questions: Was Wittgenstein, during the Tractarian period, a hard-core philosopher of language participating in the trail of Frege–Russell's logico-linguistic trend? Or, was he at the core of his very being a concerned mystic who was offering to unbosom himself in the language of the poet of *Gitanjali* by the following utterance,

> *My heart longs to join in thy song,*
> *But vainly struggles for a voice?*[2]

There are interpreters who vigorously damn any mystic interpretation of the Tractarian Wittgenstein and consider those mystic statements unwanted scribbling in the *Tractatus*.[3] But there are others who find in Wittgenstein a philosopher who seeks to

---

1 *Tractatus Logico-Philosophicus*, 1981 (repr.), tr. D.F. Pears and B.F. McGuinness, p. 3.

2 *Gitanjali*, Song Offerings, p. 3.

3 *Carnap.*

transcend the world of contingencies.[4] This is hardly to be denied that Wittgenstein himself is responsible for generating these two different sorts of reading of his enigmatic text, *Tractatus Logico-Philosophicus*. None of these interpretations is to be considered as less important in comparison with the other in its contribution towards a better unraveling of the mystery that was Wittgenstein. My objective here consists in explaining how these apparently conflicting trends merge in Wittgenstein.

This cryptic remark of Wittgenstein, with which the present discussion begins, brings out questions regarding the distinctive nature of what can be said as distinguished from what cannot be said according to the requirement of the *Tractatus*; second, what can be said, amounts to saying it clearly. A brief recapitulation of the historical background that marks the root of the text *Tractatus*, may provide some clue in this regard. There is hardly any room for doubt that Wittgenstein was thoroughly a philosopher of language in the dominant philosophical tradition of analytic philosophy and had initiated a breakthrough in the domain of Anglophone philosophy of language by the Tractarian move and a later move by his *Philosophical Investigations* and other writings of the period. G. Frege's and Bertrand Russell's inspiration was one of the major sources for Wittgenstein's venture into the philosophical domain. In the preface to the *Tractatus* Wittgenstein acknowledged his indebtedness to Frege's magnificent works and to the writings of his friend Russell. The philosophical movement known as the analytic philosophy owes its beginning to the interaction among Frege, Russell and Wittgenstein. The most important discovery of the twentieth-century analytic philosophy is the view that philosophical problems may be solved or dissolved either by the analysis of language or by understanding more about the language we use. This heralded the beginning of the linguistic turn in philosophy. Russell's *Principia Mathematica* worked out jointly with Whitehead influenced Wittgenstein to embark upon

---

[4] Suresh Chandra, 2002, *Wittgenstein New Perspectives*, p. 26.

the program of logic. He remarked, 'Philosophy consists of logic and metaphysics; logic is its basis'.[5] In fact, Frege, Russell and Wittgenstein were very much hopeful about the prospect of new logic in philosophy. It is a well-accepted truth that Frege, Russell and Wittgenstein shared a common concern for the new logic and were quite unanimous in accepting the philosophical relevance of this logic.[6]

Since our day-to-day ordinary language is often ambiguous and imprecise, it was the proposal of some philosophers of language to develop an exact and precise language which may be considered as a perfect language. Russell was of the opinion that the new logic that he had devised with Whitehead is a logically perfect language, fit to mirror the logical forms of facts. Frege also held that in a properly constructed language, no fuzziness could occur at all. Frege says:

> The law of excluded middle is just another form of the requirement that a concept should have a sharp boundary. Any object *A* that you choose to take either falls under the concept, or does not fall under it: tertium non datur.[7]

To Wittgenstein in the Tractarian period, language is a tool for description and language is a kind of picture which represents reality. In this view, the primary function that is ascribed to language is that of describing how things stand. Before we enter into a discussion about Wittgenstein's theory of language, which is known as the picture theory of language, we need to observe where Wittgenstein may be situated in the debate regarding ordinary language vis-à-vis perfect language. There is some difference of opinion among the interpreters of the *Tractatus* as to whether Wittgenstein is talking about ordinary language or perfect language in the *Tractatus* in elaborating his picture theory. There is no doubt that during the earlier phase of his career, Wittgenstein

---

5 *Notebook*, p. 106.

6 Hans Sluga et al. (eds.) 1996, *The Cambridge Companion to Wittgenstein*, p. 7.

7 G. Frege, 1964, *The Basic Laws of Arithmetic*, sect. 56.

was very much influenced by Russell's logic of *Principia Mathematica* and that must have some effect on his choice for a model of perfect language. Wittgenstein toed the path of Russell and Frege in favouring a language with its transparent syntax: Wittgenstein writes:

> In order to avoid such errors we must make use of a sign-language that excludes them by not using the same sign for different symbols and by not using in a superficially similar way signs that have different modes of signification: that is to say, a sign-language that is governed by logical grammar — by logical syntax.
>
> (The conceptual notation of Frege and Russell is such a language, though it is true, it fails to exclude all mistakes.)[8]

Wittgenstein's analysis of language, according to Russell, 'is concerned with the conditions which have to be fulfilled by a logically perfect language'.[9] According to this interpretation, Wittgenstein aimed at the construction of an ideal language, a language the words of which are precise and the sentences of which are suitable for unambiguously revealing the logical form of reality which they represent. It was felt that the task of a philosopher is to construct an ideal language in which all those defects responsible for ambiguity or lack of precision are removed by making provision for precise symbols and explicit rules for their combination. Wittgenstein says in his Tractatus:

> All philosophy is a critique of language. It was Russell who performed the service of showing that the apparent logical form of a proposition need not be its real one.[10]

But it would be too rash a conclusion to maintain that Wittgenstein was the blind supporter of perfect language for from his remark it is quite obvious that he was quite aware of its limitations. The same person in the same text *Tractatus* remarks, 'all the propositions

---

8 *Tractatus Logico-Philosophicus*, 3.325.

9 *Tractatus Logico-Philosophicus*, 'Introduction by Russell', p. x.

10 Ibid., 4.0031.

of our everyday language are in perfect order'.[11] All these remarks of Wittgenstein's really made it difficult to characterize his viewpoint on language in a straightforward manner.

In the *Tractatus*, Wittgenstein is searching for the essential core aspect of all languages, for he believes if he can find out the essence of all description, then he will be able to grasp the essential aspect of reality. Another important contribution of Wittgenstein's is his picture theory of language, his explanation of which consists in the striking idea that a sentence is a picture. He meant it literally that a sentence is a picture and not merely like a picture in certain respects. He said in his *Tractatus*:

> A proposition is a picture of reality. A proposition is a model of reality as we imagine.[12]

In any picture, according to the *Tractatus*, there has to be a one-to-one correspondence between the elements of a picture and the things in the state-of-affairs it represents. This stand does not dismiss either the possibility of different kinds of picture, or different pictorial notations or different methods of projection. One thing, however, is essentially required of a picture to be a picture of, is its having in common with reality the same logical form in order to be able to picture reality at all, either correctly or incorrectly. This logical form of a sentence, called as 'the form of reality',[13] is defined as the possibility that things in the world are related as are the elements of a picture. It has been further stated that sentences, since they are pictures, have the same form as the reality they depict. A picture can depict reality, but it cannot depict its form of representation. It depicts its subject from outside, but it cannot depict its form of representation. A picture of another form might depict the representational form of a given picture; for instance, a picture in sound might depict the representational form of a picture in colour. But in order for one to represent the

11 *Tractatus Logico-Philosophicus*, op. cit., 4.0031

12 *Tractatus*, 4.01.

13 Ibid., 2.18.

form of another, there must be something that is common to both.

> There must be something identical in a picture and what it depicts, to enable the one to be a picture of the other at all.[14]

Therefore logical form, the form of reality which all pictures must possess, cannot be depicted by any picture. This consideration must apply to sentences as well. We make assertions by means of sentences. With a sentence we say something, we say how things are. Things in the world are related in a certain way, and we try to describe these. But we cannot describe how our sentences succeed in representing reality, truly or falsely. We cannot say what is the form of representation, that makes them the picture of reality, that is common to all sentences. We cannot say how language represents the world: in other words, we cannot state in a sentence the pictorial form of all sentences. In this connection, the question may be asked as to whether language is prior to reality or reality is to be considered as prior to language in the Tractarian model. According to some interpreters of the *Tractatus*, since the metaphysics is more basic in the *Tractatus*, reality is more primitive compared to language, whereas to some it may appear that language is more primitive than metaphysics. The *Tractatus* begins with the description of the world as follows:

1. The world is all that is the case

1.1 The world is the totality of facts, not of things

In the propositions 1 to 2.063 Wittgenstein describes the most general features of the world and proceeds from these to explain the nature of propositions. Does it carry the impression that according to Wittgenstein reality is more basic than language? But there are views that assess the position of Wittgenstein in a reverse way and suggest that in the Tractarian model language should be treated as basic and reality is just an inferred and thus derived entity. In this essay however, there is very little scope for entering into all those controversies.

---

[14] *Tractatus*, 2.161.

The logical positivists did not accept the picture theory of proposition, which is the central idea of the *Tractatus*. The doctrine that was held by the thinkers belonging to the Vienna Circle was that all genuine propositions are reducible to propositions that report 'direct perception', or what is 'immediately given in experience'. Wittgenstein talks of analysis but his notion of analysis does not imply any idea of its reporting what is immediately given in experience. The logical positivists were eager to include Wittgenstein as one of the proponents of their viewpoint but Wittgenstein differed very much from their approach. A corollary to the positivist thesis is the view that 'the meaning of a statement is its method of verification'. The verification theory of meaning has not been discussed in the *Tractatus*. Wittgenstein has said in the *Tractatus*:

> To understand a proposition means to know what is the case if it is true.[15]

Nothing has been stated here about verification or anything similar to it. Wittgenstein has taken the notion of analysis in the sense of decomposition of something in its constituents: as in chemical analysis. The composition of chemical compounds is shown in terms of their constituent chemical elements, or as in micro-physical analysis the composition of a material substance is displayed in terms of sub-atomic composition of matter, so in philosophical analysis the composition of any compound proposition is displayed in terms of elementary propositions consisting of concatenated names which constitute the end point of analysis. The simple signs of the *Tractatus* are the names which figure in the elementary propositions when fully analysed, referring to the simple objects which constitute the substance of the world. The *Tractatus* thrives on the thesis that the sense of propositions be determinate and it is well understood that 'the requirement that simple signs be possible is the requirement that sense be determinate'.[16] The

---

15 *TLP*, 4.024.

16 *TLP*, 3.23.

Tractarian idea of analysis is closely linked with the idea of determinacy of sense. Every proposition, according to the *Tractatus*, is built up from elementary propositions in such a way that the truth or falsity of the whole proposition is determined by the truth or falsity of its component elementary propositions. In our ordinary language there are propositions such as, 'I believe that *p*', or '9 is necessarily greater than 7' which are not truth functions of simpler propositions they contain. Wittgenstein would not accord meaning to such propositions which on analysis also could not be shown to be truth functions of elementary propositions.

The picture theory of proposition is at the same time an account of the nature of thought. Wittgenstein's remark in the *Tractatus* is:

> 'A thought is a proposition with a sense'[17] implies that thinking is impossible without language. Since a thought is a sentence and a sentence is a picture, a thought is a picture. The totality of true thought would be a true picture of the world. In a spoken or written sentence a thought is 'made perceptible to the senses'.[18]

All thoughts can be stated in sentences and what cannot be stated are not thoughts.

The idea that permeates the *Tractatus* is that we confront the world with a language whose appropriateness is guaranteed by its deep structure that matches the world. This belief in the deep structure of thought or core aspect of thought plays a crucial role in the *Tractatus*. The early philosophy of Wittgenstein centres on the claim about the pure essence of language. Wittgenstein has equated philosophy with attempts to say the unsayable and has traced its source to our failure to grasp the 'logic of our language'. According to Wittgenstein 'most of the propositions and questions to be found in philosophical works are not false but nonsensical. Most of the propositions and questions of philosophers arise from our failure to understand the logic of our language. The basic assumption of the *Tractatus* thus consists in upholding the thesis

---

[17] *TLP*, 4.

[18] See *TLP*, 3.1.

of determinacy of sense, which implies that a proposition only has a sense, if it has an absolutely determinate sense. A meaningful proposition must be either true or false with respect to every possible situation: there must be no truth value gaps — no possible situations in which the proposition would be neither true nor false. Given the nature of language as determinate in sense and the function of language as picturing, Wittgenstein proceeds to make an important pronouncement about the limits of so-called language. It is interesting to note the following passage in which Wittgenstein himself in a letter to Russell, was summarizing his main contention of the *Tractatus* as

> the theory of what can be expressed (gesagt) by propositions — i.e. by language — (and which comes to the same thing, what can be thought) and what cannot be expressed by propositions, but only shown (gezeigt); which, I believe is the cardinal problem of philosophy.[19]

From Wittgenstein's entry in his *Notebooks* since June 1916, it is quite evident that Wittgenstein is inquisitive about our knowledge about God or about purpose of our life. In his *Notebooks* Wittgenstein commented, 'The I, the I is what is deeply mysterious'.[20] During wartime *Notebooks* (1914-16), Wittgenstein's irresolute striving between the logic of language and his pondering about ethical and mystical were striking. Later on most of these ideas were replicated in his *Tractatus Logico-Philosophicus*. The *Tractatus* works towards sharply delineating the limits of thought by delineating the limits of language — by distinguishing meaningful propositions from the realm of non-sense and what is without sense. In the *Tractatus* the logical space is conceived to be the domain of sense. No doubt, the doctrine of what shows forth but cannot be said is one of the difficult doctrines of the *Tractatus*. He writes: 'What can be shown, cannot be said'. This is the mark of solipsism in the *Tractatus*.

---

19 19 August 1919, in B. Mcguinness, ed., *Wittgenstein in Cambridge: Letters and Documents 1911-1951.*

20 *Notebooks*, p. 72.

In 5.6 we come across one of the crucial assertions of Wittgenstein's that marks the focal point of solipsism in the *Tractatus*:

> *The limits of my language* mean the limits of my world.[21]

The implication of this particular statement, which proved to be a very difficult one, is enormous in the whole of the *Tractatus*. One of the ablest Wittgenstein scholars like David Pears had commented about 5.62 as, 'one of the most difficult text in the *Tractatus* and there is very little agreement between commentators about its meaning'.[22] An enquiry into the significance of this statement may be pursued, broadly speaking, from two different, but not unrelated ways. The first question to be answered is: what in particular meant by the limits or boundaries of the world? The effort to make sense of what is meant by Wittgenstein about the limits of language necessarily leads to further explanations about the expressions like subject, self, soul, ego, etc. The interpreters often had to fall back upon *Notebooks* to make sense of his Tractarian viewpoint, though it would be rather too ambitious to think that endeavours of the interpreters had always been a bed of roses. There are also passages in the *Notebooks* which often are at variance with that of the *Tractatus*. In the *Tractatus* we find there are three sorts of things that lie beyond the limits of language. Wittgenstein had said that language cannot represent the logical form of reality.

> Propositions can represent the whole of reality, but they cannot represent what they must have in common with reality in order to be able to represent it — logical form. . . .
>
> Propositions cannot represent logical form: it is mirrored in them.
>
> . . . . Propositions show the logical form of reality. They display it.[23]

---

21 *Tractatus Logico-Philosophicus*, 5.6.

22 *The False Prison*, chap. 6, p. 164.

23 *TLP*, 4.12-4–4.121.

Second, ethics, aesthetics, the meaning of life and the mystical are beyond language. And finally, philosophy itself is also a member, if at all, of the domain of silence.

The second major issue is about the upshot of language being thus limited is solipsism in the *Tractaus*. The issues relating to solipsism, its nature, its merger with realism and many more related forceful discussions have kept Wittgenstein scholars preoccupied. Wittgenstein's solipsistic claim, '. . . The world is my world'[24] has been explained to be influenced negatively by Bertrand Russell and positively by Schopenhauer. Wittgenstein's solipsistic claim regarding the limits of the world is not the fall out of his being confronted by some impenetrable veil of mental sense-data or because of some hang-up from the inside by the relation of the world to the ego. The feature of language matters here the most and how that has come up in the writings of Wittgenstein would be mainly discussed without entering into a detailed analysis about solipsism in particular.

Let us, therefore concentrate more on the first half of the issue mentioned above. As a logician his entire search was directed towards the discovery of the essential aspect of all languages that defines the constraint of that language as such. But the above remark of Wittgenstein was startling because of its inclusion of the personal pronoun 'my' twice as qualifier in 'my language' and 'my world'. The following remark of Wittgenstein in 5.62 may be mentioned:

> . . . The world is my world; this is manifest in the fact that the limits of language (of that language which alone I understand) mean the limits of my world.

This remark of Wittgenstein has generated lots of controversy. Questions have arisen as to the exact implications of this statement. What in particular is meant by Wittgenstein by the limits or boundaries of the world? One of the important questions is how to read in 5.62 the bracketed portion, viz. 'of that language which

[24] *TL*, 5.62.

alone I understand'. Two ways of interpreting the clause, 'of that language which alone I understand' are suggested:

1. It refers to a private language, a language that I alone speak.
2. It refers to one and only language I speak.

On the first reading as derived from Anscombe,[25] Wittgenstein is defending some sort of solipsism for it suggests that in Wittgenstein's view the limits of language and the world were given in a language private to himself. This way of interpreting Wittgenstein's viewpoint matches with his remarks in the *Tractatus* as 'the world and life are one',[26] and 'I am my world'.[27] From this reading of the text, it is not unwarranted to consider Wittgenstein as a solipsist. According to Wittgenstein, in the above-quoted clause, 'my world' means 'the world which I can describe or think about'. It has been stated that my world is simply the world, just as the reality which can be described or thought of is simply the reality. The doctrine of solipsism making the claim that nothing exists apart from oneself, and the contents of one's mind are taken to imply the following claims:

1. Only what I experience exists.
2. What I do not experience does not exist.

Thus, in this interpretation, a personal limit is set to the existents. A solipsist places credence only to one's own existence.

The second alternative explanation rules out the possibility of any privacy or private domain; the phrase, 'the only language that I understand', has nothing to do with any particular language like German, English or French. In the Tractarian phase especially, for Wittgenstein, all languages are one and the same, as far as their essence is concerned, hence there cannot be any reference to any particular language like German, French, etc. All languages, as understood by Wittgenstein, are one and the same because there cannot be any language which is illogical. Logic is wholly present

---

[25] Anscombe, Introduction, p. 167, fn. 1.

[26] 5.621.

[27] 5.63.

in any language that makes sense for if a language does not have any logic then it is not to be considered as language at all. All languages, then, can be taken together in the sense that logic is wholly present in each of them, and the differences between them being merely conventional. What I conceive of as the world is given to me in my language. This particular conception is the only one that is. This conception is viewed as the only conception that is, for many other possible conceptions have been considered and are rejected on some ground or other. There is no language other than this language and so there is no possibility for any conception of the world other than this one which is provided by this language. Thus, the resulting conception is my conception. Wittgenstein draws the analogy with my visual field for it is without any second.

This view entails existence of two radically different kinds of things:

1. The subject of experience.
2. The object of experience.

How are we to make sense of the notion of subject of experience? One of the controversial terms in Wittgenstein's *Tractatus* is the *metaphysische subjekt*. He did not bother to provide any explicit clue as to the nature of this metaphysical subject. What was actually Wittgenstein's intention about a subject often appeared to be a sort of equivocation between its acceptance and denial. On closer scrutiny, it is clear that Wittgenstein is actually not contradicting himself for there is a sense in which he upholds a subject and also there is another sense in which he rejects it. He introduces the notion of philosophical self as distinguished from the psychological self. The philosophical self is according to him the metaphysical subject. Wittgenstein does not make room for any thinking, knowing, experiencing metaphysical self for in his opinion there is no such entity. An attempt may be made to collate some of the salient features of the subject and its consequences as obtained from the *Tractatus*:

1. There is no subject (in a psychological sense).

2. There is a subject (in a philosophical sense).
3. The subject is not something that entertains ideas, and thinks, analyses, synthesizes experiences.
4. The subject is not in the world.
5. The subject is a limit of the world.
6. The relation of the self to the world is analogous to that of the eye and the visual field.
7. The subject and the world are in some sense one and the same.
8. Some version of solipsism is correct.
9. Only it is a version which coincides with realism.
10. What solipsism intends is unsayable.
11. The subject is not complex or composite (5.5421)
12. The only intentionality is the intentionality of language.

We may attempt to decipher Wittgenstein's viewpoint step by step. To quote from Wittgenstein:

> There is no such thing as the subject that thinks or entertains ideas.
>
> If I wrote a book called the "World as I Found It", I should have to include a report on my body and should have to say which parts were subordinate to my will and which are not, this being a method of isolating the subject or rather of showing that in an important sense, there is no subject; for it could not alone be mentioned in that book.[28]

The position here that is being supported by Wittgenstein is really a form of the Humean argument about the non-encounterability of the self in experience. Similar points are made in the *Notebooks* on 4 August 1916, where we find him asking, 'Isn't the representing subject in the last resort mere superstition?'[29] A week later he remarks,

---

[28] *Tractatus*, 5.631.

[29] *Notebooks*, p. 80.

> The I is not an object, I objectively confront every object. But not the I. So there really is a way in which there can and must be mentioned of the I in a non-psychological sense in philosophy.

Two months later he repeats the same view in a slightly altered terminology. The illusory non-existent subject is called the 'knowing subject'. It is important to bear in mind that the Humean argument of non-encounterability was directed against the Cartesian conception of the self as res cogitans. In the *Notebooks* we have the following entry:

> The philosophical I is not the human being, not the human body or the human soul with the psychological properties, but the metaphysical subject, the boundary (not part of) the world.[30]

When Wittgenstein says that solipsism coincides with realism, a part of what he means is that the world which I am capable of representing is the real world — there is nothing possible in the world which cannot possibly be thought. But he also means that there is a sense in which the 'I' — that thing from whose point of view everything else can be represented — is not itself an item in the world. Wittgenstein says in his *Tractatus*:

> Thus there really is a sense in which philosophy can talk about the self in a non-psychological way. What brings the self into philosophy is the fact that 'the world is my world'. The philosophical self is not the human being, not the human body or the human soul, with which psychology deals, but rather the metaphysical subject, the limits of the world — not a part of it.[31]

Wittgenstein is eager to show that the metaphysical self (the supposed subject of thought and experience) is not really an item in the world, because he says in the *Tractatus*:

> The subject does not belong to the world, rather it is a limit of the world.[32]

---

30 2 September 1916.

31 *TLP*, 5.641.

32 Ibid.

D.F. Pears thinks that Wittgenstein's treatment of the self may be regarded as a critical continuation by Russell of the same topic. Initially there were certain similarities between Russell and Wittgenstein. But the two philosophers have arrived at diametrically opposite conclusions. Wittgenstein was very much close to Russell during this period. So a discussion about Russell's view in this matter may throw some light on the position of Wittgenstein. Russell detracted from his earlier position about the nature of 'ego', in 'On the Nature of Acquaintance'. For it is clearly seen that, unlike his earlier view that the ego is an object of acquaintance as maintained in his *Problems of Philosophy*, Russell in his, 'On the Nature of Acquaintance' goes to the extent of saying that the ego is not among the contents of a mind. Russell has been convinced by the Humean criticism in this regard. Wittgenstein talked about self, mind, mental states, etc. at several places in different contexts. Wittgenstein did not subscribe to the view that there is an individuative self.

A consideration of the history of philosophy shows that Descartes in the modem period made us aware of self as a substance as distinct from matter. Wittgenstein, however, reveals his anti-Cartesian attitude. In his *Blue Book* Wittgenstein clearly says that our language is responsible for creating the illusion that 'I' refers to 'something bodiless, what, however, has its seat in our body', and then concludes: 'in fact this seems to be the real ego, the one of which it was said, 'cogito ergo sum',. Prior to Wittgenstein there are many other philosophers like Hume, Kant, Schopenhauer, Freud and others who rejected the Cartesian concept of soul. Wittgenstein's anti-Cartesianism is nothing original, but there is certain unusuality in his approach. Hans Sluga in the article, 'Wittgenstein on Self' in *The Cambridge Companion to the Tractatus*, maintains that Wittgenstein's anti-objectivism lies at the root of his anti-Cartesianism. In his *Notebooks*, Wittgenstein maintains that, 'The thinking subject is surely mere illusion', but he adds to this, his anti-objectivist claims that 'I is not an object'. It has been argued by many that

Wittgenstein's argument about self bears close resemblance to Hume's analysis of the self.[33]

There is also another point to note that the *Tractatus* account of the subject has no place for the individuality we ascribe to human subjectivity. In our common sense view we suppose that human subjects are in the world, that they are distinguished by having different bodies. But Wittgenstein does not accept this notion of subjectivity. Wittgenstein's views are in this regard very close to that of Schopenhauer. Wittgenstein located the subject as the limit of the world. Hence he cannot account for the multiplicity of subjects. His view thus naturally issues into solipsism characteristic of the *Tractatus*. This is the basis of Wittgenstein's 'solipsism'. Having identified the metaphysical subject with the totality of one's language and the limits of language with the limits of the world, he could say that the limits of the subject are the limits of the world. The motive for this sort of solipsism is not like that of what is ordinarily called solipsism. It appears, rather, to portray through Wittgenstein's 'solipsism' an anticipation of the troubles of the logical positivists about other minds.

Wittgenstein is making two different claims:

1. First, that one element of truth in the statement — 'the world is my world' — that the set of metaphysical possibilities coincides with what is possible for me to represent'.
2. Second, the only way of finding a place for the metaphysical subject of thoughts and experiences is to identify it with the ineffable myness of the point of view from which these representations are formulated.

This is the basis of Wittgenstein's solipsism. Having identified the metaphysical subject with the limits of the world, he could say that the limits of the metaphysical subject are the limits of the

---

[33] Hume (1988) remarked: 'When I enter most intimately into what I call myself, I always stumble on some particular perception or other, of heat or cold, light or shade, pain or pleasure.' — *A Treatise of Human Nature*, p. 252.

world. Therefore, neither of these claims either entails or is even connected with phenomenalism. So we have found an interpretation of Wittgenstein's solipsism which is consistent with realism.

A careful study of Wittgenstein shows a close link between his notion of ethics and solipsism. The negative thesis of solipsism that the 'I' is not encountered, is a truth no doubt: but it does not give any novelty. This negative thesis taken alone fails to convey the truth of solipsism as understood by Wittgenstein. The discussion of ethics and solipsism is to be bridged. In his *Notebooks*, Wittgenstein made various remarks concerning the will, ethics and subject. It is there that the will is spoken of as 'penetrating the world' (11.6.16), as the 'bearer of good and evil' (21.7.16). His ideas are further available from his remarks dated 5.8.16 in *Notebooks*:

> The thinking subject is surely mere illusion. But the willing subject exists. If the will did not exist, neither would be there that centre of the world, which we call the 'I' and which is the bearer of ethics. What is good and evil is essentially the 'I', not the world. The 'I', is what is deeply mysterious.

Wittgenstein also says:

> The will is an attitude (Stellungnahme) to the world. The subject is the willing subject.[34]

Wittgenstein did not say much about ethics in the *Tractatus*. Ethics in his view is transcendental. According to Wittgenstein will is the bearer of value, but as such, is not a phenomenon in the world, and so cannot be spoken of. The ethical will has been taken by Wittgenstein to be like the metaphysical self; the ethical will is also supposed to lie at the limits of the world and indeed it is identical with the metaphysical subject. In his 2 August 1916 entry in the *Notebooks*, he says, 'good and evil only enter through the subject. And the subject is not part of the world, but a boundary of the world. . . .' As the subject is not part of the world but a

---

[34] *Notebooks*.

presupposition of its existence, so good and evil are predicates of the subject, not properties in the world.' Peter Hacker with a view to identifying the Tractarian subject with the ethical will, thus tried to show the connection between the two. Wittgenstein initially concentrates in his discussion on ethics and will and subsequently on will and action as Wittgenstein looks for a 'foothold for the will in the world'. In the *Tractatus*, Wittgenstein does not speak about the 'willing subject', although he speaks about 'the will'. 'The will' appears in the *Tractatus* in a dual sense, precisely parallel to the dual sense of "I' as mere psychological subject and as the world-limit. That the will in the ordinary sense, which connects willing with desires and actions, has been allotted to the cluster of facts that is the psychological subject. The bearer of ethics is no more illusory than the self which is limit of the world; they are one and the same. The text thus goes on saying about the will in its non-phenomenal sense:

> If good or bad exercise of the will does alter the world, it can alter only the limits of the world, not the facts — not what can be expressed by means of language.[35]

From Wittgenstein we derive a new conception of ethics as will. Wittgenstein does not take ethics as dealing with actions and their consequences as events or with specific motives, intentions or desires. Margaret Urban Coyue puts very nicely explaining ethics or ethical according to the *Tractatus*. 'The ethical' alludes to a character of experience as a whole which alone serves to individuate selves by individuating lives. The role of the ethical has been clarified as the individuating, perspectivizing principle which gives meaning to the world's being mine. Wittgenstein says, 'world and life are one'.[36]

Thus we find Eugene Schlossberger remarking quite rightly:

> Thus there is only one metaphysical subject, the intentionality of language itself, and it is equally common to everything. It

---

35 *TLP*, 6.43.

36 *TLP*, 5.621.

> bears, for instance, no special relation to my body.[37]

It has been further remarked by Eugene Schlossberger:

> The subject resides in language itself, not in the functioning of some bodily organism.

The main contention of this author is to highlight that Wittgenstein thought language to be pervaded by an inherent intentionality. A sentence is a picture of the world. As such it is isomorphic to the situation it portrays. What Schlossberger emphasizes is that Wittgenstein is not merely drawing our attention to the isomorphism between the language and the world, Wittgenstein is eager to establish also the intentionality of language. Schlossberger tries to clarify what is meant by the phrase 'intentionality' of language. To quote Schlossberger: 'Language is intentional; it reaches up, feels, projects, agrees, signifies and is applied.' But this is not to say that someone applies language, that someone uses language. The intentionality in language does not reside in some speaker or utterer who uses or applies language; rather it is inherent in language itself.[38]

Wittgenstein's early view of language thus consisting of basically picture theory of propositions cannot accommodate ethical propositions. Wittgenstein concludes that there cannot be any ethical propositions.[39] This implied stacking of ethical propositions to the silent realm of the inexpressible. In the *Tractatus* Wittgenstein had no scope for discussing what is right or wrong or what is the ideal. Yet Wittgenstein had a genuine interest in ethics. This is evident from the letter he wrote to Ludwig Ficker stating the purpose of the *Tractatus*:

> The book's point is an ethical one. I once meant to include in the preface a sentence which is not in fact there now but I will write out for you here, because it will perhaps be a key to the work for

---

[37] Eugene Schlossberger, 1978, 'The Self in Wittgenstein's Tractatus', pp. 148-49.

[38] Ibid.

[39] *TLP*, 6.42.

> you. What I meant to write then was this. My work consists of two parts: the one presented here plus all that I have not written. And it is precisely this second part that is the important one. My book draws limits to the sphere of the ethical from the inside as it were, and I am convinced that this is the only rigorous way of drawing those limits.[40] Wittgenstein was probably drawing attention to his remark in the *Tractatus*, 'whereof one cannot speak, thereof one must be silent'.[41]

To conclude with a quotation from Wittgenstein's 'Lecture on Ethics:

> My whole tendency and I believe the tendency of all men who ever tried to write or talk ethics or religion was to turn against the boundaries of language. This running against the walls of our cage is perfectly, absolutely hopeless. Ethics so far as it springs from the desire to say something about the ultimate meaning of life, the absolute good, the absolute valuable, can be no science. What it says does not add to our knowledge in any sense. But it is a document of a tendency in the human mind which I personally cannot help respecting deeply and I would not for my life ridicule it.[42]

---

40 Robert E. Dewey, 1967, 'Wittgenstein and His Impact on Contemporary Ethical Thought', p. 143.

41 *TLP*, 7.

42 'A Lecture on Ethics', pp. 11-12.

9

Some Observations on Builder's Language

THE *Philosophical Investigations* of Wittgenstein from its very start initiates us into the domain of builder's language for arriving at a clear view about the nature and function of language. Wittgenstein abandons the Tractarian approach of looking at language as system of signs and symbols abstracted from its uses, abstracted from the lives of its speakers as a-temporal phenomena. Wittgenstein's proposed language consisting of words, 'block', 'pillar', 'slab' and 'beam' meant to serve for communication between a builder *A* and his assistant *B*. *A* as a builder is engaged in a construction activity; he is carrying on his activities with building stones: with blocks, pillars, slabs and beams. The assistant *B* is on toes to supply blocks, pillars, slabs, stones hand in hand to *A* as per *A*'s requirement. *A* calls out, 'slab', *B* brings the slab. *A* calls out 'pillar', *B* gets the pillar for *A*. *A* calls out 'block', *B* proceeds to get the 'block'. Again hearing the call 'stone' from *A*, *B* rushes to bring stone for *A*. In all these instances *B* brings the object which he has learnt to bring at such and such call of names. The builder's language may seem to provide a fillip to the Augustinian conception of language according to which the meaning of an expression is the object named by that expression. But this way of looking at the builder's language would completely jeopardize the spirit of the whole movement in the field of philosophy of language that was heralded by the *Philosophical Investigations*. *Philosophical Investigations* begins by criticizing the Augustinian conception of language, which is also exemplified by the Tractarian conception of language with its obsession for analysis to arrive at names hooked on to simple objects and thus achieving determinacy of sense. Further, Wittgenstein's invitation to imagine this builder's language as one for which the description given by Augustine is right, turns up injudicious.

In sect. 8 of *Philosophical Investigations* Wittgenstein presents an extended version of builder's language which includes series of numerals, number of colour samples and words, 'this', 'there'. This extended version of builder's language as distinguished from its earliar non-sophisticated version brings out very clearly the points of difference between the builder's language model and the Augustinian model. With reference to the example about the slip marked, 'five red apples', some of the shortfalls of the Augustinian model comes to the surface. The belief in the essential link between the word and the object and that object is the meaning, becomes suspect. The meaning of the word, 'apple' is the thing named apples is not difficult to show. What objects are signified by words, 'red', or 'five'? Of what is 'red' the name? Of what is 'five' the name? To say that the 'apple' is the name of fruits that are round with shiny red or green skin and white flesh, 'red' is the name of colour and 'five' is the name of the number five, is to blur the distinction between different parts of speech of a language. Wittgenstein in *Philosophical Investigations* strongly criticizes the trend to magnify only names and much the same as granting abnorm al primacy to one of the parts of speech at the cost of different parts of speech. Wittgenstein repudiates referentialism of the *Tractatus* and its claim that corresponding to every name there is an object and corresponding to every object is a name. Hence the question remains how can Wittgenstein who labours hard to check the Augustinian conception of language as the only model of language and suggests another alternative model of language such as the builder's language makes such un-meticulous comments? Wittgenstein's stark remark regarding the builder's language as the language regarding which 'the description given by Augustine is right', needs to be reconsidered.

At the very beginning of sect. 2 he persists on talking about the role of the concept of meaning in the primitive idea of language.

Augustine has not succeeded in deciphering the whole truth about the function of language but undoubtedly he pointed at one of the very important functions of language, that is the mechanism ot referring. The primordial task of language is to reach out to the world, to relate to the object and that is being performed by the referring function of the language. Wittgenstein does not endorse in *Philosophical Investigations* the Augustinian conception of essence of language, hence in the example of builder's language, which is a variant of language game, he is not after any quest for the essence of language. If we again look at the example, we find that he begins with an alternative paradigm of language where the description of Augustine regarding the functional activity of language in terms of word reaching to objects also holds. There need not be any hesitation to concede this for we have already seen in the builder's language the word 'pillar' stands for pillar, the word 'slab' stands for the thing slab, the word 'beam' stands for the beam and so on and so forth. Baker and Hacker point out that Wittgenstein describes a language . . . for which the description given by Augustine is right. Note that it is not contended that the Augustinian conception of the 'essence of language' is right for this protolanguage, merely that Augustine's description is appropriate for it.[1] The moral of Wittgenstein's remark here is this: to say that a word signifies an object is nothing objectionable in stating the function of some words say nouns and like. It is quite pertinent to add here that Wittgentein's rejection of the claim that every word is a name and every word signifies something or other is in no way inconsistent with the endorsement of the previous claim.

As the builder's language is a protrayal of a primitive language and its functioning, Wittgenstein does not provide with any well-defined syntax and formation rules for sentences. The builder's language though presented as a very naïve sort of language, some of its important features are not to be left unnoticed. The very characterization as a builder's language indicates that the language has been specified with reference to the building activities of some

[1] Wittgenstein *Understanding and Meaning*, vol. 1, p. 65.

members of a society. In fact, we know that in *Philosophical Investigations* Wittgenstein's approach towards language is very concrete and empirical. Gone are the days of the *Tractaus Logico-Philosophicus,* when Wittgenstein was on the look out for the common essence of all language whatsover. Second, the builder's language presupposes a speech-community specific approach. This language contains vocabulary 'slab', 'pillar', 'block' and 'beam'. Another important feature is that of criterion of understanding. We have seen that if the builder calls, 'stone' , the assistant brings the stone. This implies that the assistant hears the word or sentence from the utterer and understands what is meant by such utterance. Hence the question arises how do we know what we have understood by hearing a word or sentence. In other words, what is the criterion of understanding? In this essay, I would like specifically to dwell on the idea of understanding that is the last but not the least important component of builder's language in our discussion. In *Philosophical Investigations* we come accross a clear demarcation in his approach: as a critique endeavours to clear all sorts of misconception surrounding the idea of understanding and establish what are not implied by the idea of understanding; second, more confidently in his assertive approach opens up sheath by sheath his idea on understanding. The readers of *Philosophical Investigations* are not unfamiliar with the unceasing deliberations between the interlocutor and the *Philosophical Investigations* endorser throughout the pages of *Philosophical Investigations.*

The Tractarian model is regulated by the idea that the sense of a sentence is a function of the meaning of its constituents and their mode of combination. On this model to understand the utterance of sentence is quite discerning. If one does not understand the words of a sentence or their mode of combination, then one will not understand the sentence. In the builder's language the understanding of an utterence, indeed, plays a very crucial role. But how do we explain this very concept of understanding?

In *Philosophical Investigations*, 138, Wittgenstein asks us in what sense the meaning of a word (what is grasped in coming to understand it, or on hearing it and understanding it) can 'fit' the use that a speaker subsequently makes of the word. It has been maintained by some thinkers that the meaning a word is grasped 'in a flash', when we hear it. Thus, the act of grasping the meaning of a word consists of hearing the word and understanding it and the use that is subsequently made of the word. If the meaning of a word is grasped in a flash when we hear it, then it has to be presumed that meaning is something that is grasped by the mind in an instant. In contrast to the above fact, the use that a speaker of the word makes subsequently is extended in time. The use of the word, thus explained, presupposes hearing of the word and understanding of it. No doubt, it remains a quagmire to explain the connection or the link between the two, of which one occurs in an instant and the other spreads over in time. How is it to make sense of the link of an instantaneous occurrence with another occurrence extended in time? Does it follow therefrom that the totality of all possible uses comes before the mind just by hearing the word and grasping its meaning? Or, alternatively, is it just that much grasped which fits one particular use of the word? Many such obnoxious and tricky questions come before us.

It may be answered straightforwardly that there is a connection between what occurs in a speaker's mind when he hears the word and understands it and the subsequent use that he makes of it. There are various approaches to answer this question. But Wittgenstein does not consider many of these interpretations to be correct. It may be said that a speaker's understanding the meaning of a word is a sort of mental state and that mental state is at the root of the speaker's making subsequent correct uses of the word. Any speaker's ability to use the words of his language correctly is explainable in terms of a mental state. How do we understand that someone has understood the meaning of a word in a flash? Is there any criterion for determining that the meaning of a word has been grasped in a flash? It is answered in terms of a speaker's avowal and subsequent applications of the word. So the phenomenon of grasping the meaning of a word in a flash does not show that the meaning grasped is something different from the use 'which is extended in time'; rather it may be stated that to grasp the meaning is to have accquired the ability to use the word.

The view that is presently under consideration suggests that meaning determines use. But we find some philosophers totally reverse this position as put by Wittgenstien in *Philosophical Investigations* 139 '. . . Well, but isn't the meaning of the word also determined by this use?'[2] Thus abandoning the earlier approach suggesting meaning determines use, in this case the reverse position has been upheld wherein meaning is taken to be determined by use. Granted that the meaning is determind by use, it may be asked how can any object of instantaneous understanding accord with a case?

According to some thinkers understanding is closely connected with the formation of mental pictures or images. In the history of philosophy, reference is often made to the imagist view, a version of which is available in the theory of ideas of Locke and Hume. According to them thought is made up of mental images copied from experiences. It may be said that something comes before one's mind when one understands the word. Thus, what comes before one's mind when one understands, say, the word 'cube' is a pcture of a cube. For the proponent of this view, the answer will be the same in the context of builder's language, when the communication takes place between the builder and his assistant. When the builder utters the word 'slab', his assistant understands that he would have to bring the slab. In this view, understanding an order involves forming image of what one has been ordered to do. Similar viewpoint has been explored by Wittgenstein in his passages of *The Blue and Brown Books*:

> If I give someone the order, fetch me red flower from that meadow,

---

[2] *Philosophical Investigations*, sect. 139.

> how is he to know what sort of flower to bring, as I have only given him a word?
>
> Now the answer one might suggest first is that he went to look for a red flower carrying a red image in his mind, and comparing it with flowers to see which of them had the colour of the image.[3]

About this mental picture, we have two possibilities to take into consideration: the first is the possibility of the picture to fit the use and the second is its possibility of failing to fit the use. Naturally, the question will arise as to how these two possibilities regarding the match of the picture with the use or its mismatch with the use are to be decided. One is inclined to say that the mental picture fits the use, when the word is applied to the object of which the mental picture is a picture. Thus, when one applies the word 'cube' to those objects of which the mental picture is that of cubes and not of pyramids, the mental picture is said to fit the use.

> In what sense can this picture fit or fail to fit a use of the word, 'cube'? Perhaps you say: 'its' quite simple; — if that picture occurs to me and I point to a triangular prism for instance, and say it is a cube, then this use of the word doesn't fit the picture.[4]

Wittgenstein asks further, 'but doesn't it fit?'[5] The very question raised by Wittgenstein makes us aware of certain hidden implications which are overlooked in this account. The method of projection plays a crucial role, for depending on a method of projection the word cube may be the representative of a pyramid. What comes out clearly is that a mental picture is suggestive of a use but it cannot be held to determine one particular use.

> The picture of the cube did indeed suggest a certain use to us, but it was possible for me to use it differently.[6]

---

3 *The Blue and Brown Books*, 3.

4 *Philosophical Investigations*, p. 54e.

5 Ibid.

6 Ibid.

Wittgenstein does not commit to the view that having mental images is necessary for understanding. He leaves it open for somebody to understand and carry on order without having a mental image of what one has been ordered to do. For the elaboration of Wittgenstein's position in this connection reference to his *The Blue and Brown Books* would be helpful.

Another important argument from Wittgenstein against the imagist view is that a mental picture, like any other pictures, has scope for various interpretations. But it should not be supposed that Wittgenstein is absolutely negating the scope for having mental images. In spite of his providing arguments against the imagist view, Wittgenstein does not deny the popularity of this viewpoint in accounting for intentionality of thought. Wittgenstein reminds us of popular belief which is in favour of the imagist view. Sometimes attempts are made by replacing the idea of mental images, to reinstate ideas of some kind of 'queer' or 'superlative images'. It has been supposed that such superlative images are not susceptible to multifarious interpretations. The supporters of mental image hypothesis would like to establish that it is an intrinsic feature of mental image that it is the image of this and nothing else. This is taken to establish super-likeness of the image and the object of which it is the image. Wittgenstein does not seem to support any such viewpoint for he dubs any such consideration as mythical. As an explanation for the intentionality of thought or understanding, the approach suggested by the imagist is not logical. But Wittgenstein himself is clearly against any such theorization for he is strongly against the move to account for intentionality in terms of 'queer' or 'superlative images'.

Wittgenstein thinks that any picture admits of multifarious interpretations and this is equally true about mental images. In cases where understanding involves invoking of images, it may be not due to any inherent or intrinsic nature of the picture, but because of how it has been understood or applied. We have already dealt with the instance of the word, 'cube'. This particular example of the word, 'cube', is relevant for the present discussion for it shows us that although 'the picture of the cube did indeed suggest a certain use to us . . . it was possible for me to use it differently'. Then we need to ponder over the nature of the connection between the picture and the use that led me to overlook possibility of any alternative application. Wittgenstein asks 'is there such a thing as a picture, or something like a picture, that forces a particular application on us? In some quarters there is a tendency to consider picture of a 'cube' to be such a picture which has forced upon us a particular application of 'cube'.[7] But this is not universally accepted. We must realize that when we are talking about the application of a picture, there is an element called 'applying the picture of a cube'. Our idea that a particular use is forced on us amounts to admitting 'only the one case and no other occurred to us'.[8]

At the end of *Philosophical Investigations* 140, Wittgenstein draws the following conclusion:

> What is essential is to see that the same thing can come before our minds when we hear the word and the application still be different. Has it the same meaning both times? I think we shall say not.

Wittgenstein's interlocutor does not, however, abandon the idea of a picture that forces a particular use on us. Couldn't it be the case, he asks, that not merely the picture but also the method of projection comes before my mind when I hear the word and understand it? Thus for the assistant *B* it may be presumed, when he understood the word 'slab', the method of projection also occurs to the mind of *B*?

Wittgenstein's position is quite clear for he does not concede to the view that the mental 'meaning-picture' carries any application with it, and forces on us either an application or varied applications in different ways. Wittgenstein's view, however, has not received universal acceptance. Wittgenstein also does not deny

---

7 *Philosophical Investigations*, sect. 140.

8 Ibid.

the possibility of a collision between a picture and its application. Since according to Wittgenstein's viewpoint there cannot be any forcible imposition on us regarding any particular application, the possibility of a variance between a picture and its application prevails. Wittgenstein has a candid reply: the possibility of a collision arises simply in so far as:

> The picture makes us expect a different use, because people in general apply this picture like this.[9]

Wittgenstein goes on:

> I want to say: we have here a normal case, and abnormal cases.

Wittgenstein also puts before us the other possibility of explaining the concept of understanding as a determinate state lying behind the correct use:

> The understanding itself is the source of the correct use.[10]

Wittgenstein asks us to imagine an instance where we are teaching a pupil how to construct different series of numbers according to particular formation rules. He asks when will we say that this pupil has mastered a particular series, say the series of natural numbers?

> Suppose the pupil now writes the series 0 to 9 to our satisfaction. And this will only be the case when he is often successful, not if he does it right, once in a hundred attempts.[11]

What is being successful? Wittgenstein explains:

> Now, however, let us suppose that after some efforts on the teacher's part he continues the series correctly, that is, as we do it.[12]

But how far need he continue the series for us to have the scope

---

9 *Philosophical Investigations*, sect. 141.

10 Ibid.

11 Ibid., sect. 145.

12 Ibid.

for saying that the student is successful? To this also Wittgenstein has a reply: 'clearly you cannot state a limit here'.[13]

Thus we find that Wittgenstein in all such cases does not provide us with any definite yes/no answers. This fact should not be viewed as an incapability on the part of Wittgenstein to arrive at any final answer. Rather by drawing attention to this fact, Wittgenstein tries to bring to light the inherent vagueness in our criteria of judging whether a pupil has mastered the system in connection with his how often carrying on it rightly. This vagueness is the characteristic of our psychological state. Thus for Wittgenstein the picture of the link between understanding and use is empty. There is also another angle from where understanding as a mental state is the source of the correct use may be emphasized. The interlocutor urges:

> When I say understand the rule of a series, I am surely not saying so because I have found out that up to now I have applied the algebraic formula in such-and-such way! In my own case at all events I surely know that I mean such-and-such a series; it doesn't matter how far I have actually developed it.

This remark suggests that one must grasp something which already anticipates the use that one goes on to make of a word. This remark further carries the suggestion that we do know what we mean by a word independently of watching ourselves use it. Wittgenstein, however, adds that still the question remains as to:

> What is the grammar of the concept of 'the state of knowing the meaning'?

This leads some to suppose that there must exist some state that somehow anticipates my future use of a word. But this sort of presumption is difficult to uphold for we have already seen similar difficulty in the case of 'cube'. This sort of presumption regarding the existence of a mental state seems to be vacuous. In that case, if one insists on admitting a mental state, he will have to admit, as maintained earlier, that this state is the source of correct use.

---

[13] *Philosophical Investigations*, sect. 158.

In fact, in the context of builder's language, as proposed by Wittgenstein, the notion of understanding plays a predominant role. The assistant *B* needs to understand what is meant by the utterence of words by his supervisor. This has to be accepted that in *Philosophical Investigations*, one of the important question that kept Wittgenstein preoccupied is regarding the actual implication of the concept of the state of knowing/understanding. The question of the grammar of the concept of understanding is the main thrust of Wittgenstein's investigations. As a philosopher of language, he makes it his point to be cautious about probable misconception and misunderstanding about the grammar of language. It is not uncommon on our part to misunderstand the functioning of language and drawing inappropriate analogies, irresponsible comparisons and irrelevent questions. His endeavour consists in giving the appropriate characterization of the concept of understanding. If the concept of understanding is regarded as a sort of mental state, how it is to be distinguished from the concept of other mental states like the concept of being in pain, of being depressed, of hearing a buzzing sound, etc.?

These concepts distinctively carry some sense of time in terms of duration, interruption and continuity. But with regard to the concept of understanding we do not find any link with occurrence. Wittgenstein suggests the concept of understanding conveys the idea of disposition or ability. When we talk about pain, we talk in terms of greater pain or less pain. This shows that talk about pain involves some talk about intensity. When we talk about degrees or intensity with regard to understanding we do not use these concepts in the same sense. Wittgenstein goes on asking what sort of mental state, if it is, is understanding? Wittgenstein remarks, in sect. 149:

> Nothing would be more confusing here than to use the words, 'conscious' and 'unconscious' for the contrast between states of consciousness and disposition. For this pair of terms covers up a grammatical difference.

If we lack any clear-cut explanation about the concept of

understanding, some suggestions for explaining the concept of understanding in terms of the internal structure of a mental apparatus like brain may be posited to account for the ability or disposition. Wittgenstein, however, does not accept this view also. For him in our investigation about the concept of understanding we are not describing the determinate state of an internal mechanism. Now we may refer to Wittgenstein's own comment.[14] The grammar of the word 'knows' is evidently closely related to that of 'can', 'is able to'. But also closely related to that of 'understands'. ('Mastery of a technique.') Thus, in Wittgenstein's view the idea of understanding is quite closer to that of the idea of 'can', 'is able to'. The sort of ability that is being emphasized here is certainly the ability to use words correctly. The question that has cropped in this connection as to whether Wittgenstein is in favour of taking the idea of understanding in a dispositional sense as distinguished from an occurrent sense of understanding. Wittgenstein does not seem to be favourably inclined towards accepting the existence of some neurological structure underlying the ability to use words. Even if it is admitted that there is some underlying neurological structure, Wittgenstein would strongly reject the claim that neurological structure is the ability. Granted that structure is not ability, at most it may be supposed to be the causal foundation.[15] According to Wittgenstein, our use of the concept of understanding shows that we are not describing the determinate state of an internal mechanism. Wittgenstein in sect. 150 writes 'mastery' in scare quotes perhaps to convey that the sense of the verbal roots know and understand is related to that of mastering a technique.

In *Philosophical Investigations* 151, Wittgenstein is occupied with the exploration of the grammar of understanding:

> *A* writes series of numbers down: *B* watches him and tries to find a law for the sequence of numbers. If he succeeds he exclaims: "Now I can go on".

---

[14] *Philosophical Investigations*, sect. 150.

[15] Ibid., sect. 153.

This example may suggest that understanding is a state of mind that makes its appearence in a moment and also provides explanation for *B*'s ability to go on with the series cor- rectly. Again Wittgenstein draws our attention to some other instances where we are tempted to conceive understanding as a mental state. Let us consider the instance as follows: '*A* has written down the number 1, 5, 11, 19, 29': at this point B says he knows how to go on. What happened here? It is possible that *B* might come up with the algebraic formula. But is this coming up with a formula to be equated with understanding? This coming up with a formula may be considered as 'characteristic accompaniments or manifestations of understanding'. It may be held that the state of understanding must contain something more than the formula that occurs to him, for that is just an instance of manifestation of understanding.

> We are trying to get hold of the mental process of understanding which seems to be hidden behind those coarser and therefore more readily visible accompaniments.

But this account does not find favour with Wittgenstein. Wittgenstein brings out very categorically that 'how can the process of understanding has been hidden, when I said 'Now I understand because I understood!' Wittgenstein brings out clearly when I use words, 'Now I understand because I understand, it is of course from a particular background or history'. He is not subscribing to the view that the mental process of understanding lies hidden, unmanifest. 'If there has to be anything behind the utterance of the formula', it is particular circumstance which provides justification for saying that I can go on when the formula occurs to me. This background history has to be given due recognition to find out the grammar of the concept of understanding. We need not search for the grammar of the concept in some hidden domain. According to Wittgenstein the concept of understanding is closely linked with a speaker's participation in the form of life. In his search he comes to the conclusion that the grammar of the concept of understanding covers our practices and connects those practices with complex patterns of our forms of life. The circumstances in which the words are uttered, 'now I understand' matters most. The use of language is embedded in the practice of language.

10

The Structural Universals
Arguments For and Against

METAPHYSICS is as old as philosophy and many of its basic questions and issues remain alive till today. One such problem is, broadly speaking, the problem about universals, and one of its highly sophisticated and intriguing upshots, particularly, is the problem about structural universals, which is the main subject for discussion in this essay. Here, I would like to cover the views of two distinguished analytic philosophers of the latter half of the twentieth century — David Malet Armstrong (1926–2014) and David Kellog Lewis (1941–2001). Armstrong was committed to a kind of immanent realism, often nicknamed by him as scientific realism, whereas Lewis, in this context prefers to characterize himself as a nominalist, which is much closer to a variety of nominalism called as class nominalism. Armstrong is very much committed to the existence of universals and he has offered mainly his views in *A Theory of Universals: Universals and Scientific Realism* (1978). Lewis as critique of Armstrong presents his views mainly in *On the Plurality of Worlds* (1986) and in 'New Work for a Theory of Universals' and 'Against Structural Universals'. This concern for structural universals is not the result of any ad hoc decision. Demands for an adequate theory for structural universals have come from various quarters, from science, from commonsensical macroscopic account of the world and also from combinatorial theorization about modality.

To start from the common sense level, everybody agrees that particulars have properties and particulars stand in relations to other particulars. Plato, however, was the first to point out that there was a puzzle underlying this situation. Two things clearly emerge from the analysis of the above pre-analytic common-sense view:

a. The same property can belong to different things.

b. The same relation can relate different things.

To be precise, something can be the same in things which are not numerically identical. The question is: how to account for this? In the history of Western metaphysics, this is one of the baffling issues that brings in the divide between realism, on the one hand, and anti-realism on the other, including nominalism and conceptualism as well. Realists answer the question by positing objective universals, whereas nominalists claim all things that exist are only particulars. There are the following three possibilities in all debates centring the existence of universals:

a. *ante res,* i.e. before things universals exist independently as in Plato's Forms.

b. *in rebus,* i.e. in things universals exist as in Aristotle.

c. *post res,* i.e. after things universals exist as in conceptualism and nominalism.

In the context of Indian philosophy also the problem of universals recurs as one of very hotly debated issues especially among the Nyāya-Vaiśeṣikas, the Mīmāṁsakas and the Buddhists. However, it is not possible to accommodate all these discussions, interesting and illuminating though they are, within the scope of this essay.

Generally, in the Western tradition words like 'universal', 'property', 'quality', 'attribute', 'feature', 'type', 'kind' and 'sort', and perhaps some others are used interchangeably. In the context of Armstrong–Lewis debate on universals, we must note that Armstrong's account of universals prevails. Armstrong is against the accepted position which holds that predicates stand in a one–one correlation to universals, implying thereby for each predicate type, there exists one universal and for each universal there exists one predicate type. Armstrong maintains;

> Given a predicate, there may be none, one or many universals in virtue of which the predicate applies. Given a universal, there may be none, one or many predicates which apply in virtue of that universal.[1]

Lewis maintains quite sarcastically, 'let me reserve the word "universal" for those entities, if such there be, that mostly conform to Armstrong's account'[2] for finally in his nominalistic scheme no room would be left for universals.

Armstrong makes it clear that predicates are mainly of two types depending on their applicability; he talks about the distinction between open predicates and predicates which are closed. An open predicate is such that it applies to any number of finite particulars.

It may as a matter of fact apply to one or to any number of finite particulars. If a predicate is not open, it is said to be closed; 'identical with the planet Venus' and 'the wisest of men' are closed predicates. Predicates are also said to be pure and impure; if there is nothing in the semantics or meaning of the predicate which prevents its applicability to an infinite number of particulars, then the predicate is pure. If it is not pure, then the applicability of the predicate is restricted essentially to a particular, hence it is said to be impure.

> From the standpoint of theory of universals, it is, of course, predicates which are both pure and open which are of especial interest.[3]

While commenting on Armstrong's conception of universals, Lewis has pointed out very rightly that one of the distinctive features of this theory is that universals are sparser compared to the properties. According to Armstrong universals are there to ground objective resemblances and the causal powers of things. So many alleged universals will not find room in the scheme of Armstrong.

---

[1] 'Predicates and Universals', in *A Theory of Universals*, vol. II, p. 9.

[2] 'New Work for a Theory of Universals', ibid., p. 164.

[3] 'Predicates and Universals', p. 15.

But there are properties in immense abundance. According to Armstrong because properties are so many and do nothing to discriminate between things they are not suitable for capturing objective resemblance.

Universals capture 'an elite minority of special properties' which are also called natural properties by Lewis, whose sharing makes for resemblance. A nominalist on the other hand, would like to account for resemblance in terms of 'primitive objective resemblance among things'.[4] According to the nominalists all things that exist are particulars.

According to the nominalism, an object's possession of the property being white, is completely determined by the fact that the predicate 'white' applies to this object. They make it clear that this argument is not a priori, but depends on experience.

Two aspects, both negative and positive, need to be clarified of this argument.

1. This argument does not establish that the predicate 'white' applies to the object in virtue of the objective property of whiteness.
2. This argument does establish that there must be something about the particular, besides the fact that it is a particular, to explain why the predicate 'white' applies to it.

Armstrong thus shows that even a nominalist in spite of his rejecting objective universals makes a covert appeal to the notion of property or to certain kind or sort. All that the nominalist can provide in place of primitive universals a reductive analysis of what it is for some thing to have property or to be of a certain kind or sort.

Armstrong, as we have seen, adopts an immanent realism about universals. This version of realism distinguishes the particularity from the properties of the particular. This comes closer to the Aristotelian realism which proposes that the thing capable

---

[4] D.K. Lewis, 'New Work for a Theory of Universals', p. 166.

of independent existence is 'this-such' , which conveys a real distinction between the haecceity (Duns Scotus) of a particular and its forms. Thus there is no separation between particulars and universals. Universals are nothing without particulars and particulars are nothing without universals. From this observation of Armstrong, two more important principles[5] are to be drawn:

I. Principle of Instantiation: For each *N*-adic universal, *U*, there exist at least *N* particulars such that they *U*.

II. The Weak Principle of the Rejection of Bare particulars.

Armstrong claims that his realism about universals is not a priori or rationalistic, rather it draws its sustenance from science for as we have already noted that in Armstrong there is an attempt to link universals with causality. He suggests four identity conditions for properties:[6]

a. The active and passive powers of particulars are determined by their properties.

b. Every property bestows some active/passive power upon the particulars of which it is a property.

c. A property bestows the very same power upon any particular of which it is a property.

d. Each different property bestows a different power upon the particulars of which it is a property.

Are There Complex Properties?

Armstrong admits that there are properties which appear to be complex.[7] According to him complex properties must have parts and these parts or relations are also properties. These are called constituents of the complex property. However, it is maintained further, it should not be supposed that the ultimate constituents of a complex property are necessarily simple properties and simple relations. Armstrong has in mind two sorts of complexity for

---

5 *A Theory of Universals*, p. 113.

6 *Universals and Scientific Realism*, vol. I.

7 'Properties and Relations', in Armstrong, vol. II, p. 67.

ultimate constituents of a complex property may be (1) finite, or (2) infinite.

Now, what is a structural property? A structural property is a complex property and he clarifies the notion of a structural property by utilizing an old distinction, due to Anaxagoras, between homoeomerous and anomoeomerous properties.[8]

A property is said to be homoeomerous if and only if for all particulars, *x*, which has that property, then for all parts *y* of *x*, *y* also has that property. A structural property is a species of anomoeomerous property. A property *S* is structural if and only if proper parts of particulars having *S* have some property or properties *T*, □ not identical with *S*, and this state of affairs is, in part at least, constitutive of *S*. Structural properties are of two types: relational and non-relational structural properties.

What is meant by structural universals?

1. Being universals, these are something that do, or at least can, occur repeatedly.
2. These structural universals are instantiated by different particulars, at different spatio-temporal positions; and wherever these are instantiated, these structural universals are considered to be non-spatio-temporal parts of particulars that instantiate these.
3. These are said to be distinctive universals. The structural universals involve other universals.
4. There is a necessary connection between the instantiating of the structural universals by the whole and instantiating of other universals by the parts.

Example of a structural universal is methane.

a. Necessarily something instantiates methane if and only if it is divisible into five spatial parts — *c*, *h*1, *h*2, *h*3 and *h*4.
b. *C* instantiates the other universal carbon, each of *h*s

---

8 'Properties and Relations', in Armstrong, pp. 68-71.

instantiates hydrogen, and each of *c–h* pairs instantiates bonded.

Arguments in Favour of Admitting Structural Universals

The realists who are sympathetic towards universals need some arguments to defend structural universals. Following are the major arguments advanced by different proponents of structural universals:[9]

- It is assumed that a predicate, a man-made thing, is applied to certain particulars and is applicable to an indefinite number of particulars. It is further maintained that there is a universal for every predicate, whether simple or complex, we can formulate. There are such predicates as 'is a methane molecule'; so there are the corresponding universals, and these must be structural. Armstrong, however, does not support this sort of argument.
- Universals are postulated because we have knowledge of similarity. Things may resemble one another by being alike in their structure, by being composed of like parts arranged in a like way. To give an account of this sort of structural resemblance we need to postulate structural universals. The basic presupposition of this argument is that structural similarity between two things should be explained in terms of a shared universal. But Lewis is not much convinced by this argument.
- Structural universals can serve as ersatz possible world or individuals, affording an objectual treatment of modality without requiring us to believe in an implausible abundance of other-worldly concrete particulars. This argument is mainly derived from Peter Forrest, claiming himself to be a realist about possibility; he admits independent existence of what is possible from what we think. He does not believe in the existence of merely possible particular but he admits

[9] Lewis, 'Against Structural Universals', pp. 200-03.

existence of uninstantiated properties. Armstrong, however, would not endorse Forrest's programme for Forrest talks of uninstantiated particulars.

- Can we be sure that there are any simples? If not, then we cannot dispense with structural universals in favour of simples they involve. 'May be there is no end to the complexity may be there are no simples, just structures of structures ad infinitum.' Lewis further argues even if there are simples, does it imply one should adopt a theory of universals that presupposes simple? Should we prefer putting an end to all speculation about infinite complexity? For Lewis this argument is the most strong argument in support of structural universals. But the adherents of structural universals will have to account for infinite complexity.

Different Conceptions of Structural Universals[10]

1. *The Linguistic Conception*: A structural universal is a set-theoretic construction out of simple universals, just as a linguistic expression is taken to be as set-theoretic construction out of its words. In this view, structural universals are complex predicates and words are the simple universals. To satisfy the predicate is to instantiate the universal. But Lewis is not at all sympathetic to this view of structural universals. Because according to this linguistic conception, structural universals are constructed out of simples. But so far the most strong argument about structural universals is concerned it need to cover the possibility that there are no simples or not enough simples. Hence the worry about infinite complexity remains unanswered by this linguistic conception.
2. *The Pictorial Conception*: On the pictorial conception, a structural universal is isomorphic to its parts. We may take the structural universal, say methane, be pictorially

---

[10] Lewis, 'Against Structural Universals', p. 203.

represented by a ball-and-spring model containing one large central ball and four smaller balls attached to it by springs. But this sort of conceptualization leads to many questions. The ball-and-spring model itself is a particular, and so is distinct from each of the methane molecules to which it is isomorphic. And while considering the pictured, that is the structural universal methane is an immanent universal and is isomorph. As a universal, the structural universal methane is wholly present as a non-spatio-temporal part of each methane molecule that instantiates it. Lewis points out that in this conception a structural universal is no longer a set but it becomes a mereological composite. Thus understood the simpler universals may be present as parts and there may be no simples. One advantage of this conception is that it may permit infinite complexity. This is one way of understanding structural universals wherein we do not require them to be reducible to simples. The other alternative is that there are simples and thus understood structural universals are nothing over and above their parts. Just molecule is nothing over and above its atoms, so in this conception structural universals are nothing over and above their simple parts. According to this ontological viewpoint the whole is an extra item only in a minimum sense that it is not identical with any of its parts, but it is not distinct from either. Thus structural universals are nothing over and above their simpler parts, whether or not any of its parts are simple simpliciter.

Lewis himself at one time was drawn to this conception of structural universals. But he subsequently was worried by associated inconsistency of this conception. Lewis concludes: '. . . no version of the pictorial conception is satisfactory.'

3. *The Magical Conception*: The magical conception carries an unacceptable price in mystery.[11]

[11] Lewis, 'Against Structural Universals', p. 214.

Lewis thus wants to establish that there are no cogent argument in favour of admitting structural universals nor are there any adequate explanations to account for how do structural universals come into being. Here most of the arguments of Lewis are directed towards Armstrong and other proponents of structural universals. Though Armstrong talks about structural universals he very much differs from Forrest for the latter admits uninstantiated structural universals. Lewis does not accept uninstantiated structural universals either.

Bibliography

Adam, Robert, 1979, 'Theories of Actuality', in *The Possible and the Actual*, ed. Michal Loux, Ithaca and London: Cornell University Press.

Alston, William P. and Jonathan Bennett, 1984, 'Identity and Cardinality: Geach and Frege', *The Philosophical Review*, XCIII(4), October.

Anscombe, G.E.M., 1959, *An Introduction to Wittgenstein's Tractatus*, London: Hutchinson University Library.

Armstrong, D.M., 1980, *A Theory of Universals: Universals and Scientific Realism*, vols. I-II, Cambridge: Cambridge University Press, 1st paperback edn.

Aurobindo, Sri, 2004, *Kena and Other Upanishads*, Pondicherry: Sri Aurobindo Ashram.

Backer, G.P. and P.M.S. Hacker, 1980, *Wittgenstein: Understanding and Meaning*, vol. 1, part II, Oxford: Basil Blackwell.

Bealer, George, 1998, 'Universals and Properties', in *Contemporary Readings in the Foundations of Metaphysics*, ed. Stephen Laurence and Cynthia Macdonald, Oxford: Blackwell Publishers.

Bigelow, John and Pargetter Robert, 1998, 'A Theory of Universals', in *Contemporary Readings in the Foundations of Metaphysics*, ed. Stephen Laurence and Cynthia Macdonald, Oxford: Blackwell Publishers.

Bostock, David, 1984, *Aristotle: Metaphysics Z and H: A Commentary and Tanslation*, Oxford.

Bricker, Philip, 1987, 'Reducing Possible Worlds to Language', *Philosophical Studies*, 52: 331.

Butchvrov, Panayot, 1979, 'Identity' in *Contemporary Perspectives in the Philosophy of Language*, ed. Peter A. French, Theodore E. Uehling and Howard K. Wettstein, Minnesota: University of Minnesota Press, pp. 159-78.

Carnap, Rudolf, 1946, 'Modalities and Quantification', *Journal of Symbolic Logic*, 11: 33-64.

———, 1947, *Meaning and Necessity*, Chicago: University of Chicago Press.

Carruthers, Peter, 1989, *Tractarian Semantics*, Oxford: Basil Blackwell.

———, 1990, *The Metaphysics of the Tractatus*, Cambridge University Press.

Chandra, Suresh, 2002, *Wittgenstein New Perspectives*, New Delhi: Indian Council of Philosophical Research.

Devitt, Michael, 1974, 'Singular Terms', *Journal of Philosophy*, 18 April, LXXI(7): 183-205.

Dewey, Robert E., 1967, 'Wittgenstein and His Impact on Contemporary Ethical Thought', in Paul Engelmann, *Letters from Ludwig Wittgenstein with a Memoir*, New York: Horizon Press.

Donnellan, Keith S., 1979, 'The Contingent A Priori and Rigid Designators', in *Contemporary Perspectives in the Philosophy of Language*, ed. Peter A. French, Theodore E. Uehling and Howard K. Wettstein, Minnesota: University of Minnesota Press, pp. 45-60.

Donnellan, Keith S., 1972, 'Reference and Definite Descriptions', in *New Readings in Philosophical Analysis*, ed. H. Feigl, W. Sellars and K. Lehrer, New York: Appleton Century Crofts, pp. 59-71.

Dummett, M., 1973, *Frege: Philosophy of Language*, chap. 16, London: Duckworth.

Dunn, J.M. and N.D. Belnap (Jr.), 1968, 'The Substitution Interpretation of the Quantifiers', *Nous*, 2(2): 177-85.

Engelmann, Paul, 1967, *Letters from Ludwig Wittgenstein with a Memoir*, New York: Horizon Press.

Feldman, F., 1969, 'Geach and Relative Identity', *Review of Metaphysics*, 22: 547-55.

Fitch, F.B., 1949, 'The Problem of the Evening Star', *Philosophy of Science*, 17: 137-40.

Forrest, Peter, 1998, 'Ways Worlds Could Be', in *Contemporary Readings in the Foundations of Metaphysics*, ed. Stephen Laurence and Cynthia Macdonald, Oxford: Blackwell Publishers.

Frege, G., 1950, *The Foundations of Arithmetic*, tr. J.L. Austin, Oxford: Blackwell.

———, 1960, *Translation from the Philosophical Writings of Gottlob Frege*, ed. and tr. P. Geach and M. Black, Oxford: Blackwell, 2nd rev. edn.

———, 1964, *The Basic Laws of Arithmetic*, tr. M. Furth, Oakland, CA: University of California Press.

Fϕllesdal, Dagfinn, 1971, 'Quantification into Causal Contexts', in *Reference and Modality*, ed. L. Linsky, London: Oxford University Press, pp. 52-62.

———, 1975, 'Quine on Modality', in *Words and Objections*, ed. D. Davidson and J. Hintikka, Dordrecht: D. Reidel, pp. 175-85.

Geach, P.T., 1962, *Reference and Generality*, Ithaca, NY: Cornell university Press.

———, 1972, *Logic Matters*, Oxford: Basil Blackwell.

———, 1973, 'Ontological Relativity and Relative Identity', in *Logic and Ontology*, ed. Milton K. Munitz, New York: New York University Press.

———, 1976, 'Why Logic Matters', in *Contemporary British Philosophy*, Fourth Series, ed. H.D. Lewis, London: George Allen & Unwin.

———, 1977, 'Names and Identity', in *Mind and Language*, ed. Guttenplan, Oxford: Clarendon Press, repr.

Griffin, Nicholas, 1977, *Relative Identity*, Oxford: Clarendon University Press.

Haack S., 1977, 'Lewiss Ontological Slum', *The Review of Metaphysics*, March, XXX(3): 415.

———, 1978 *Philosophy of Logics*, Cambridge: Cambridge University Press.

Hacker, P.M.S., 1996, *Wittgenstein's Place in Twentieth Century Analytic Philosophy*, Oxford: Blackwell Publishers Ltd.

Hintikka, Jaakko, 1969, 'Existential Presuppositions and Their Elimination'; 'Modality and Quantification'; 'The Modes of Modality'; 'Existential Presuppositions' and 'Uniqueness Presuppositions', *Models for Modalities*, 23: 23-44, 57-70, 71-86, 112-47.

Hirsch, Eli, 1982, *The Concept of Identity*, New York/Oxford: Oxford University Press.

Hughes, G.E. and M.J. Cresswell, 1972, *An Introduction to Modal Logic*, London: Methuen and Co.

Hume, David, 1988, *A Treatise of Human Nature*, ed. L.A. Selby Bigge, Oxford and London: Clarendon Press.

Jeffery, Richard, 1965, *The Logic of Decision*, New York: McGraw-Hill, 2nd edn. 1983, Chicago: University of Chicago Press.

Kaplan, David, 1971, 'Quantifying in', in *Reference and Modality*, ed. L. Linsky, London: Oxford University Press, pp. 112-44.

Kanger, Stig, 1957, *Provability in Logic*, Amsterdam: Almquist and Wiksell.

Kripke, Saul, 1963, 'Semantical Considerations on Modal Logic', in *Acta Philosophica Fennica* (*Proceedings of a Colloquium on Modal and Many-Valued Logics*), pp. 83-94.

———, 1971, 'Identity and Necessity', in *Identity and Individuation*, ed. Melton K. Munitz, New York: New York University Press, pp. 135-64.

———, 1972, 'Naming and Necessity', in *Semantics of Natural Language*, ed. D. Davidson and G. Harman, Dordrecht: D. Reidel, pp. 253-355.

———, 1976, 'Is There a Problem about Substitutional Quantification', in *Truth and Meaning*, ed. Gareth Evans and John McDowell, Oxford: Clarendon Press, pp. 325-419.

Leibniz, G.W., 1969, *Philosophical Papers and Letters*, tr. L.E. Loemaker, Dordrecht: Reidel.

Leinfellner, Elisabeth et al. (eds.), 1978, *Wittgenstein and His Impact on Contemporary Thought*, Vienna: Holder, Pitcher and Tempsky.

Lewis, David, 1986, *On the Plurality of Worlds*, Oxford: Blackwell Publishers.

———, 1998, 'Against Structural Universals', 'New Work for a Theory of Universals', in *Contemporary Readings in the Foundations of Metaphysics*, ed. Stephen Laurence and Cynthia Macdonald, Oxford: Blackwell Publishers.

Linsky, Leonard (ed.), 1971, *Reference and Modality*, London: Oxford University Press.

———, 1977, *Names and Descriptions*, Chicago: The University of Chicago Press.

Loux, Michael (ed.), 1979, *The Possibile and the Actual*, Ithaca and London: Cornell University Press.

Marcus, Ruth Barcan, 1972, 'Quantification and Ontology', *Nous*, VI(3): 240-49.

———, 1946, 'A Functional Calculus of First-Order Based on Strict Implication', *Journal of Symbolic Logic*, 11: 1-16.

———, 1962, 'Interpreting Quantification', *Inquiry*, 5: 252-59.

———, 1963, 'Classes and Attributes in Extended Modal Systems', in *Acta Philosophica Fennica*, Modal and Many-Valued Logics, pp. 123-35.

———, 1963, 'Modalities and Intensional Languages', *Boston Studies in the Philosophy of Science*, ed. M.W. Wartofsky, Dordrecht: D. Reidel, pp. 77-96.

———, 1967, 'Essentialism in Modal Logic', *Nous*, March, I(1): 91-96.

———, 1971, 'Essential Attribution', *Journal of Philosophy*, 8 April, LXVIII(7).

———, 1971, 'Extensionality', in *Reference and Modality*, ed. L. Linsky, London: Oxford University Press, pp. 44-51.

———, 1972, 'Quantification and Ontology', *Nous*, September, VI(3): 240-49.

———, 1976, 'Comment' on D. Wiggins' paper, 'Identity, Necessity and Physicalism', in *Philosophy of Logic*, ed. Stephen Körner, Oxford: Basil Blackwell, pp. 132-46.

McGuinness, B. (ed.), 2008, *Wittgenstein in Cambridge: Letters and Documents, 1911-1951*, Oxford: Blackwell.

Munitz, Milton K., 1971, *Identity and Individuation*, New York: New York University Press.

Nelson, J., 1971, 'Relative Identity', *Nous*, 4: 241-60.

Noonan, Harold W., 1980, *Objects and Identity*, The Hague: Martinus Nijhoff.

———, 1986, 'Relative Identity: A Reconsideration', *Analysis*, pp. 6-10.

Odegard, D., 1972, 'Identity Through Time', *American Philosophical Quarterly*, **9**: 29-38.

Parsons, T., 1974, 'Essentialism and Quantified Modal Logic', in *Reference and Modality*, ed. L. Linsky, Oxford: Oxford University Press, p. 75.

Pears, David, 1978, *The False Prison: A Study of the Development of Wittgenstein's*

Philosophy, vol. I, Oxford: Clarendon Press.

Pelletier, Francis Jeffry, 1979, 'Mass Expressions', in *Hand Book of Philosophical Logic*, vol. IV, ed. D. Gabbay and F. Guenthner, Dordrecht: D. Reidel Publishing Co.

———, (ed.), 1979, *Mass Terms: Some Philosophical Problems*, Dordrecht: Reidel Publishing Co.

Perry, John R., 1970, 'The Same F', *Philosophical Review*, 79: 181-200.

Plantinga, Alvin, 1974, *Nature of Necessity*, Oxford: Clarendon Press.

Prior, 1963, A.N., 'Is the Concept of Referential Opacity Really Necessary?', in *Acta Philosophica Fennica* (Societas Philosophica Fennica), pp. 189-98.

Quine, W.V., 1949, 'Designation and Existence', in *Readings in Philosophical Analysis*, ed. H. Feigl and W. Sellars, New York: Appleton Century Crofts, pp. 44-51.

———, 1953, 'Identity, Ostension and Hypostatis', 'On What There Is', in *From a Logical Point of View*, Cambridge, MA and London: Harvard University Press.

———, 1960, *Word and Object*, Cambridge, MA: M.I.T. Press.

———, 1963, 'On What There Is', 'Logic and Reification of Universals', 'Reference and Modality', in *From a Logical Point of View*, New York: Harper and Row Publishers, pp. 1-9, 10-129, 139-59.

———, 1963, 'Reference and Modality', *From a Logical Point of View*, Cambridge, MA: Harvard University Press.

———, 1964, 'Review of Geach, Reference and Generality', *Philosophical Review*, 73: 100-05.

———, 1971, 'Quantifiers and Propositional Attitudes', in *Reference and Modality*, ed. L. Linsky, London: Oxford University Press, pp. 101-11.

———, 1972, 'Notes on Existence and Necessity', in *Semantics and the Philosophy of Language*, ed. L. Linsky, Illinois: University of Illinois Press, pp. 77-91.

———, 1975, 'Replies to Hintikka', 'Replies to Follesdal', 'Replies to Kaplan', in *Words and Objections: Essays on the Work of W.V. Quine*, ed. D. Davidson and J. Hintikka, rev. edn., Dordrecht/Boston: D. Reidel Publishing Co.

———, 1976, 'On Multiplying Entities', in *The Ways of Paradox and Other Essays*, rev. and enlarged edn., Cambridge, MA and London: Harvard University Press.

———, 1976, 'Three Grades of Modal Involvement'; 'Reply to Professor Marcus'; 'A Logistical Approach to Ontological Problems'; 'The Variable', in *The Ways of Paradox and Other Essays* (rev. edn.), Harvard: Harvard University Press, pp. 158-76, 177-84, 197-202, 272-82.

———, 1979, 'Intensions Revisited', in *Contemporary Perspectives in the Philosophy of Language*, ed. Peter A. French, Theodone E. Uehling and Howard K. Wettstein, Minnesota: University of Minnesota Press.

Rescher, Nicholas, 1975, *A Theory of Possibility*, Oxford: Basil Blackwell.

———, 1979, 'The Ontology of the Possible', in *The Possible and the Actual*, ed. Michael Loux, Ithaca and London: Cornell University Press.

Sanyal, Indrani, 1983, Philosophical Problems of Quantified Modal Logic' Unpublished Ph.D. dissertation, Jadavpur University, Kolkata.

———, 1984, 'The De Re Modality and Essentialism', *Indian Philosophical Quarterly*, July, XI(3): 365-72. (Chap. 2 of this book.)

———, 1987, 'How Is "(∃*x*) (*x* Is Necessarily Greater than 7)" Possible?', *Journal of Indian Council of Philosophical Research*, Spring, IV(2): p 1-33. (Chap. 1 of this book.)

———, 1990, 'Modality and Possible Worlds', in *Foundations of Logic and Language: Studies in Philosophical and Non-Standard Logic I*, Jadavpur Studies in Philosophy, second series, ed. Pranab Kumar Sen, Allied Publishers in collaboration with Jadavpur University, Calcutta, pp. 193-242. (Chap. 3 of this book.)

———, 1998, 'Youktik Parivyāpti', in *Wittgenstein*: *Jagat Bhasa O Cintan* (in Bengali), ed. Tushar Kanti Sarkar, Indrani Sanyal and Shefali Moitra, Kolkata: Allied Publishers and Jadavpur University. (Chap. 7 of this book.)

———, 2000, 'Sen's Views on Reference and Quantification and Their Implications in a Modal Context', in *Realism*: *Responses and Reactions*, in modal context, *Essays in Honour of Pranab Kumar Sen*, ed. D.P. Chattopadhyay, Sandhya, Basu, Madhabendra Natha Mitra and Ranjan Mukhopadhyay, New Delhi: Indian Council of Philosophical Research. (Chap. 5 of this book.)

———, 2000, 'Pragmatic Ambiguity', in *Rabindra Bharati Journal of Philosophy*, VI. (Chap. 6 of this book.)

———, 2002, *On Essentialist Claims*, Allied Publishers in collaboration with Jadavpur University, Kolkata.

———, 2007, 'The Structural Universals: Arguments For and Against', *Indian Journal of Analytic Philosophy*, II(1). (Chap. 10 of this book.)

———, 2010, 'Some Observations on Builder's *Language*', *The Journal of Indian Academy of Philosophy*, 49(1-2). (Chap. 9 of this book.)

———, 2015, 'The Limits of Language and the Unlimited Beyond', in *Philosophy, Science and Analysis*: *The Festschrift Volume in Honour of Sibajiban Bhattacharya*, ed. Dikshit Gupta and Dilip K. Basu, New Delhi: New Delhi Publishers. (Chap. 8 of this book.)

———, forthcoming, 'A Taranscendental Argument for Essentialism', in *Mind and Cognition*: *An Inter-Disciplinary Sharing — The Festschrift Volume in*

Honour of Amita Chatterjee, ed. by Madhuchanda Sen, Kuntala Bhattacharya and Smita Sarkar, New Delhi: D.K. Printworld. (Chap. 4 of this book.)

Schlossberger, Eugene, 1978, 'The Self in Wittgenstein's Tractatus', in *Wittgenstein and His Impact on Contemporary Thought*, ed. Elisabeth Leinfellner et al., Vienna: Holder, Pichler and Tempsky.

Sen, Pranab Kumar, 1980, 'Variables and Quantification'; 'The Necessary and the A Priori', in *Logic, Induction and Ontology*, Jadavpur Studies in Philosophy, vol. II, New Delhi: The Macmillan Co. of India, pp. 56-91, 159-79.

———, 1991, 'Reference, Modality and Predication', 'Some Notes on Singular Reference', 'Non-Singular Reference', in *Reference and Truth*, Allied Publishers, pp. 56-81, 17-33, 34-55.

Sluga, Hans and David G. Stern (eds.), 1996, *The Cambridge Companion to Wittgenstein*, New York: Cambridge University Press.

Smullyan, A.F., 1971, 'Modality and Description', in *Reference and Modality*, ed. L. Linsky, London: Oxford University Press, pp. 35-43.

Stenius, E., 1960, *Wittgenstein's Tractatus*, Oxford: Blackwell.

Stewenson, L., 1972, 'Relative Identity and Leibniz's Law', *Philosophical Quarterly*, 22: 155-58.

Strawson, P.F., 1959, *Individuals*, London: Methuen.

———, 1976, 'Entity and Identity', in *Contemporary British Philosophy*, Fourth Series, ed. H.D. Lewis, London: George Allen & Unwin.

Tagore, Rabindranath, 2003, *Gitanjali*, in English, New Delhi: UBSPD in association with Visva Bharati, Santiniketan, 2003.

Tarski, A., 1970, *Introduction to Logic and to the Methodology of Deductive Sciences*, Oxford: Oxford University Press.

Tharp, L.H., 1971, 'Truth, Quantification and Abstract Objects', *Nous*, V: 363.

Wallace. J., 1971, 'Convention T and Substitutional Quantification', *Nous*, V: 199.

———, 1972, 'On the Frame of Reference', in *Semantics of Natural Language*, ed. D. Davidson and G. Harman, Dordrecht: Reidel, p. 219.

White, Roger, 1977-78, 'Wittgenstein on Identity', in *Proceedings of the Aristotelian Society*, New Series, LXXVIII: 158-74.

Whitehead, A.N. and Bertrand Russell, 1957, *Principia Mathematica*, vol. I, Cambridge: Cambridge University Press, pp. 30-31, 171-74.

Wiggins, David, 1971, 'The De Re, "Must": A Note on the Logical Form of Essentialist Claims', in *Truth and Meaning*, ed. Gareth Evans and John Mcdowell, London: Oxford University Press, 1971.

———, 1974, 'Essentialism, Continuity and Identity', *Synthese*, 23(3).

———, 1976, 'Identity, Necessity and Physicalism', in *Philosophy of Logic*, ed. S. Korner, Oxford: Basil Blackwell.

———, 1980, *Sameness and Substance*, Cambridge, MA and London: Harvard University Press.

———, 2001, *Sameness and Substance Renewed*, Cambridge: Cambridge University Press.

Williams, C.J.F., 1989, *What Is Identity?*, Oxford: Clarendon Press.

Wittgenstein, Ludwig, 1958, *The Blue and Brown Books*, Oxford: Blackwell.

———, 1961, *Tractatus Logico-Philosophicus*, tr. D.F. Pears and B.F. McGuninness, London: Routledge Kegan Paul.

———, 1961, *Note Books 1914-1916, ed.* G.H. von Wright and G.E.M. Anscombe, tr. G.E.M. Anscombe, Oxford: Blackwell.

———, 1965, 'A Lecture on Ethics', *The Philosophical Review*, 74: 3-12.

———, 1971, *Proto-Tractatus*: *An Early Version of Tractatus Logico-Philosophicus*, ed. B.F. McGuinness, T. Nyberg and G.H. von Wright, tr. D.F. Pears and B.F. McGuinness, London: Routledge and Kegan Paul.

———, 2001, *Philosophical Investigations*, tr. G.E.M. Anscombe, New York: Blackwell Publishers.

Zemach, Eddy M., 1974, 'In Defence of Relative Identity', *Philosophical Studies* 26: 207-18.

Index

absolute
  actuality, 91
  conception of identity, 139
  identity theory, 162
  predication, 71, 73

act of
  grasping the meaning, 249
  individuation, 140-41
  language use, 191

Adams, Robert, 107, 114-16, 126-28

alternative
  account of possible worlds, 6
  interpretations, 40
  way of referring, 40
  worlds, 130

amphibious ontological basis, 109

analysis of
  identity statements, 148
  language, 201, 225, 227
  substitutional quantification, 179

analytic
  philosophers, 2, 11-12, 187, 191, 196
  philosophic tradition, 202
  philosophy, 1-2, 14, 16, 18, 187, 196, 225
  tradition of philosophy, 187

Anaxagoras, 265

anecdote of history, 188

Anglo-American Analytic Philosophy, 1

Anscombe, G.E.M., 235

anti-Cartesianism, 239

anti-constructivists, 158

anti-essentialist, 69, 132

applied semantics, 83

Aristotelian, 154
  essentialism, 133
  realism, 263

Aristotle, 22, 49, 93-94, 102, 137, 158, 203
  counterparts of, 93

Armstrong, D.M., 17, 133, 260-64, 266-67, 269
  scheme of, 262

Armstrong–Lewis debate, 261

Augustine, St., 247

Augustinian,
  conception of
    essence of language, 247
    language, 219, 245-46
  model, 246
  temptation, 191

axiomatic
  development of modal calculus, 76
  system of mathematics, 76

axioms and rules of modal logic, 87

Ayer, A.J., 137, 142-43

Baker, Gordon P., 247
basics of truth-functional logic, 212
best candidate theory, 161-62
bipolarity of truth and falsity, 223
bivalence, 223
bi-valued logics, 219
Black, Max, 216
boundaries of language, 244
Bricker, Phillip, 120-22, 126
Brouwerian system, 79
Buddhists, 261
builder's language, 245-48, 250

calculus model, 202
canonical conception of properties, 100, 102-03, 106
Carnap, Rudolf, 117
Cartesian concept of soul, 239
Castaneda, Carlos, 116
causal theory of proper names, 189
charge of essentialism, 4, 65, 134
Cicero, 22-23
class nominalism, 260
classical
  conception of identity, 148
  mathematics, 33
classification of semanticists, 90
cognitive act of
  individuating, 168
  individuation, 138-39
combinatorial theorization, 260
common essence of all language, 248
concept of
  containment, 205
  interpretation, 77
  logical space, 12, 197-98, 203
  material substances, 161
  meaning, 246
  model structure, 77
  necessary identity, 52
  pragmatic ambiguity, 176
  possibilia, 143
  reference, 8, 172
  satisfaction, 77, 181
  tātparya, 12
  understanding, 254, 256-58
conception of
  a variant description, 112
  individuation, 140
  modality, 163
  supernumerary, 112
  universals, 262
conjunction, 223
construction of
  an ideal language, 227
  modality, 165
contingent proposition, 215
contradiction
  in essentialism, 70
  of essentialism, 73
contradictory propositions, 215
conventional
  approach to essentialism, 7
  reading of essentialism, 167
  understanding of language, 119
co-referential terms, 194
counterpart
  theorist, 93

theory, 92-94
Coyue, Margaret Urban, 242
Cresswell, M.J., 78
critics of quantified modal logic, 44, 65
cry for determinacy of sense, 15

definite description, 189, 195
definition of a model, 77
delink existential generalization and substitution, 174
depraved semantics, 85
Descartes, René, 128, 203, 239
descriptive
apparatus of language, 121
phrase, 190
uses of language, 37
determinacy of sense, 231
determinate individuative practices, 143, 153, 155
development of
modal logic, 26
quantification logic, 169
Devitt, Michael, 177, 189
different kinds of incompossibility, 110
discussion of ethics and solipsism, 241
dispositional sense, 257
distinct types of semantics, 86
doctrine of
essentialism, 65, 136
Lewis, 93
linguistic ersatzism, 127
plurality of real worlds, 94
relative predication, 73
solipsism, 235
domain of
possibilia, 142
set theory, 166
silence, 234
Donnellan, Keith, 11, 49-50, 61, 176-77, 188-89
language of, 194
Donnellian scheme, 8
Dummett, Michael, 49
Dummettian view of objectivity, 87

Eiffel Tower, 166
elementary proposition(s), 222-23, 231
eliminative reduction of possible worlds, 107
espousal of epistemological argument, 168
essence of language, 202
essential core aspect of all languages, 228
essentialism, 4, 8, 25, 66-68, 132-34, 137-39, 142, 162, 165, 168
modest form of, 166
type of, 7
essentialistic qualification, 113
ethical propositions, 243
existence of
possible worlds, 109
unactualized possibilia, 75
uninstantiated properties, 267
existential
generalization, 32, 37, 53, 56-57, 62-63, 170, 174, 186, 192-93, 195-96
presupposition, 37-38, 58

quantification, 38
quantifier, 24, 28-29
existents and possibilia, distinction between, 96
explication of modal notions, 5, 74
exploration of grammar of understanding, 257
extension of logical space, 206
extensional
logicians, 46
point of view, 46
extensionality principle, 166
extreme realism of Lewis, 107

failure of existential generalization, 61, 175
failure of
quantification, 165
substitutivity, 58, 138
faith in formalism, 83
falsity of
a contingent proposition, 217
an elementary proposition, 217
feature of
a model structure, 77
language, 234
Russellian theory, 47
Follesdal, Dagfinn, 59-60
Ficker, Ludwig, 243
first type of essentialism, 4
Fitch, F.B., 3, 42-43, 47, 60
force of gravitation, 97
formal semantics, 84-85
formalization of modal talks, 92
formation of
mental pictures, 250
pseudo-propositions, 14
Forrest, Peter, 266-67, 269
foundation of
logic, 210, 219
reality, 219
modal calculus, 76
framework of
possible world, 81, 92, 113
substitutional quantification, 31, 183
Frassen, Van, 167
Frege and Russell, 227
Frege, G., 13, 146, 149, 219-22, 226-27
Fregean and the Russellian convictions, 219
Frege–Russell's logico-linguistic trend, 224
Freud, Sigmund, 239
function of language, 247
functional calculus, 27

Geach, Peter, 148-49, 154, 163
Geachian interpretation of identity, 154
general notion of a model, 76
generalizations of tautologous propositions, 221
genuine interest in ethics, 243
Gödelian theorem, 123
grammar of concept of understanding, 256, 258
grammatical
structure, 189, 191

syntax, 213

Haack, Susan, 85, 94, 124
Hacker, Peter, 242, 247
haecceity, 133
Hazen, Allen, 94
hidden logic, 211
hierarchy of sortals, 151
Hintikka, Jaakko, 4, 27, 36-39, 41-43, 53, 58-60, 74, 76-77, 87, 170
history of
philosophy, 16, 239, 250
Western metaphysics, 261
Western philosophy, 199
Hughes, G.F., 78
Hume, David, 239-40
Humean
argument, 237
criticism, 239

inclusion and exclusion of states of affair, 98
incompleteness theorem, 123
indexical
analysis of actuality, 91, 95, 99, 127
theory of actuality, 128
Indian philosophy, 12, 261
individuative essentialism, 138, 162
influence of
Russell upon Wittgenstein, 199
Wittgenstein, 14, 16
insistent brand of essentialism, 150
intentionality of
language, 243
thought, 252
interpretation of quantification, 26
intersubstitution of
co-designative terms, 63
two co-referential terms, 56

Jackson, Frank, 124
Jeffrey, Richard, 114, 125

Kanger, Stig, 5, 74
Kant, Immanuel, 167, 205, 239
Kaplan, David, 170
Kripke, Saul, 4, 10, 47-51, 53, 59-60, 74-78, 80-81, 84-85, 101, 113, 134-37, 142-43, 163, 167, 179, 181, 208
formal semantics of, 82
semantical argument of, 6
set-theoretical presentation of, 84
Kripkean
semantic representation of modal logic, 79
semantics, 78, 80, 83
of possible worlds, 116
viewpoint, 163

language infinite, 120
language-independent propositions, 115
later Wittgensteinian legacy, 12
Leibniz's law, 154, 157
Leibnizian
idea, 159

schema, 157
Lewis, David, 90-91, 94-95, 107-08, 119-25, 127, 192, 208-09, 260, 262-63, 266-69
doctrine of, 93
full-blooded realism of, 96
ontology of possible worlds of, 93
realism of, 94
robust realism of, 106
system, 79
technical language of, 94
theory of, 92
lexical categories, 184
limits of
language, 232-33, 240
metaphysical subject, 240
linguistic
and non-linguistic entities, 185
conception, 267
construction, 119, 121, 125
entity(ies), 5, 30, 91, 114, 118, 120-21, 125-26, 182, 184, 186
ersatzer(s), 118, 121-22, 124
ersatzism, 114, 118-19
expression, 176
intentions, 50
items, 185
reductionist, 127
world-surrogates, 114
logic, 223
logic of
identity, 139
language, 211, 231-32
modality, 79, 89
logical
anomalies, 101
argument, 58
of Quine, 3, 22
atomism, 198, 199
atomist, 198
clarification of thought, 202
concept, 203
constants, 222-23
form, 203
of a sentence, 228
of all languages, 210
of facts, 226
of reality, 233
formula, 83
grammar, 213, 227
implication, 83
impossibility, 24
incompossibility, 110
objects, 222-23
part of the language, 121
Positivism, 15
positivist(s), 15, 230, 240
proposition(s), 218, 220-21
relation of axioms, 76
source of language, 220
space, 197-98, 200, 203-09, 215-19, 223, 232
space and language, relation between, 210
structure, 14
syntax, 213-14, 227
techniques of substitutional quantification, 170
truth, 219
logically independent elementary propositions, 202
Lycan, William, 116

magical conception, 268
Mīmāṁsakas, 261
manifestation of understanding, 258
Marcus, Ruth Barcan, 3, 9-10, 27-28, 31-33, 42-43, 51-53, 58-60, 68-69, 170, 178, 182

mark of weakness in logic, 7
maximal
  consistent set, 127, 129
  state of affairs, 98
meaning of
  an expression, 189
  sortal concepts, 145
meaningfulness of modal logic, 90
mechanism of language, 8, 169
mental
  image hypothesis, 252
  images, 17, 252
  process of understanding, 258
metaphysical
  argument, 6, 58, 137
  atomism, 198
  idea, 223
  incompossibility, 110
  jargons or theories, 199
  jungle of Aristotelian essentialism, 66
  justification of quantified modal logic, 21
  perspective, 92
  subject, 241
  thesis, 209
metaphysics of
  essence, 6
  objects, 205
miscarriage of quantification, 23, 138
modal
  calculus, 74-76
  compatibility, 117
  context(s), 8, 28, 36, 53, 75, 163, 169, 172, 175, 186, 192-93, 195
    is referentially opaque, 193
  distinctions, 95
  logic, 42, 59, 63, 84, 86, 136
  logicians, 70
  notions, 5, 103, 123, 129
  operator, 60
  possibilism, 90
    of Lewis, 96
  proposition, 60
  realism, 90, 93, 96, 106
  reasoning, 84
  sentence, 49
  statement, 40, 88
  systems, 74, 84, 101
mode of characterization, 25, 135
model
  calculus, 77
  concepts, 135
  proposition, 48, 64
  structure, 77
    of a modal calculus, 77
    of Kripke, 78
    of modal calculi, 79
  systems, 77
  theory, 74-76
model-theoretic
  approach to modal logic, 75
  representation, 76, 78
modern logical techniques, 140
modest realism, 96
Mondadori, Fabrizio, 87-88
monolithic view of logical necessity, 124
Moore, G.E., 13, 219
Morgan, Augustus De, 223
Morton, Adam, 87-88
multiplicity of reference, 41
mutual incompossibility, 110
mystic interpretation, 224
mythical tie, 193

nature and function of language, 245

nature of
- elementary propositions, 216
- language, 232
- logic, 219
- ordinary proper names, 47
- possibilia, 97
- possible world(s), 103, 113, 129-30
- quantification, 9, 27
- realism, 209
- relation between logic and the world, 210
- substitutional quantification, 179
- tautologies, 218

needless multiplication of entities, 209

neurological structure, 257

nomic incompossibility, 110

non-circular explanation of modality, 125

non-denumerable infinity, 35

non-denumerably infinite objects, 36

non-derivativeness, 129

non-existent possibles, 108-09

non-linguistic
- entities, 184, 186
- things, 191

non-logical vocabulary, 123-24

non-modal
- logic, 135
- properties, 89

non-singular reference, 187-88

non-spatio-temporal entities, 117

non-truth functional, 52

notion of
- a possible individual, 81
- a possible world, 75
- a structural property, 265
- absolute actuality, 128
- actuality, 91, 127
- analysis, 202, 230
- concordance, 154
- consistency, 124
- converse of modal compatibility, 117
- counterparts, 92
- epistemological independence, 85
- essence, 18, 137, 166
- essentialism, 65, 142
- ethics and solipsism, 241
- identity, 51, 102
- internal principle of distinction, 132
- language, 120
- logical
  - space, 14, 203, 206, 209, 216
  - truth, 218
- maximal consistent sets of propositions, 126
- mind-independent existence, 131
- möglichkeit, 209
- multiple references, 39
- non-existing possible individuals, 81
- objectivity, 131
- philosophical self, 236
- possible world(s), 74, 99, 122, 129, 142
- possibility, 6, 130
- *prakaraṇa*, 12
- quantification, 3, 26
- scope–ambiguity, 48, 50
- strict equivalence, 53
- subject of experience, 236
- *tātparya*, 196
- tautology, 218

truth, 32, 115
understanding, 16-17, 256
unique reference, 39

Nyāya-Vaiśeṣikas, 261

object of reference, 188

objectivity of a modal statement, 81, 88

objectual
interpretation of quantification, 3, 26-27, 42, 75, 171, 178
quantification, 10, 28, 30, 37, 179-83, 185-86

Occam's
principle, 5, 75
razor, 94

ontic status of the possibilia, 108

ontological
basis, 109
categories, 31, 182-83
entity, 83
issues regarding possibilia, 84
slum, 94

ontology of
possible worlds, 114, 127
relative existents, 157
substance, 152
this-such substantive continuants, 154
three-dimensional continuants, 152

outcome of essentialism, 67

paradox of quantified modal logic, 51, 60

parallel system of modal logic, 92

Parsons, T., 68, 116

Passmore, John, 199

Pears, David, 233, 239

perfect logical language, 220

philosophers of
language, 145-46, 188, 208
logic, 208

philosophical
illness, 201
logic, 192

philosophy
consists of logic and metaphysics, 226
is a critique of language, 14, 201, 227

philosophy of
language, 2, 15, 176
logic, 2
mind, 2
Wittgenstein, 231

physical laws of the actual world, 158

pictorial
conception, 267-68
form of all sentences, 229

picture theory of
language, 226, 228
proposition, 231, 243

pillar of salt, Lot's wife, 153-54

pioneers of the modern analytic philosophy, 199

Plantinga, Alvin, 69, 81-84, 96-105, 107, 116

Plato, 260

Platonic
ideas, 104
realist, 108
realm, 131

plurality of
  full blooded worlds, 91
  possible worlds, 129
  worlds, 91
poet of *Gitanjali*, 224
positivist thesis, 230
possibilism, validity of, 122
possibility of
  pragmatic ambiguity, 176
  quantification, 80, 193
  quantified modal logic, 4, 27
possible
  languages, 210
  truth value combinations, 217
  world(s), 6, 89-90, 93, 95-98, 100-01, 105, 107-08, 110-11, 113-18, 121-22, 125-28, 130-31, 135-36, 143
practice of language, 259
pragmatic ambiguity, 12, 193, 196
pragmatics, 191, 194
presupposition of
  quantification, 41
  uniqueness, 38, 59
presuppositionless logic, 38, 42
primitive
  idea of language, 246
  language, 16
  modality, 5
  notion of possible world, 126
primordial task of language, 247
principle of
  bivalence, 81
  compossibility, 109
  epistemological independence, 86
  existential generalization, 25, 63, 135, 171
  identity of the indiscernibles, 110
  individuation, 75, 112
  instantiation, 264
  reducibility to acquaintance, 198
  sortal continuity, 156
  substitution, 51-52
  substitutivity, 22-24, 43, 51, 55-56, 58, 60, 175, 192-93
    of identicals, 25
Prior, A.N., 43, 53, 59-60
problem of
  cardinality, 119
  quantification, 2
  Theseus's ship, 161
  trans-world identity, 136
  reference, 187
pro-Fregean thinkers, 149
proponents of quantified modal logic, 58
propositions, 197, 218
protagonists of essentialism, 142
pro-Wittgensteinian thinkers, 149
purely possible substances, 142
pure semantic, 83

quantification, 28, 178
quantification in modal contexts, 26
quantificational model structure, 80
quantified modal
  context, 50
  logic, 6, 9-10, 12, 22, 26-27, 33, 37-38, 41-42, 51-52, 58-60, 64-65, 68-69, 80, 134, 170, 179, 192
quantified sentence, 36
question of truth and falsity, 31

Quine, W.V., 2, 8-10, 12, 21-28, 32-34, 36-37, 41, 46, 54-62, 65-66, 68, 72-73, 75, 97, 132, 137, 149, 162, 165, 171, 175, 178, 181, 186, 192, 193
  weakness of, 42
Quine's
  antithetical attitude, 170
  objection, 3-4, 35
Quinean, 170
  accusation, 165
  framework, 3
  jargon, 163
  notion of quantification, 59
  objection, 8, 170
  stricture, 6, 170
  thesis, 27

real essences of concrete things, 167
realism of
  Lewis, 96
  Wiggins, 162
reference, 32, 196
  failure, 190
referential
  expression, 177, 190
  function, 194
  opacity, 22-25, 59, 163
  transparency, 22
  use, 193
    of a descriptive phrase, 189
    of an expression, 191
    of descriptive phrases, 196
referentially opaque, 193-94
relation between
  logical space and language, 210
  world and logic, 211
relation of identity, 92
relative
  identity theory, 154
  predication, 71
replacement of possible worlds, 120
repugnant to the intellect, 99
Rescher, Nicholas, 107-12, 131
Richards, Tom, 96
richness and complexity of the phenomenon of language, 192
rival theories of quantification, 179
role of
  context, 190
  pragmatics, 196
Roper, Andrew, 116-17
rule of
  inference, 69
  logic, 220
Russel, Bertrand, 13, 44-45, 137, 173, 189, 198-99, 219-22, 225-27, 232, 234, 239
  and Wittgenstein, similarities between, 239
  theory of definite description of, 187
  upon Wittgenstein, influence of, 199
Russellian
  tradition, 11, 187
  view, 48

salient features of the doctrine of Aristotelian essentialism, 68
satisfactory theory of propositions, 116
Schlick, Moritz, 14

Schlossberger, Eugene, 242-43
Schopenhauer, Arthur, 234, 239-40
scope–ambiguity, 43, 47
self-contradictory propositions, 212
semantic
 notion of consistency, 123
 representations, 184
 account of modal logic, 87
 analysis of modal logic, 93
 argument, 137
  of Kripke, 6
 distinctions, 185
 properties, 115
 question, 175
 representation of modal logics, 134
 treatment of
  modal logic, 74
  modality, 143
semantics of
 modal logic, 81, 93
 modal system, 84
 possible worlds, 87, 93, 134
semanticists, 5
Sen, P.K., 4, 8-12, 18-19, 31, 49, 169-70, 172-77, 179-82, 184-89, 196
sense of quantification, 37
sentential function, 28-33, 180-83, 185
set(s) of linguistic
 constructions, 118, 121
 marks, 122
set-theoretic construction, 121, 267
set-theoretical
 construct, 93
 construction, 86
 presentation of Kripke, 84
set-theory, 121, 165
Sheffer, Henry M., 223
silent realm of the inexpressible, 243
similarities between Russell and Wittgenstein, 239
simple property theory, 128
Sluga, Hans, 239
Smullyan, Arthur, 3, 42-44, 47, 50-51, 53, 60, 62, 170
Socrates, 32, 99, 102, 104, 163
sortal
 concept(s), 146-48, 150-51, 160-61
 dependency of identity, 7
 substantive predicate, 154
spatial interpretation, 148
speciality of substitutional quantification, 180
speculative metaphysicians, 187
Spinoza, Baruch, 203
spirit of transcendental philosophy, 196
Stalnaker, Robert, 96-97, 106-07
Stenius, Erik, 206
strata of ontological realms, 89
Strawson, P.F., 148, 176
structural universals, 17-18, 260, 265-69
structure of language, 187
sub-atomic composition of matter, 230
subject of logical atomism, 198

sub-language of a natural
  language, 121

sublimity of logic, 13

substance
  concept, 155
  ontology, 152

substantival discontinuity, 156

substantive sortal concept, 153

substitutional quantification, 9, 182

substitution, 53
  instance, 34
  type of, 31

substitution of
  co-designative terms, 59
  co-referential terms, 43, 56-57, 175, 193

substitutional
  interpretation of
    quantification, 9, 27-29, 31, 33, 58, 75, 177, 186
  quantification, 9-10, 28-32, 34, 36, 178, 180-86

substitutivity of
  co-designative terms, 25, 61
  co-referential terms, 26

superlative images, 252

supernumeraries, 112

supplementation of identity
  statements, 154

surface grammar of language, 14, 201

syntactic
  delineation, 185
  notion of consistency, 123
  rules, 213-14

syntax of
  language, 191
  linguistic expressions, 173

system(s) of
  elementary propositions, 200
  modal logic, 78
  quantified modal logic, 80

(a) synthetic whole, 200

Tarski, Alfred, 77

Tarskian semantic theory of truth, 181

Tarski-like notion of satisfiability, 123

tātparya, 196

tautological proposition(s), 215, 217-18, 222

tautologies, 219

tautologous proposition, 212, 220

technical language of Lewis, 94

techniques for inferring
  sentences, 185

ten subsidiary formulations of D-thesis, 8

tenet of essentialism, 137

terminological
  modification, 177
  revolution, 95

terminology of logic, 212

Tharp, Leslie, 10, 179

theorem of logic of Cantor, 126

theories of actuality, 114

theorization of identity, 8

theory of
  identity, 144
  individuation, 7, 137
  Lewis, 92
  meaning, 200

picturing, 191
universal, 262

thesis of
concordance, 155
essentialism, 18
modal realism, 124
relative identity, 149, 157, 160
sortal dependency of identity, 144, 147-50
sortal-relative identity, 153

three
grades of modal involvement, 163
of modal operators, 165
stalwarts of European philosophy, 13

tone of fatalism, 70

totality of
actualized combinations of objects, 207
actualized states of affairs, 207
all the possibilities, 207
elementary truth possibilities, 216
existents, 96

Tractarian, 197
approach, 245
conception of language, 202, 245
essentialist and referentialist framework, 18
idea of analysis, 231
model, 12, 229, 248
language, 229
of language, 191
move, 225
period, 210, 224, 226
phase, 235
philosophy, 13
of language, 200
position, 199, 201
proposition, 214
scheme, 211
standpoint, 191
subject, 242

tradition of analytic philosophy, 209

trajectory of epistemology, 7, 168

transcendental argument, 7, 137

transparent syntax, 227

trivialization of sortal predication, 156

truncated descriptions, 47

truth
and falsity of the substitution instances, 30
and structure of the possible worlds theory, 120
conditions, 135
function, 222
functions of elementary propositions, 216, 231
of a modal statement, 89
or falsity of the modal statements, 88

truth-functional
context, 45-46
logic, 212, 214, 219
proposition, 45

truth-value, 24, 45, 79, 88

twentieth-century analytic philosophy, 200, 225

two notions of existence, 130

type of
essentialism, 7
substitution, 31

unanalysable truths of logic, 220

understanding, 257

uninstantiated structural universals, 269
uniqueness
  and singular, subtle distinction between, 173
  of reference, 41
  presupposition, 58
universal quantifier, 28-29
Unlimited Beyond, 16

vague identity theory, 162
vaktur icchā, 196
Venus, 262
verification theory of meaning, 230
Vienna Circle, 14, 202, 230

Wallace, John, 10, 179
Wallace–Tharp, 181
  Thesis, 10, 179
weak principle of the rejection of bare particulars, 264
well-formed
  formulae of a language, 214
  ideography to cure philosophy, 213
Western
  analytic tradition, 11
  metaphysics, 261
  philosophy, modern, 198
  tradition, 261
Western Philosophy, 16, 239, 250
  history of, 199
Whitehead, A.N., 44-45, 225-26
Wiggins, David, 6-8, 137-44, 147-50, 155, 152-59, 161-68
  epistemological argument of, 6
  essentialism of, 167
Wittgenstein, Ludwig, 13-16, 18, 103, 191-92, 198-99, 201-03, 205-10, 212-15, 217-47, 249-55, 257-58
  influence of, 14, 16
  interpreters of, 15
  main contention of, 216
  main intention of, 211
  objective of, 211
  philosophy of, 231
  repudiates referentialism of the tractatus, 246
  totality, 204
Wittgenstein's
  concept of form of life, 17
  idea of logical space, 200
  notion of logical space, 216
  solipsism, 240-41
  theory of language, 226
Witgensteinian
  concept of possible worlds, 209
  tradition, 191
world
  and life are one, 242
  and logic, relation between, 211
  of contingencies, 225

zero ontological status, 108-09
Zweir, Paul K., 67